MacRuby in Action

MacRuby in Action

BRENDAN G. LIM
WITH JERRY CHEUNG
AND JEREMY MCANALLY

MANNING

SHELTER ISLAND

For online information and ordering of this and other Manning books, please visit
www.manning.com. The publisher offers discounts on this book when ordered in quantity.
For more information, please contact

Special Sales Department
Manning Publications Co.
20 Baldwin Road
PO Box 261
Shelter Island, NY 11964
Email: orders@manning.com

Manning Publications Co.
20 Baldwin Road
PO Box 261
Shelter Island, NY 11964

Development editor: Sara Onstine
Technical proofreader: Nick Howard
Copyeditors: Lianna Wlasiuk, Tiffany Taylor
Proofreader: Melody Dolab
Typesetter: Marija Tudor
Cover designer: Marija Tudor

ISBN: 9781935182498
Printed in the United States of America
1 2 3 4 5 6 7 8 9 10 – MAL – 18 17 16 15 14 13 12

brief contents

contents

preface

When I was first learning Ruby, I immediately fell in love with the language. I knew early on that I wanted to work with Ruby professionally, which became possible later when I created my first startup using Ruby on Rails.

I later worked for a Ruby on Rails consulting company where I spent a few years focusing on Ruby before I headed up the mobile development department. I've had an interest in mobile development since I was young and it was a very exciting time to work on iOS and Android applications. With iOS development came the need to learn Objective-C, which ultimately led me into the world of Cocoa for Mac development.

I developed a few Mac applications personally and professionally and thought how great it would be if I could write Mac applications using Ruby. I'd heard of Ruby-Cocoa, but I knew of its shortcomings. Then I learned about MacRuby: it was the solution I'd been waiting for.

When I was contacted by Manning to work on this book, I knew I'd be able to reach many other individuals who were Rubyists and who wanted to create rich Mac applications without having to use Objective-C. This book is meant for you if you love the Ruby language and want to get into Mac development

BRENDAN G. LIM

acknowledgments

Putting together a book like this is no easy feat, and many people behind the scenes worked countless hours to get the book into your hands. First and foremost, everyone at Manning deserves all the thanks we can give them. Without them, we wouldn't have been able to create such a great book for you.

We interacted frequently with a few individuals from Manning and would like to specifically mention them. We'd like to thank Troy Mott, our acquisitions editor, who originally came to us to work on this book and helped us through thick and thin. Sara Onstine, our development editor, guided us through the formalities of writing a book like this. And Marjan Bace, our publisher, always challenged us to find ways to improve the book's content and organization.

We'd also like to thank our book's production team. Lianna Wlasiuk, Tiffany Taylor, and Melody Dolab, our copyeditors and proofreader, read the entire manuscript and made sure everything was organized and presented properly. Nick Howard, our technical proofreader, caught errors that we didn't know were there.

Over the course of the development of the book, many people generously volunteered to review it to help make it as good as it could be. These reviewers deserve a tremendous amount of credit for the impact they made through their feedback. Our thanks to Pradeep Elankumaran, Brent Collier, Adam Bair, Philip Hallstrom, Mike Stok, Alex Vollmer, Coby Randquist, Jerry Cheung, Greg Vaughn, Warner Onstine, and Daniel Bretoi.

BRENDAN would like to thank his father, Chhorn, his mother, Brenda, and his two brothers, Chhorn and Chhun, for their support and encouragement. He also wants to thank his wife, Edelweiss, for her love and support and for letting him spend night and day working on this book. Last but not least, thanks to Pradeep Elankumaran, who let Brendan spend so much time writing this book after they both quit their jobs to focus on their startup, Kicksend.

JERRY would like to thank his parents, Margaret and Kevin, and his wise-guy brother Randall. He'd also like to remind Wendy that he beat her to her thesis (thanks, love, for letting me win this one). A special shout-out goes to Brendan for getting Jerry interested in MacRuby and Mac development in the first place.

JEREMY would like to thank his wife, friends, and dogs for sustaining him through yet another writing project. Without their support, he would likely end up a raving maniac under an overpass tapping out code examples while throwing cans at passing cars.

about this book

MacRuby in Action was written to give Rubyists the ability to create rich Cocoa applications for the Mac OS X platform without having to learn Objective-C. Our goal is to have you, the reader, creating amazing Cocoa applications using MacRuby by the end of the book. Throughout the book, you'll learn in the ins and outs of MacRuby while exploring the Cocoa framework, design patterns, system scripting, testing, and getting your application into the Mac App Store. We know that sometimes the best way to learn is to get your feet wet. That's why you'll be creating useful Mac applications along the way so you can apply the key topics as you learn them.

Who should read this book

This book is aimed at developers interested in writing software for the Mac platform. It doesn't matter if you're new to both the Mac and the Ruby language or you're an experienced Ruby developer looking to learn how to write Mac apps. If you have the desire to create beautiful Cocoa applications for the Mac platform and want to do so using the elegant and highly productive Ruby language, then this book is for you. If you're new to Ruby, we give you a brief overview of the language so you'll feel comfortable enough to take on the rest of the book.

MacRuby in Action is also a more approachable introduction to Cocoa development than traditional Objective-C books. Throughout the book, we explore practical code examples that you'll face when creating your own applications. *MacRuby in Action* can act as a guide for using MacRuby and Cocoa from the ground up, or you can use it as a reference if you're looking to dive deeper into MacRuby.

Roadmap

The book has 11 chapters divided into three parts as follows:

Chapter 1 explores the inner workings of MacRuby and how to set up your development environment. There's also an introduction to Ruby and an overview of Objective-C syntax. We then go into the MacRuby syntax, give a few examples, and end with two "Hello World" examples.

Chapter 2 takes a deeper dive into MacRuby with more in-depth examples. We look into using external frameworks, Ruby gems, and the MacRuby console. At the end of the chapter, you build a MacRuby Pomodoro application.

Chapter 3 talks about Apple's development environment tools. You spend more time using Xcode's Interface Builder to create rich Cocoa user interfaces. You then use your Interface Builder knowledge to create an application to manage to-do lists.

Chapter 4 introduces and explains a code design technique known as *delegation*. This design pattern is used often in the Cocoa framework and is important to know because it's a core concept. You explore delegation by creating a web browser with MacRuby.

Chapter 5 covers Cocoa's notification system, which lets you set observers throughout an application to listen for and react to changes. This is another pattern that is used frequently in Cocoa. At the end of the chapter, you build an iTunes notification observer.

Chapter 6 explores key value coding (KVC) and observing. KVC is a mechanism in Objective-C that's used throughout Cocoa. You learn about KVC, bindings, and key-value observing.

Chapter 7 introduces the Core Data framework. Core Data is Apple's answer to object-relational mapping. We compare Core Data with other persistence solutions that you may be familiar with. At the end of the chapter, you use Core Data to add persistence to the Todo List application you built in chapter 3.

Chapter 8 discusses image manipulation, animation, and much more with Core Animation. Throughout the chapter, we go through examples to showcase what you can do with Core Animation once you scratch the surface.

Chapter 9 dives into the MacRuby-oriented mapping library HotCocoa. HotCocoa gives developers an alternative to Interface Builder by making it easy to create interfaces in code. You end up building a small application of your own.

Chapter 10 discusses testing with MacRuby. Testing is an essential part of software development, and it has gained a strong focus within the Ruby community. We look at different ways to test with MacRuby.

Chapter 11 explains how to release a MacRuby application to the world with the Mac App Store. We go into detail about the different review guidelines, how to provision your application for submission, and finally how to submit it for review.

Appendix A talks about scripting with MacRuby. We first provide a little history and an introduction to AppleScript. We then look at how you can use MacRuby to create scripts to automate functionality.

Code conventions

There are many code examples throughout this book. These examples always appear in a `fixed-width code font`. If we want you to pay special attention to a part of an example, it appears in a **`bolded code font`**. Any class name or method within the normal text of the book appears in code font as well.

Many of Cocoa's methods have exceptionally long and verbose names. Because of this, line-continuation markers (➡) may be included in code listings when necessary.

Not all code examples in this book are complete. Often we show only a method or two from a class to focus on a particular topic. Complete source code for the applications found throughout the book can be downloaded from the publisher's website at www.manning.com/MacRubyinAction.

Software requirements

An Intel-based Macintosh running OS X 10.6 or higher is required to develop Mac-Ruby applications. You also need to download MacRuby, but it's freely available at http://macruby.org.

The book offers full coverage of MacRuby and Xcode 4.

Author Online

Purchase of *MacRuby in Action* includes free access to a private web forum run by Manning Publications where you can make comments about the book, ask technical questions, and receive help from the authors and from other users. To access the forum and subscribe to it, point your web browser to www.manning.com/MacRubyinAction. This page provides information on how to get on the forum once you're registered, what kind of help is available, and the rules of conduct on the forum.

Manning's commitment to our readers is to provide a venue where a meaningful dialog between individual readers and between readers and the authors can take place. It's not a commitment to any specific amount of participation on the part of the authors, whose contribution to the AO remains voluntary (and unpaid). We suggest you try asking the authors some challenging questions lest their interest stray!

The Author Online forum and the archives of previous discussions will be accessible from the publisher's website as long as the book is in print.

about the authors

BRENDAN G. LIM is a professional Ruby and Objective-C developer. He is also a noted conference speaker who specializes in developing Ruby on Rails, Android, iOS, and Mac applications. Brendan graduated from Auburn University where he studied Wireless Software Engineering. He is also a Y Combinator alum and cofounded the file-sharing startup Kicksend. During his free time, Brendan enjoys rock climbing and taking photos and videos.

JERRY CHEUNG loves creating software. He started experimenting with Ruby on Rails in 2007 and has been hooked on Ruby ever since. Upon graduating from Berkeley, he joined Coupa, and later he went on to start his own company, Outspokes, with several friends from Berkeley. He currently works as a Rails engineer at Intridea and experiments with emerging technologies like MacRuby and Node.js. When he's not furiously typing, Jerry might be out running, brewing beer, or enjoying a BBQ and getting a serious sunburn.

JEREMY MCANALLY is founder and principal at Arcturo, a web and mobile development firm. He spends his days hacking Ruby and Objective-C.

about the cover illustration

The figure on the cover of *MacRuby in Action* is captioned "A man from Ubli, Dalmatia." The illustration is taken from a reproduction of an album of Croatian traditional costumes from the mid-nineteenth century by Nikola Arsenovic, published by the Ethnographic Museum in Split, Croatia, in 2003. The illustrations were obtained from a helpful librarian at the Ethnographic Museum in Split, itself situated in the Roman core of the medieval center of the town: the ruins of Emperor Diocletian's retirement palace from around AD 304. The book includes finely colored illustrations of figures from different regions of Croatia, accompanied by descriptions of the costumes and of everyday life.

Ubli is a town on the island of Lastovo, one of a number of small islands in the Adriatic off the western coast of Croatia. The figure on the cover wears blue woolen trousers and a white linen shirt, over which he dons a blue vest and black jacket, richly trimmed with the colorful embroidery typical for this region. A red turban and colorful socks complete the costume. The man is also holding a pistol and has a short sword tucked under his belt.

Dress codes and lifestyles have changed over the last 200 years, and the diversity by region, so rich at the time, has faded away. It's now hard to tell apart the inhabitants of different continents, let alone of different hamlets or towns separated by only a few miles. Perhaps we have traded cultural diversity for a more varied personal life—certainly for a more varied and fast-paced technological life.

Manning celebrates the inventiveness and initiative of the computer business with book covers based on the rich diversity of regional life of two centuries ago, brought back to life by illustrations from old books and collections like this one.

Part 1

Starting with MacRuby

MacRuby is a combination of technologies that together create a powerful and very usable new technology. Part 1 of this book provides the basics needed for new MacRuby users to understand the background and underlying details of how MacRuby works so the development environment, language, and platform make sense. With this grounding, you'll be able to pick any sections in the rest of the book and learn about the areas that are most interesting or relevant to you.

Introducing MacRuby

This chapter covers

- Exploring and installing MacRuby
- Important Cocoa concepts
- Objective-C and Ruby fundamentals
- MacRuby syntax and methods
- Developing with the Xcode IDE

MacRuby gives you the ability to write full-fledged Mac applications while enjoying the benefits of the Ruby language. You won't take a deep dive into writing your first releasable application worthy of the Mac App Store just yet—you'll do that in chapter 2. To write great MacRuby applications, you first need to become familiar with its foundation. The MacRuby language is deeply rooted in the Ruby and Objective-C languages so it's important to have a good understanding of both of these to fully leverage all that MacRuby offers.

In this chapter, we'll briefly cover the Cocoa framework, Ruby, and Objective-C. After you have an understanding of these topics, we'll dive into some real MacRuby code. You'll even get a chance to write a Hello World application; we'll show you two approaches to user interface development.

To get started, let's learn what MacRuby is all about and get it installed on your system.

1.1   Introducing MacRuby

MacRuby is an Apple-sponsored development project. Over the years, Apple has shown support for Ruby as a language, and, since 2002, Apple has included Ruby as part of the Mac OS X operating system. Apple bundled a Ruby Scripting Bridge implementation called RubyCocoa with Mac OS X Leopard. Prior to MacRuby, RubyCocoa was the only way to work with Ruby and the Cocoa framework together.

In this section, you'll learn how MacRuby is different from past attempts at combining Ruby and Objective-C and what makes it such a great language. We'll also jump right into getting MacRuby installed onto your system and introduce you to MacRuby's class structure.

Let's set the stage for MacRuby.

1.1.1   The MacRuby difference

The goal of MacRuby is to provide an implementation of the Ruby language on top of core Mac OS X technologies, such as the Objective-C runtime, garbage collection, and Core Foundation. In MacRuby, all classes are Objective-C classes, all methods are Objective-C methods, and all objects are Objective-C objects. Unlike RubyCocoa, you don't need a bridge between Ruby, Objective-C, and the Cocoa framework. MacRuby is implemented on top of the Objective-C runtime as shown in figure 1.1.

MacRuby gives you the ability to do almost anything you want with the Mac platform—all while giving you the clean, concise syntax of the Ruby language. Another thing that sets it apart from RubyCocoa is that you get this functionality without making performance sacrifices because MacRuby doesn't rely on a bridge implementation.

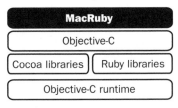

Figure 1.1   MacRuby is built on top of the Objective-C runtime.

MacRuby is similar in concept to the IronRuby and JRuby projects in that it's an implementation of Ruby on top of another runtime. IronRuby runs on the .NET runtime for Windows, and JRuby runs on the Java Virtual Machine (JVM) runtime. MacRuby is currently under active development by Apple, which gives the language a great deal of support and momentum.

Think of MacRuby as the child of two languages: Objective-C and Ruby. MacRuby is rooted in the Objective-C object hierarchy, but it also has the Ruby 1.9 core functionality layered on top. Syntax-wise, MacRuby resembles Ruby more than Objective-C. Theoretically, you could write a Ruby 1.9 script and run it under MacRuby. The key difference in MacRuby is that you can directly access Objective-C frameworks, classes, objects, and methods.

Before you write any code, you'll want to install MacRuby and Xcode on your system. Xcode is Apple's suite of developer tools needed to create Mac OS X applications. After all, what good are code examples if you can't follow along?

1.1.2 *Setting up your environment*

Install the Xcode development environment first. It's best to install MacRuby *after* you have Xcode set up on your machine. If you don't install in this order, tools such as Interface Builder (which is now built into Xcode 4) won't be able to recognize your MacRuby code.

INSTALLING XCODE

Registered Apple Developers can download the latest version of Xcode for free at https://developer.apple.com/xcode/. If you don't have an Apple Developer Account, you can purchase Xcode for $4.99 from the Mac App Store.

> **TIP** Xcode is a big file; take a break while you wait for it to download.

After the download is complete, run the installer to set up Xcode on your system. Xcode will be available from your /Developer/Applications folder.

INSTALLING MACRUBY

Installing MacRuby is a simple two-step process:

> **NOTE** Make sure that you're running an Intel-based system with Mac OS X 10.6 or higher, which is the minimum requirement for MacRuby.

1 Download the latest stable release. From http://macruby.org, proceed to the download section. A self-installable binary should be available for you to save and run, which should install the latest version of MacRuby on your system.

2 Test the MacRuby installation. Open the Terminal application, type `macirb`, and then press Enter. You should see something similar to the following code:

```
$ macirb
irb(main):001:0>
```

This puts you directly into Macirb, the MacRuby console, which is a great tool for experimenting with MacRuby. You'll learn about Macirb in more detail in chapter 2.

Next, type this command:

```
p "Hello World!"
```

If your installation was successful, you'll see the words Hello World! printed out without any errors. If you see errors, try installing again.

> **NOTE** If Xcode doesn't recognize MacRuby files, return to this page and re-install MacRuby.

If everything went as planned, congratulations! You've written your first line of MacRuby! You can now follow along throughout the book. Let's start with a MacRuby script.

1.1.3   *Hello World, part 1*

The MacRuby scripting runtime provides a way to
execute MacRuby scripts as Cocoa applications,
without the need for any other tools. To get a taste
of MacRuby, you're going to write a script that,
when run, looks like figure 1.2.

Open your favorite text editor, and create a file
and save it with the name hello.rb. The .rb indicates

**Figure 1.2   The MacRuby script in
action**

that it's a Ruby source file. MacRuby uses the same file extension as standard Ruby,
but it uses its own command to run scripts, as you'll soon see.

The Hello World application shown in listing 1.1 is 25 lines long because you're
creating it programmatically rather than using the interface development tools built
into Xcode. Most of the code is for the user interface, which is why most people
choose to use HotCocoa or Xcode.

Let's start by looking at the code in the script, and then we'll break it down into
digestible bits.

Listing 1.1   MacRuby Hello World script

```
framework 'cocoa'

app = NSApplication.sharedApplication        ①  Initializes
                                                 NSApplication

win = NSWindow.alloc.initWithContentRect
  ([300,500,400,200],
  styleMask:NSTitledWindowMask | NSClosableWindowMask
  | NSMiniaturizableWindowMask | NSResizableWindowMask,     ②  Sets up
  backing: NSBackingStoreBuffered, defer:false)                NSWindow

label = NSTextField.alloc.initWithFrame
  CGRectMake(0,0,250, 45))
label.setStringValue "Hello World!"
label.drawsBackground = false
label.bezeled = false                              ③  Creates
label.font = NSFont.fontWithName("Arial", size:45.0)   label
label.editable = false

label.frameOrigin = NSMakePoint
  ((win.contentView.frameSize.width/2.0)
  -(label.frameSize.width/2.0),                    ④  Centers
  (win.contentView.frameSize.height/2.0)              label
  -(label.frameSize.height/2.0) )

win.contentView.addSubview(label)                    Adds
                                                  ⑤  subview

win.title = "Hello World"
win.display                                   ⑥  Configures
win.orderFrontRegardless                          app window
win.makeKeyWindow

app.run
```

The first line uses the `framework` method to load the Cocoa base framework for Mac-Ruby. This method loads both the Foundation and AppKit frameworks into your environment so that your application has access to the core Cocoa classes.

You start by initializing the `NSApplication` singleton ❶ for the app. Every Cocoa program has a singleton instance of `NSApplication` responsible for managing the application's run loop. You create a variable, `app`, and assign it a reference to the `NSApplication` singleton.

Next, you set up the application window. At ❷, you create an instance of `NSWindow` with parameters and assign it to the `win` variable for reference. To add subviews to the application, you reference the main window (`win`). You also specify the size of the window as the first parameter of the `NSWindow` instance.

To display the Hello World! message, you need an element to display the text. You create an instance of `NSTextField` ❸ and then set the text for it to `Hello World!` You also set its bounds so that it displays centered in the window ❹. The frame origin of the text field is set to roughly the center of the window based on the window's dimensions.

Next, you add the text field as a subview of the application window's content view ❺. The view hierarchy in Cocoa lets you easily add views on top of existing views.

You finish by setting the application window title, and telling the window to display and then become the front key window ❻. Finally, you tell the `NSApplication` instance to run the application.

That may have felt heavy for a Hello World, but that's because there was a good amount of setup for the interface elements. To run the script, type the following in the terminal (assuming you've named your script hello.rb):

```
macruby hello.rb
```

When the application runs, you'll see the application window appear (see figure 1.2). You created a simple Hello World application using a single MacRuby script. In reality, you aren't likely to write too many apps like this. But this is a great way to initially dip your toes into Cocoa and MacRuby. This script uses a few of the core classes from the Cocoa frameworks—the most important of these are `NSApplication` and `NSWindow`. Every Cocoa application works with `NSApplication`. It's also likely that you'll be dealing with `NSWindow` in your applications. To get a feel for the common operations and functions available to these two classes, we recommend that you read the Cocoa API documentation for both of them. You'll build several applications throughout this book that use these classes.

Before we look any further at MacRuby, it's important that you learn (or, in some cases, review) a few concepts about Cocoa, Objective-C, and Ruby.

1.2   Cocoa: *What you need to know*

To fully understand and appreciate MacRuby, you'll need to learn a little about Cocoa development. If you're already familiar with Cocoa, feel free to skip this section. Cocoa is the high-level programming API for Mac OS X and is widely considered the best programming environment for writing native Mac applications. As an API, Cocoa provides an elegant way to interact with the operating system and the window manager. Cocoa consists of a powerful set of libraries. Known as *frameworks,* they cover virtually every task imaginable to work with the operating system, and they provide a great set of tools for writing desktop applications.

In this section, we'll first discuss Cocoa's important classes and concepts, and then give you a brief overview of frequently used design patterns.

1.2.1   Important classes and concepts

What makes an application a Cocoa program? Is it the language? The tools you use? The platform it's running on? The answer to all these questions is no. What makes a program a Cocoa program is that all the objects inherit from the root class NSObject and can run on the Objective-C runtime.

The NSObject class is defined in the Foundation framework. In Cocoa programming, the two core frameworks are Foundation and Application Kit (AppKit for short), which provide the core set of libraries that you need to write a Mac application. When you wrote your Hello World script, you may have noticed that both frameworks are required for Mac application development. All other frameworks that you may include in your project can be viewed as optional.

> ### About the NS name prefix
>
> The classes, data types, constants and functions defined in Foundation and AppKit have a name prefix of NS. The NS is a holdover from Steve Jobs' old company, NeXTSTEP, and—you guessed it—it stands for NeXTSTEP. You'll see more of the NS name prefix as you develop in Cocoa and MacRuby.

Let's take a closer look at the Foundation framework.

FOUNDATION FRAMEWORK

The Foundation framework provides a set of classes that act as the support layer for your Cocoa applications. Whether a class is in Foundation or in AppKit is determined by one factor: its role in the user interface. If a class doesn't exclusively interact with the user interface then it's part of Foundation; if it does, it's part of AppKit.

Foundation supports several paradigms that include the following:

- *Object retention and disposal*—Foundation and the runtime provide two ways for Cocoa applications to manage objects: the older style of manual management using retain/release memory references and the newer garbage collection technology. For our purposes, all you need to know is that garbage collection is available in Objective-C 2.0, because MacRuby, at least for now, relies on it to manage memory under the hood.
- *Mutable class variants*—Many of the data-handling classes in Foundation have both an immutable base class and mutable subclasses—these include NSArray,

NSDictionary, NSString, and many more classes. To modify the data after initialization, you need to use a mutable variant. You'll find that MacRuby does this for the classes that underlie its array, hash and string classes.

- *Notifications*—Notifications are used heavily in Cocoa, and we'll discuss the Cocoa view of the design pattern in the next section. In general, notifications provide a broadcast mechanism for inter-object communication in synchronous, asynchronous, and distributed modes.

Foundation is the framework responsible for handling the base value objects in your Cocoa application. These include primitive types, structures, and pointers. Foundation is responsible for collection objects such as arrays and hashes (NSArray, NSDictionary). The framework provides enumerators and, as already mentioned, both mutable and immutable variants.

As a quick overview, Foundation framework also supports these functional areas:

- Operating system services—File system, threading, networking
- Archiving and serialization
- XML processing
- Scripting
- Expressions
- Many more

The other important framework we mentioned was the AppKit framework, which is short for Application Kit. Let's see how this framework can help you with your UI-based Mac applications.

APPLICATION KIT FRAMEWORK

The Mac OS X user interface is an event-driven system, and AppKit provides the classes you need to interact with this event-driven GUI. AppKit provides a large number of UI components; its classes indirectly support the UI components.

AppKit provides the Application object that each Cocoa app will have as a singleton instance for running in the main event loop. AppKit also gives you access to UI objects such as windows, views, menus, cursors, table views, and most anything needed to create a robust user interface.

You're interacting with AppKit when you use MacRuby code to manipulate the UI. You can also interact with AppKit with different tools, such as Xcode and HotCocoa. If you're not familiar with HotCocoa, it's a layer of Ruby mappings on top of Cocoa that allow you to quickly construct interfaces programmatically. We'll introduce HotCocoa in more detail in chapter 9. Some of the other functions that AppKit provides are graphics and color, internationalization, printing, and faxing.

NOTE For a full description of the capabilities of Foundation and AppKit, see Apple's *Cocoa Fundamentals Guide* (http://mng.bz/HT7j).

1.2.2   *How Cocoa implements common design patterns*

Cocoa often applies a design pattern to make use of the language and runtime capabilities that Objective-C provides. According to Apple, Cocoa puts its own distinctive spin on a pattern because its designs are influenced by factors such as language capabilities or existing architectures. Some of Cocoa's variations on common design patterns may differ from their canonical usage or how you're used to seeing them applied. Cocoa relies on three common patterns.

DELEGATION

Delegation is a huge part of Cocoa. In the time that I've (Brendan) been programming with Cocoa, I've used delegation more than I think I ever have in my life. Delegation is a mechanism that's leveraged throughout the API's; if you understand and make use of delegation, it can be a great tool in writing Cocoa applications.

The delegation mechanism relies on two objects, a host and a delegate. The host object delegates a task to the delegate object.

To delegate certain actions/methods, the host object passes the messages it receives to the delegate object. Delegate methods are defined in classes that serve as protocols, which are declared methods that can be implemented by any class.

In Cocoa, you can define a protocol as either *formal* or *informal* when you're defining the interface that an object can delegate to another. A formal protocol requires you to implement the protocol in the delegate. Informal protocols, however, allow you to implement only the methods you want to respond to.

When the host receives a delegate message, it first sends the `respondsToSelector:` message to check with its delegate whether the method has been implemented. If so, the host invokes that method. This check allows the host to avoid exceptions when passing along the message.

> ### Warning: delegate method signatures
>
> When you work with delegates you have to be extremely careful that you're defining the delegate method signatures correctly in your delegate objects. The host won't pass on the message to the delegate if the delegate has a typo or the wrong method name because it will fail the `respondsToSelector:` check. You won't see any errors if this happens, but you should notice that your delegate method is never getting called. If you have trouble with delegates, remember to double-check the method signature!

NOTIFICATIONS

Notifications in Cocoa are a variation on the Observer pattern. Notifications are a one-to-many broadcast mechanism in which objects can add themselves or other objects to a list of observers of notifications. An object can observe many notifications, where each notification is identified using a global string identifier.

To post a notification, an object creates a notification object and sends it to a notification center to be broadcast. To observe a notification, you give the notification center a selector (reference to a specific method) on the object that it's going to be observing. When the notification is received, this selector is then called on the object that is performing the observations. An observer's selector should conform to the notification method signature, which takes one parameter, the NSNotification object itself:

```
- (void) somethingHappened:(NSNotification*):notification {...}
```

It's standard practice for all methods that are given as receivers of notifications to use this parameter.

MODEL-VIEW-CONTROLLER

The world of web development has brought the model-view-controller (MVC) design pattern to the forefront in recent years. If you're a Rubyist (or an aspiring Rubyist), you've likely had some exposure to this pattern via the Ruby on Rails web framework, which makes heavy use of this pattern. Ruby on Rails provides a full MVC architecture right out the box every time you start a new project. The MVC pattern is well defined and easy to recognize in a Rails application—right down to the folder structure, which has separation for models, views, and controllers. In Cocoa applications, the separation between roles and the function of each isn't always as clear-cut.

Ideally, models are responsible for encapsulating data and handling the business logic related to that data. Views are responsible for presenting information to the user and, often, for formatting and styling that presentation. Controllers act as the intermediary between the models and the views, often controlling access and telling views when data in a model changes.

In general, when applying MVC, you should have objects that play each of the three roles distinctly. Cocoa is much more apt than Rails to have objects play dual roles, often either as controller-views or controller-models. Cocoa's tendency to enforce less strict separation in the application and folder structure itself plays a big part in why it tends toward dual roles.

Cocoa makes use of many other design patterns, although the three described here are probably the most common in day-to-day Cocoa programming. You can dig into more information on Cocoa and its design pattern usage in the *Cocoa Fundamentals Guide.*

COCOA WRAP-UP

We touched on enough parts of the Cocoa development framework for you to be familiar with the framework. Both the Apple developer sites and the API documentation provide ample information about Cocoa. To learn more about the framework, we recommend looking there first.

Now that you've been introduced to Cocoa, we'll turn our attention to the two languages MacRuby development depends on—Objective-C and Ruby.

1.3   *Objective-C and Ruby: what you need to know*

MacRuby is interesting in that it's literally a combination of Objective-C and Ruby. The goal of this section is to introduce you to both Ruby and Objective-C. We'll survey each language and show you its syntax. We'll also cover the key parts of each language that you should be aware of when working with MacRuby. Because MacRuby is written in and sits on top of Objective-C, the more you understand Objective-C and how it works the better off you'll be. Likewise, the more you know about standard Ruby, the quicker you'll pick up MacRuby. As you'll soon see, it pays to know a bit about both of these great languages.

1.3.1   A shared heritage

Smalltalk is an object-oriented language that pre-dates Ruby and Objective-C. A *dynamically typed, reflective* programming language, Smalltalk is historically significant because of its influence on languages, such as Objective-C and Ruby. A language is said to be dynamically typed when it does most of its type-checking at runtime rather than during compilation. For instance, in Ruby, you don't need to explicitly specify whether something is an integer or a string. A reflective language allows you to write code that can effectively observe and modify its own behavior.

At a high level, Objective-C and Ruby share a surprising number of features also found in Smalltalk. Both languages provide a dynamic runtime, use message passing, allow runtime access to class and object information, and support metaclasses, to name a few.

Message passing

Message passing is similar to method calling. The main difference is that message passing requires a lookup to make sure the method exists before jumping to it during runtime, whereas message calling calls the method directly without doing a check. Message-passing support is one of the reasons that languages such as Smalltalk, Objective-C, and Ruby are considered dynamic.

If you're familiar with one language and not the other, you'll find that, at a conceptual level, you can solve problems similarly in either Objective-C or Ruby.

One of the most significant similarities between Ruby and Objective-C is the dynamic runtime, which makes it much easier to model Ruby in Objective-C. Sharing a dynamic runtime allows MacRuby to fully support both standard Ruby and Objective-C functionality. You get two for the price of one. Also, the dynamic nature that makes Ruby so flexible is available in MacRuby.

One of the standout features of Objective-C is its dynamic runtime, which still provides the speed advantages of a native compiled language and has access to both C and C++ as needed. The ability to make runtime class modifications and handle message redirection (both of which could be considered advanced programming topics) are also key features of the Ruby language.

If this is new to you, don't worry. As we revisit these concepts throughout the book, you'll understand why and where the dynamic runtime comes into play.

1.3.2 *Objective-C 101*

Objective-C was developed as an extension to the C language. It's object-oriented and is the primary language of Apple's Cocoa API. We'll go over the basics of the language: its syntax, class structure, methods, frameworks, and how to use the documentation. If you're already familiar with Objective-C, feel free to jump to the next section.

BASICS

Unlike Ruby, Objective-C is a compiled language. The IDE of choice is Apple's Xcode, which allows you to create, compile, debug, and package your applications. Xcode 4 comes with Interface Builder built in, which allows you to create user interfaces for your Cocoa applications.

Although it's best to stick with the Xcode development environment, you have other choices. If you're a TextMate fan, you can use a bundle to write Objective-C, but the bundle still needs to utilize Xcode for compilation and packaging. The KDevelop IDE is also an option, but it's not widely adopted.

SYNTAX

The message-passing syntax is the most important Objective-C concept you need to know. Because MacRuby can call all the Objective-C API functions, it's beneficial to know how to call those functions and what the method signatures look like. You'll often have to translate an Objective-C method signature into the appropriate MacRuby equivalent to call the API function you want to use. Let's go over a few operations using Objective-C to get familiar with its syntax. First, create an instance of an array:

```
NSArray *myArray = [NSArray alloc];
[myArray init];
```

What's this code doing? You call a class method, `alloc`, on the `NSArray` class and then assign the result to a pointer of type `NSArray`. In the next line, you call the instance method, `init`, on the resulting `NSArray` object.

The following code shows the same example, but this time, you're using message passing, and you need only one line of code:

```
NSArray *myArray = [[NSArray alloc] init];
```

The important thing to take away from this example is the message-passing syntax. In Objective-C, you can invoke a method on an object using the bracket syntax you just used. To illustrate how the syntax works, consider the following code:

```
[[someObject someMethod] anotherMethod];
```

In this example, `someObject` is the receiver of the message, `someMethod`. The result of this message then becomes the receiver of the message, `anotherMethod`.

You can also pass parameters with a message.

CALLING METHODS

Objective-C uses a *named-parameter* approach, which might seem strange at first if you're not familiar with it. After you get used to it, though, you'll find reading the

Apple developer documentation simple. In Objective-C, the parameters are part of the method name; you don't need to pass in a separate parameter list as you do in many other languages. A parameter is denoted by a colon at the end of its name.

Let's take a typical example of instantiating an `NSTimer` that fires once after a 40-millisecond delay. The following method has five parameters:

```
scheduledTimerWithTimeInterval:target:selector:userInfo:repeats:
```

Yes, that whole line is the name of one single method. The parameters and colons make up the name of the function. It might take a little getting used to, but if you take the time to understand the syntax, you'll quickly amass the Cocoa API documentation, which is a necessary resource for Mac development.

To use the method in an application, it looks like this:

```
[NSTimer scheduledTimerWithTimeInterval:0.40f target:self
 selector:@selector(doSomethingOnTimer) userInfo:nil repeats:NO];
```

You first call a class method on the `NSTimer` class. As you can see, `NSTimer` is the receiver of the method call. You then call the method that we just described, but this time using real parameters:

- `scheduledTimerWithTimeInterval:0.40f` is passed a float value of 0.40.
- `target:self` is passed the value `self`, which lets the method know that the class that's making this method call is the target for the following `selector` parameter.
- `selector:@selector(doSomethingOnTimer` specifies a selector (we'll be going over this in detail next).
- `userInfo:nil` is passed a value of `nil`, which is a null value.
- `repeats:NO` is passed a BOOL (Boolean) value, `NO`.

Let's discuss selectors so that we can further explain that `selector` parameter.

METHOD SELECTORS

Objective-C supports dynamic message-passing using something called a *method selector*. In strict terms, a method selector can be thought of in two ways. First, it's the name of the method as referred to in source code. Second, the method selector is the unique identifier that replaces the method name when you reference the method. Simply put, selectors allow you to dynamically denote method names and identifiers. Objective-C uses a specific data type, `SEL`, to represent the unique selector ID. You can use a selector to invoke an `SEL` method on an object. This technique supports the target-action design pattern used heavily in Cocoa development. You'll learn more about target-action in chapter 2.

In code, you can refer to a compiled selector using the `@selector()` directive. The most common use for this is when you invoke a method that expects a callback method as a parameter. To specify which method should be invoked, you use the `@selector` reference.

Look again at the method signature for the `NSTimer` example, and examine the `selector` parameter:

```
[NSTimer scheduledTimerWithTimeInterval:0.40f target:self
  selector:@selector(doSomethingOnTimer) userInfo:nil repeats:NO];
```

You pass the `@selector` directive a method name; in this case, it's doSomethingOn-Timer. When the timer hits its time threshold, it's going to call that method.

Remember the second parameter, `target`? You pass in `self`, which means that the object from which you call this function is the target for the doSomethingOnTimer selector. You define the doSomethingOnTimer method in the same class from which you call the NSTimer method because you're passing the class as the target for the selector. The combination of the `target:` and `selector:` parameters is the equivalent of having the timer run this line of code:

```
[self doSomethingOnTimer];
```

Selectors are a powerful feature when implementing dynamic functionality in your applications. They also map well to the Ruby dynamic evaluation techniques, such as send(), eval(), class_eval(), instance_eval(), and so on.

The importance of colon placement

When working with selectors, be aware of a common error. Consider the following two `@selector` directives:

```
@selector(someMethod)
@selector(someMethod:)
```

Notice the difference? The second has a trailing colon, which is a critical distinction. A selector with no trailing colon indicates a method with no parameters, whereas a selector with a trailing colon indicates a method with one parameter.

Be aware of this difference because it's all too easy to forget or to mistakenly add an extra colon to your selector, which causes errors and potential bugs.

CLASSES

Creating classes in Objective-C requires two files. One file acts as the interface and the other acts as the implementation. The interface file, typically saved with a .h extension, is where you define your instance variables and your public methods. The implementation file, saved with a .m extension, is where you implement the code for methods defined in the interface as well as any private methods you want to include.

Let's create interface and implementation files for a class called Book. First, let's examine the interface file, Cocoa.h:

```
#import <Cocoa/Cocoa.h>

@interface Book : NSObject {
  NSString *title;
  NSString *authors;
}
```

```
- (NSString *) title;
- (NSString *) authors;

@end
```

You first import the Cocoa framework to pull in the resources you need for a Cocoa application. On the next line, you can see that you call this class `Book` and that it's a subclass of the `NSObject` class. Inside the curly braces, you define two instance variables, which are of class `NSString`. The next two lines outside the curly braces are getter methods for the instance variables, `title`, and `authors`. Notice how `NSString` is inside parentheses on these two lines? That's the return type for that specific method. Also, in Objective-C, it's conventional to leave out the `get` prefix for getter methods.

The following code is the implementation file, Book.m:

```
#import "Book.h"

@implementation Book

- (NSString *) title {
  return [NSString stringWithString:@"MacRuby in Action"];
}

- (NSString *) authors {
  return [NSString stringWithString:@"Brendan G. Lim & Paul Crawford"];
}

@end
```

In the implementation of the `Book` class, you first import the interface file you created. You then declare the implementation and specify the class name, `Book`. The next lines are custom getters for the instance variables, implemented in a simple fashion. You return a new `NSString` for each method.

Dealing with garbage collection and memory management

If you've developed iOS or Cocoa applications before, you've probably had to worry about releasing memory that was allocated for certain objects in your application. Manual memory management can certainly be a big barrier to entry for those who are new to iOS development. Not many people like having to make sure they're properly freeing up memory; they expect this to be automated for them. Luckily for us, MacRuby uses the Objective-C garbage collection engine, which has been available since Objective-C 2.0. With garbage collection, you don't need to worry about manually releasing objects created throughout your application.

Let's move on to frameworks, which play a large part in Objective-C development.

FRAMEWORKS

Frameworks are collections of classes that provide a set of functionality. *Frameworks* is the term Cocoa uses for libraries. Apple provides many different frameworks, and you

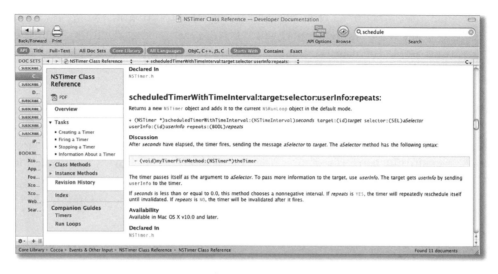

Figure 1.3 Documentation for the `NSTimer` class

can make use of Objective-C frameworks directly in MacRuby using the framework directive, which we'll explain in chapter 2. Frameworks provide an efficient code-organization mechanism for separation of disparate functionality. Some of the most common frameworks include Foundation, AppKit, and CoreGraphics. As you make use of different OS X capabilities in your applications, the variety of frameworks that Apple provides will come in handy.

APPLE DEVELOPER DOCUMENTATION

The Apple developer documentation is a great tool for learning about the methods available on any of the Cocoa classes. Figure 1.3 shows the documentation for the method you used on the `NSTimer` class in the previous examples.

In figure 1.3, the documentation lists the five parameters for this method, and indicates their data types in the description. To access other API documentation, start up Xcode and choose Help > Documentation. Use the search bar to search for common classes. We recommend looking at something like `NSString` or `NSArray` to see how Objective-C defines common-operation functions for strings and arrays.

OBJECTIVE-C WRAP-UP

We've only scratched the surface of Objective-C development, but you've learned enough to understand the Objective-C code examples throughout the book. Because MacRuby's usefulness is heavily reliant on the Cocoa API, it's important to be able to read Objective-C code, especially when diving through the developer documentation. Now, let's turn to the Ruby language.

1.3.3 *Ruby 101*

Because MacRuby's syntax is much like Ruby, it's important that you spend a little time understanding it. More than likely, you're already experienced with the Ruby language and can feel free to skip this section. If you're not, it's important to continue learning about Ruby because you'll be using it to write MacRuby. Ruby is a concise and simple language. Let's take a look at a few operations in code so you can see what we mean.

BASICS

Ruby classes are defined in a single class file ending with a .rb extension; in fact all Ruby source files end in a .rb extension. Typically, to run a Ruby script, you use the Ruby executable (`ruby`) to run the script. Ruby, like many programming languages, doesn't require much in terms of tools. You can use any text editor to write and edit Ruby source files. At the least, we recommend using a text editor that supports syntax highlighting for Ruby (which will work for most MacRuby syntax as well). When you're working with MacRuby, you always have the option of using Xcode.

OBJECTS

Ruby is all about objects. Everything in Ruby is an object, and we mean everything! Other languages use simple data types that aren't first-class objects. For example, a number literal might be a data type of `integer`, but it isn't, in fact, an object of class `Integer`.

In Ruby, when you type `1`, you have an object of class `Fixnum`, and you can call methods directly on what looks like a literal. Let's try this out in Irb.

Open Irb (or if you prefer, use Macirb, which we'll explore in chapter 2), and type the code as shown in the following listing.

Listing 1.2 Inspecting Ruby classes and methods

```
>> 1.class
=> Fixnum
>> 1.methods
=> ["%", "odd?", "inspect", "prec_i", "to_yaml",
"taguri", "<<", "tap", "div", "", "po", "clone", ">>",
"public_methods", "object_id", "__send__", "taguri=",
"denominator", "instance_variable_defined?", "equal?"...
```

To get a feel for Ruby, try out a few more things in Irb right now. Use the method, `methods`, to see what methods are available on an object; use the method, `class`, to see what the class of an object is. Explore a little, and call some methods on the string `"Ruby"` to see what you get.

CALLING METHODS

Ruby is a flexible language. So what, right? Many programming languages are flexible. What makes Ruby stand out is that the language provides more than one way to do something, even important things like calling methods. When you're reading someone else's Ruby code, it's helpful to know that Ruby provides various ways to accomplish common tasks. Consider the most common operation you can do in Ruby: calling methods. There are a few ways you can do this.

Suppose you have a string, and you want to reverse the characters in it. You can use the `String#reverse` method to accomplish this. In message-passing terms, the string `racecar` is the *receiver* and the method `reverse` is the *message*. All three of these statements are equivalent:

```
"racecar".reverse()
"racecar".reverse
"racecar".send(:reverse)
```

The second option is the most typically used way to call methods. In Ruby, parentheses are optional on method calls, and, often, you need to use them only to help with readability when you make nested method calls. The third option uses one of Ruby's metaprogramming features, the `send` method, which allows you to specify a string or symbol that will be treated as a method name.

Ruby uses a dot notation for method calls that looks like this: `receiver.message`. If you don't use the dot notation, then it's implied by Ruby that the receiver for that message will be `self`, the current object.

Determining what `self` is in any given context can be confusing, although the most common cases are either the class or instance context for a given object. If you're working in a class definition, you'll likely be dealing with `self` either when `self` is the class or when `self` is an instance of the class. This example calls the kernel method `puts` to output a string to `stdout`:

```
puts "Hello World!"
```

You can call many kernel methods without an explicit receiver. They're made available to every Ruby object. The most common kernel methods are used for raising exceptions, requiring other Ruby source files, and accessing metaprogramming functionality, such as creating anonymous functions. See the Ruby documentation for kernel to get an idea of what's available.

CLASSES

Ruby classes are simple to define. They don't require a lot of boilerplate code, and with shortcut methods, it's easy to create getter and setter methods for attributes. A class is defined by the kernel method `class`, which behaves like a keyword in other languages and takes a Ruby *block* that defines the class functionality (we'll discuss blocks shortly).

Let's create a Ruby class file that creates the class `Book` and gives it some attributes and methods:

```
class Book
  attr_accessor :title, :price

  def initialize(title, price)
    @title = title
    @price = price
  end

  def increase_price(amount)
```

```
    @price += amount
  end
end
```

After you define the class Book, you call the method attr_accessor, which sets up the instance variables title and price. The result is that you have getter and setter behavior on Book instances for those two attributes and a local variable for each in the Book class. You can take an instance of Book and call book.title or book.title = "foo" without having to define the getter and setter methods yourself.

In Ruby, the new method is used to create a new instance of an object, and it's the standard constructor for Ruby objects. When you define a Ruby class, you don't implement a new method; instead, you implement the initialize method. This is the method used to initialize the instance of the object. Here you implement an initialize method that sets the title and price of the Book variables to the values that are passed in.

Methods are defined using def, which is given the method name, a parameter list, and a block that defines the functionality of the method. In this case, you define the method increase_price with the parameter amount. This is an instance method available to instances of the Book class.

Let's see what you can do with this Book class. If you instantiate a new Book without passing any parameters to new, you get the following error:

```
>> book = Book.new
ArgumentError: wrong number of arguments (0 for 2)
from (irb):15:in 'initialize'
from (irb):15:in 'new'
from (irb):15
```

When you initialize a new Book, you need to pass in the title and price parameters:

```
>> book = Book.new("MacRuby in Action", 10.00)
=> #<Book:0x1077514 @price=10.0, @title="MacRuby in Action">
```

You now have an instance of Book, let's try out the accessors:

```
>> book.title
=> "MacRuby in Action"
>> book.price
=> 10.0
>> book.title = "Foo"
=> "Foo"
>> book.title
=> "Foo"
```

You can now access and modify the values of the Book's attributes using the accessor methods. What about the increase_price method?

```
>> book.increase_price(5.00)
=> 15.0
>> book.increase_price(5)
=> 20.0
```

To add amounts to the price, you can use float or integer values.

RUBY WRAP-UP

We've introduced you to a good bit of Ruby basics. You'll learn more Ruby code and concepts as we work our way through the key concepts of MacRuby and Cocoa programming. Take advantage of the plethora of Ruby resources out there because a solid understanding of Ruby will help you write MacRuby applications.

We've covered the basics of Objective-C and Ruby—the two languages that, together, make up MacRuby. At this point, you can read Objective-C method signatures, and you understand Ruby syntax. Next, we'll move on to MacRuby itself.

1.4 Diving into MacRuby

You're already familiar with MacRuby's foundation, so we can jump into the language itself. In this section, we'll first show you how classes are represented, and then move onto method signatures. You'll also learn how to create user interfaces and experiment with calling Ruby and Objective-C methods from MacRuby.

1.4.1 Class structure

Each MacRuby object is implemented directly on top of its Objective-C equivalent. For instance, suppose you want to create a string. Ruby has the class `String` and Objective-C has the class `NSString`. In MacRuby, when you create a Ruby `String`, you're also creating an Objective-C `NSString`. What's great is that the `String`/`NSString` has access to the methods from *both* classes. Suppose the content of your Ruby `String` is the all-lowercase phrase `i am short`. To modify the phrase to all uppercase, you can use either a Ruby or Objective-C method. Both approaches shown in table 1.1 produce the same result: `I AM SHORT`.

Table 1.1 Both Ruby and Objective-C have a method for capitalizing the letters in a string.

Ruby	Objective-C
`"i am short".upcase`	`"i am short".uppercaseString`

This behavior is true for all MacRuby classes. In fact, if you do a little digging into the classes, you'll see that each MacRuby class inherits from an Objective-C class as well as the Cocoa base class `NSObject`. An example using Macirb illustrates how you can display the ancestors of the MacRuby `String` class:

```
>> "i am short".class
String
>> "i am short".class.ancestors
[String, NSMutableString, NSString, Comparable, NSObject, Kernel]
```

Because of this inheritance, you can use the existing Cocoa and Objective-C APIs with MacRuby. If you have a Ruby background, you can take advantage of your favorite features of Ruby and vice versa for Objective-C. The approach that Apple has taken in this implementation gives you a great deal of flexibility when working with MacRuby. For instance, you can use both Ruby and Objective-C libraries in your MacRuby project, which gives you double the amount of resources.

Let's look again at the Objective-C Class structure. Remember the class hierarchy you saw previously (see figure 1.1)? Table 1.2 shows a slightly modified version that includes the MacRuby classes.

Table 1.2   MacRuby classes and the equivalent Objective-C classes

MacRuby class	Objective-C class
String	NSMutableString
Number	NSNumber
Array	NSMutableArray
Hash	NSMutableDictionary
Object	NSObject

To illustrate the underlying implementation of the MacRuby classes, let's look at an example:

```
>> o = Object.new
=> #<NSObject:0x800818420>
>> o.class
=> NSObject
```

In the first line, you create a new `Object`. To find out what class it is, you call the `class` method on the `Object` instance, and you can see that it returns back `NSObject`. (Remember, every object in MacRuby inherits from `NSObject`.) You could do the same thing with any of the other MacRuby classes shown in table 1.2 to see their respective Objective-C class. Figure 1.4 shows how everything in MacRuby is inherited from `NSObject`.

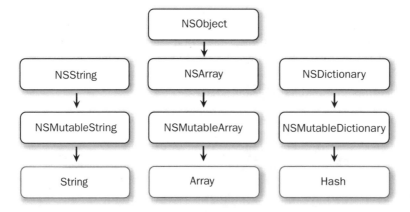

Figure 1.4   In the MacRuby class hierarchy, everything is inherited from NSObject.

Now that you have an overview of the MacRuby class structure, we can show you some real MacRuby code. We'll start by going over the syntax and method signatures.

1.4.2 *Creating MacRuby classes*

In MacRuby, everything is an object, and classes define all objects. Creating your own classes in MacRuby is as simple as creating classes in Ruby. Unlike Objective-C, you don't need a separate interface. Let's create a MacRuby class. Open a text editor and enter the following class definition:

```
class Book
end
```

You define a class with the `class` keyword and end it with the `end` keyword. By convention, you'll name this file book.rb. The class has no instance methods and is as basic as can be. By default, the `Book` class is a subclass of `NSObject`. If you want it to be a subclass of a different class, you define it as shown:

```
class Book < OtherObject
end
```

You declare `Book` a subclass of a fictional class named `OtherObject`, which gives the `Book` class access to all its functionality.

Let's remove this subclass declaration and instantiate the `Book` class in the book.rb file. To customize instantiation of the class, you'll define an `initialize` method. In the following code, you initialize the `Book` class outside the class declaration:

```
class Book
  def initialize
    puts "Hello, I'm a book"
  end
end

  Book.new
```

From the terminal, run book.rb to see if the `Book` class gets properly initialized when you call `Book.new`:

```
$ macruby book.rb
Hello, I'm a book
$
```

As you can see, the `Book` class was properly instantiated, and the custom `initialize` method ran, printing out `Hello, I'm a book`.

You probably noticed that you initialized the class the same way you did in Ruby, by using the `.new` function. MacRuby classes should be instantiated this way, whereas Objective-C/Cocoa classes should be instantiated using `alloc.init`. Instead of using `NSString.new`, always use `NSString.alloc.init`. Both functions will work, but using `alloc.init` is how Objective-C classes are expected to be initialized.

Now that you have an understanding of how to create MacRuby classes, let's look further into its syntax and method signatures.

1.4.3   *Syntax and method signatures*

MacRuby syntax is Ruby 1.9 syntax. If you know Ruby, you'll find MacRuby familiar. If you're not that familiar, don't worry—MacRuby looks just like the code you saw in the Ruby introduction (see section 1.3.3) because it's Ruby that you're writing.

You can use both the Ruby and Objective-C methods on a given MacRuby object. Although this ability gives you a good deal of flexibility, you must be aware of the coding styles in Ruby and Objective-C.

Method names in Ruby use snake-case letters (`to_s`), whereas Objective-C method names use camel-case letters (`stringWithFormat:`). When writing MacRuby code, you'll see a mix of camel case and snake case in the code. Throughout this book, you'll use snake case in your custom method names because you're writing Ruby 1.9. When writing Objective-C methods in MacRuby, though, you must use camel case to match the original method signature.

Calling Objective-C methods in Ruby can sometime feel unnatural and verbose because Objective-C uses a parameter/method name approach. The best way to get a grasp of this naming convention is to practice with a few examples. Consider an Objective-C method, such as the following:

```
[NSTimer scheduledTimerWithTimeInterval:0.40f target:self
➥ selector:@selector(doSomethingOnTimer) userInfo:nil repeats:NO];
```

Now let's call this same method in MacRuby. After all, you have access to all the Cocoa methods in MacRuby, right?

```
NSTimer.scheduledTimerWithTimeInterval(0.40, target:self,
➥ selector:"doSomethingOnTimer".to_sym, userInfo:nil,repeats:true)
```

You may have noticed the absence of brackets in MacRuby and the use of dot notation. Pay attention to how you pass in the arguments to this method. You can see that the named parameters in the original Objective-C method are treated like hash keys in MacRuby. This syntax, in which you use colon syntax to create a hash, is new in Ruby 1.9

Ordered and unordered hashes/sets

In previous versions of Ruby, a hash is unordered. This means that you can't count on your hash returning its objects in the order in which they were added.

In Ruby 1.9, a hash has an order attached to its behavior. For example, if you add items A, C and B to a hash in that order, they'll remain in that order when you retrieve the keys from that hash.

MacRuby is built on top of Ruby 1.9, but in MacRuby, hashes are *unordered*. MacRuby hashes are implemented on top of the Objective-C class `NSMutableDictionary`, which doesn't support ordered sets. This is something to pay attention to if you're porting code from a standard Ruby 1.9 script or class to MacRuby.

as opposed to the old way of using hash rockets (=>). Note also that when you pass arguments to an Objective-C method, you must preserve the order of the arguments.

In Ruby 1.9, hash keys are symbols, so the old way of creating a hash is still valid. The following example shows how to create a hash using the older hash rocket syntax that many people are familiar with:

```
h = {:a => 1, :b => 2, :c => 3}
```

To get the same result in Ruby 1.9, use the new colon syntax as shown:

```
h = {a:1, b:2, c:3}
```

Let's refactor the NSTimer example using the traditional hash syntax:

```
NSTimer.scheduledTimerWithTimeInterval(0.40, :target => self,
➡ :selector => "doSomethingOnTimer".to_sym, :userInfo => nil,
➡ :repeats => true)
```

Either syntax is valid. Deciding which of the two you prefer is a matter of personal preference.

Method names and parameters in MacRuby

Parameter names can affect the method names in MacRuby. When you're using hash-based named parameters to call Objective-C methods, *all* the parameter names must match the Objective-C method signature. This can be a tricky-to-catch issue because a typo in one of the parameter names can make it appear as though the method you're calling doesn't exist on the object you're calling. The following Objective-C Class method invocation includes an incorrect parameter name:

```
NSTimer.scheduledTimerWithTimeInterval(0.40, :target => self, :selector =>
➡ "doSomethingOnTimer".to_sym, :userInfo => nil, :repeat => true)
```

Can you see the error? The :repeats parameter is missing the s. Calling this produces the following error:

```
NoMethodError: undefined method
"scheduledTimerWithTimeInterval:target:selector:userInfo:repeat:"
for NSTimer:Class
```

That one missing character is considered a name error because of the way Objective-C methods handle parameters.

You've seen how to transform an Objective-C method to the appropriate syntax for MacRuby, but what about method passing? In section 1.3.2, we showed you how to create a new NSArray using the alloc and init methods. As a refresher, here's that code:

```
NSArray *myArray = [[NSArray alloc] init];
```

In MacRuby, the equivalent code looks like the following:

```
my_array = NSArray.alloc.init
```

Instead of chaining with brackets, you use the Ruby dot-syntax. Also, as a matter of personal preference, you changed `myArray` to `my_array`, but either syntax is correct in MacRuby.

Suppose you want to turn the following Objective-C example, which combines message passing with named parameters, into MacRuby code:

```
[@"Paul" stringByReplacingOccurrencesOfString:@"Paul"
➥ withString:@"Brendan"];
```

Here's the equivalent MacRuby code:

```
"Paul".stringByReplacingOccurrencesOfString("Paul", withString:"Brendan")
```

In MacRuby, the first parameter isn't named. Every following parameter is expected to be named using the `withString` parameter, as shown in the example.

Now that you have an understanding of MacRuby syntax and how to convert Objective-C methods, let's take a look at how MacRuby gives you a choice of which methods you can use.

1.4.4   *Using Ruby and Objective-C methods*

MacRuby is unique in that it's so transparent in exposing its underlying implementation. When you create a new MacRuby string, you can easily see both the Ruby and Objective-C methods available to that `String` object. Standard Ruby provides the `methods` function, which lists the methods on an object.

The version of `methods` that MacRuby provides has two optional parameters: the first defaults to `true`, and the second defaults to `false`. If you call `methods` with both parameters set to `true`, it returns not only the Ruby methods, but also the underlying Objective-C methods available on an object.

The following code lists the Ruby methods available to a MacRuby `String` object:

```
>> "Hello".methods
=> [:to_yaml, :is_binary_data?, :is_complex_yaml?, :taguri, :taguri=, :to_c,
   :to_:ascii_only?, :valid_encoding?, :force_encoding, :encoding,
   :rpartition, :partition, :delete!, :tr_s!, :tr!, :count, :squeeze,
   :delete, :tr_s, :tr, :rstrip!, :lstrip!, :chop, :gsub, :sub, :center,
   :rjust, :ljust, :scan, :end_with?, :start_with?, :include?, :reverse,
   :chars...
```

What happens if you set the second parameter of the `methods` function to `true`? Run a count and examine the length of the array that's returned. Changing the parameter value returns more methods:

```
>> "Hello".methods(true, false).length
=> 160
>> "Hello".methods(true, true).length
=> 584
```

The first line returns the number of methods available to the `String` object. The second returns the number of methods available to the `String` object *and* includes the

Objective-C/Cocoa methods from `NSString`. You'll see that there are quite a few Cocoa `NSString` methods!

One of the best things about MacRuby is that you get to choose if you want to use Ruby or Objective-C/Cocoa methods. If you'd rather use one over the other, nothing stops you from doing so. It's a matter of personal preference and what will get the job done. This example uses the Ruby method `capitalize` and the Cocoa `NSString` method `capitalizedString`:

```
>> "small string".capitalize
=> "Small String"
>> "small string".capitalizedString
=> "Small String"
```

Both methods accomplish the same thing: capitalize the first letter in each word. You can also use both Ruby and Objective-C methods on the same line:

```
>> "small string".gsub(/sma/, "ta").capitalizedString
=> "Tall String"
```

You call the Ruby `string` method `gsub`, and then chain it with the Objective-C `NSString` method `capitalizedString`. You have the freedom to mix and match these methods as you like.

Most people are drawn to MacRuby because they want to develop Mac applications with great user interfaces. Let's learn about the options for UI development.

1.4.5 *Creating user interfaces*

Writing command-line tools is fun, but one of the biggest benefits of MacRuby is the ability to use the Cocoa framework to develop applications that have nice user interfaces.

PROGRAMMATICALLY WITH NO TOOLS

One way to create user interfaces is to code them without any external tools or libraries. Not many people will find this option appealing, mainly because of the verbose and complicated syntax required. Let's quickly examine the MacRuby code required to create a graphical window, known as an `NSWindow`:

```
win = NSWindow.alloc.initWithContentRect([300,500,400,200],
  styleMask:NSTitledWindowMask | NSClosableWindowMask
  | NSMiniaturizableWindowMask | NSResizableWindowMask,
  backing: NSBackingStoreBuffered, defer:false)
```

This code creates a window that's 400x200 pixels in size and positions the window 300 pixels to the right and 500 pixels from the bottom of the *origin*. The origin is at the top-left of your screen. To create the interface elements, you write similar code that specifies exact positioning, size, and any other options.

Another way to create user interfaces is to use HotCocoa.

HOTCOCOA

With HotCocoa, you can still programmatically create user interfaces, but you can do the same in much fewer lines of code. HotCocoa provides a set of mappings that wrap the standard Objective-C Cocoa API in a more Ruby-friendly and easy-to-configure set of methods. HotCocoa is available as a Macgem and can be installed by running the following from your terminal:

```
sudo macgem install hotcocoa
```

You'll learn HotCocoa in-depth in chapter 9. For now, let's see what it would take to create the same window in the previous MacRuby example:

```
win = window :frame => [300,500,400,200]
```

Much easier, isn't it? Now, let's take a look at one more option for user interface development: Interface Builder.

XCODE INTERFACE BUILDER

Interface Builder has long been the interface tool of choice for Cocoa development. Interface Builder, previously a separate application, is now built in to Xcode 4, which allows you to work on your code and interfaces all in the same IDE.

Interfaces are created in .xib files. To create a window, you find an NSWindow from the library. NSWindow contains a set of interface elements that you can use. Then you drag the window over to your Interface Builder workspace and resize it to the correct proportions. We'll explore how to create advanced interfaces in chapter 3. For now, we'll show you how to use Xcode to build an interface for the second iteration of your Hello World application.

1.5   *Hello World, part 2*

You've already seen the not-so-quick-and-dirty way to create a Hello World application using a MacRuby script. If you build applications with more complex user interfaces, you don't want to have to do it with straight MacRuby code alone.

In this section, you'll create a more complex application using Apple's Xcode IDE. You could use HotCocoa, but we'll be going more in-depth into that in chapter 9 to build something much better than a simple Hello World application. Throughout this book, you'll use Xcode to construct your Cocoa applications, so it's important for you to get a good feel for it from the start.

When you write Cocoa applications, you spend most of your time in Xcode (Interface Builder has been integrated into Xcode), which is our development environment of choice for writing MacRuby Cocoa applications. With Xcode, you can edit and view source code, build and compile applications, and test using the built-in graphical debugging interface. It's a robust IDE that we'll use throughout this book to create MacRuby Cocoa applications.

You can also use Xcode to create user interfaces for your Cocoa applications. The files that are associated with Xcode Interface Builder often have the extension of .xib or .nib. You don't always need to use Xcode to create UI elements, but you'll see that it's much easier than programmatically creating your views.

Figure 1.5   The finished Hello World application that you'll create using Xcode

Let's get started. When you're finished, you'll have a one-window application like the one shown in figure 1.5.

The first step is to create a project file.

1.5.1   Creating an Xcode project

After you fire up Xcode, choose File > New Project to create a new application. Depending on which version of Xcode you're using and which SDKs you have installed, the window that appears may look different than what is shown in figure 1.6. What you're looking for is the Application option under the Mac OS X templates. After you've located this, find and click the MacRuby Application template and then click Next.

You'll be prompted to name the project, select an App Store category, and specify whether it's a Core Data application. For now, name the project Hello World.

After the application is created, one of the files that has been created for you is MainMenu.xib. Double-click this file to launch Interface Builder within Xcode. You

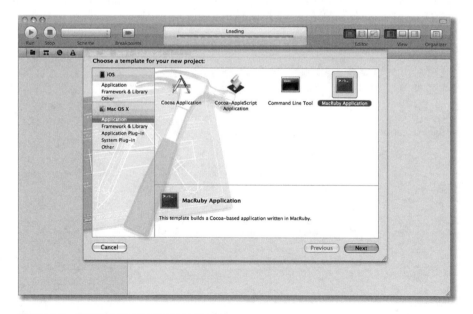

Figure 1.6   Starting a new project in Xcode

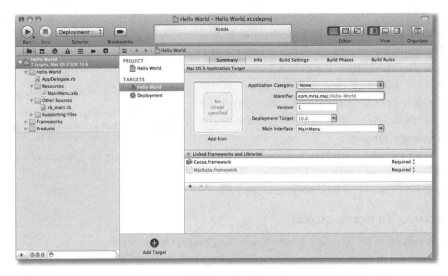

Figure 1.7 A new project in Xcode. Double-clicking MainMenu.xib launches Interface Builder.

can see in figure 1.7 that the template created quite a few files for you. We'll be diving deeper into some of these files later in chapter 3.

Next, let's focus on building the interface.

1.5.2 Creating the interface

Click on MainMenu.xib to edit the interface in Xcode. You should see something that looks similar to figure 1.8.

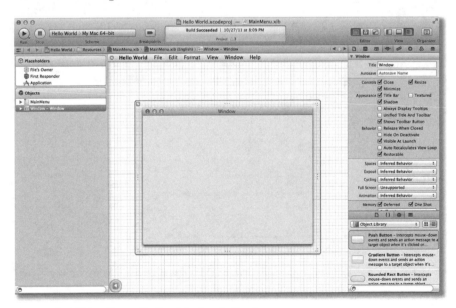

Figure 1.8 Editing the application interface in Xcode

You'll need to get acquainted with several utilities and windows, but we won't go into much detail about them yet. You'll learn more about them in later chapters.

You may have noticed in figure 1.8 that the project navigator doesn't appear at the left of the window and a new pane appears at the right of the window. We hid the navigator and chose to display the utility area using the View options at the top-right of the window (see figure 1.9).

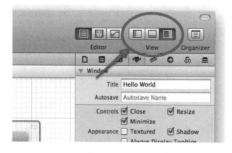

Figure 1.9   To hide/show panes, click items in the View selector.

Let's go over the tools shown in figure 1.8.

- *Library pane*

  The Library pane, which is at the lower-right of the document window in the utility area, lists the available UI elements that you can add to your view. To add any of these elements to your view, drag them into place.

- *Inspector pane*

  The Inspector pane, which is at the top-right of the document window, lets you modify objects. Use the Inspector selector bar to modify attributes, effects, size, bindings, connections, and the identity of the currently selected object.

TIP   If you happen to close either of these tools, choose View > Utilities to re-open them.

- *Dock*

  The other tool to pay attention to is the dock at the left of the document window. This shows the Interface Builder objects in your interface and displays them in either an icon or outline (hierarchical tree) view. Use the outline view to add new objects to your interface.

Because you're building a simple user interface, it isn't much trouble to create it first. Double-click the window object in the document window and resize it. Make it smaller by dragging the bottom-right corner and let go when it's small enough. The window should be just big enough to fit a button and a label that will display a small amount of text.

From the Object library (in the utility area), search for a push button object. After you've located it, drag it to the bottom of the window. Click the button then bring up the Attributes tab in the Inspector pane. From the Attributes tab, change the title from its default `Button` to `Good-bye`.

From the Object library, find a label object and drag it to the window. Place it slightly above the button. From the Attributes tab, change the title of the label to `Hello World`. Set the text to be center-aligned.

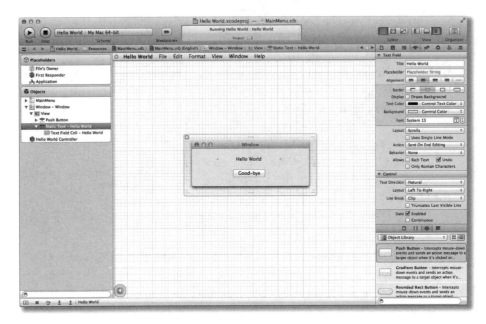

Figure 1.10   The finished Hello World interface

This will do for the Hello World interface (see figure 1.10).

Now that the interface is in place, you can start working on the controller.

1.5.3   *Creating the controller*

Right-click the Hello World group (it looks like a folder), and choose Add > New File. Choose Ruby File and name the new file HelloWorldController.rb.

To be able to connect pieces of your interface to your code you'll need to create an IB (Interface Builder) outlet. To create outlets in the controller for the label and button, you'll use the `attr_accessor` method. Outlets can be interacted with in Interface Builder, which also sets up instance variables for these objects so that you can access them from the controller.

While you're at it, let's also create a class instance variable named `hello`. This instance variable serves as a Boolean that checks the current state of the application. Your code should look similar to the following:

```
class HelloWorldController
  attr_accessor :hello_label, :hello_button, :hello
end
```

Next, you'll add a protocol method named `awakeFromNib`, which sets the default value of the `hello` instance variable to `true`. This function is called when the controller is initialized from the user interface. You set the default to `true` because this value determines which text to display on the label and button.

```
def awakeFromNib
  @hello = true
end
```

The last piece of code you need to add to the controller is a method that the push button calls. This type of method is commonly referred to as an action, or an IB (Interface Builder) action. These actions always take one parameter named sender. The sender parameter is an instance of the object that called the specific method. In this case, the sender is the button. Without this sender parameter, Interface Builder won't recognize this method as an action, and you won't be able to connect it to the button. If your action isn't listed in Interface Builder, it's always wise to check if you're missing the sender parameter.

The changeLabel method does the following:

- If the hello instance variable is true, it updates the label text to Good-bye and changes the title of the button to Hello.
- If the hello instance variable is false, it does the opposite, and updates the label text to Hello World and changes the title of the button to Good-bye.
- In each case, you also make sure to change the value of the hello instance variable to reflect the state of the application.

Here's the code :

```
def changeLabel(sender)
  if @hello
    @hello_label.stringValue = "Good-bye"
    @hello_button.title = "Hello"
    @hello = false
  else
    @hello_label.stringValue = "Hello World"
    @hello_button.title = "Good-bye"
    @hello = true
  end
end
```

The completed controller code is shown in the following listing.

Listing 1.3   HelloWorldController.rb

```
class HelloWorldController
  attr_accessor :hello_label, :hello_button, :hello

  def awakeFromNib
    @hello = true
  end

  def changeLabel(sender)
    if @hello
      @hello_label.stringValue = "Good-bye"
      @hello_button.title = "Hello"
      @hello = false
```

```
      else
        @hello_label.stringValue = "Hello World"
        @hello_button.title = "Good-bye"
        @hello = true
      end
    end
end
```

Next, you'll connect the outlets and actions in Interface Builder.

1.5.4   *Connecting the interface and controller*

From the Object library, look for an NSObject, which is represented as an object in the library. Drag it to the bottom of the document window. You'll use this NSObject to represent the HelloWorldController. (In case you forgot, you're using an NSObject because everything in MacRuby is a subclass of an NSObject.)

With the NSObject selected, open the Inspector pane to update the class identity of the NSObject. Click the third tab at the top-right of the Inspector pane (see figure 1.11), type HelloWorldController in the Class field, and then press Enter.

Next, from the Inspector pane, click the tab with the arrow icon (third tab from the right). This tab lists the outlets and actions that you have access to from the controller. If you don't see anything listed, make sure you typed the correct name of the class. Next to each outlet and action is a circle/dot icon that connects each item to an interface element. Use the icon to connect outlets and actions to the interface.

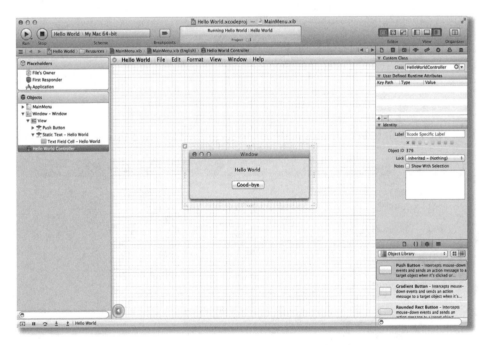

Figure 1.11   Adding HelloWorldController as an NSObject to the interface

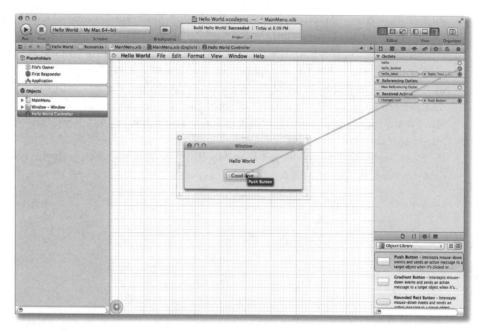

Figure 1.12 Creating a connection between the `hello_button` outlet and the push button

To connect the `hello_button` outlet to the button, click the circle/dot and then drag the line over to the button. Do the same for the `hello_label` outlet, but drag the connection directly to the label that you created. Last, drag the `change_label` action to the push button. This tells the button to execute this action when it's clicked (see figure 1.12). Without this connection, the button won't execute any code when it's clicked.

Save the interface, and then open the project navigator pane (use the View selector as shown in figure 1.9). You can now run the application!

From Xcode, click Run at the top-left of the window (the Play icon). If you set everything up correctly, you should be presented with the Hello World label and a button that displays Good-bye. Click Good-bye, and the label text changes to Good-bye and the button displays Hello.

Congratulations! You've just created Hello World using Xcode. That wasn't too bad, was it? This application may have seemed more tedious to create in Xcode compared to your self-contained MacRuby Hello World script, but if you write more complex MacRuby Cocoa applications, having tools like Xcode and Interface Builder will make things exponentially easier in the long run.

1.6   Summary

You now have a basic understanding of MacRuby and know more than enough to be dangerous in the language. You've also learned Ruby and Objective-C concepts and how to combine the best of both languages in MacRuby. This material will help you further understand MacRuby application development. You've even created your first MacRuby script, and dived right into Xcode to create your first application.

With MacRuby, you have the power to do practically anything you want on the Mac platform. You can write Cocoa applications as if you were writing in Objective-C, but with the ease and simplicity of Ruby's syntax. As we get further into the book, we'll dive deeper into MacRuby and go beyond the core concepts of the language. You'll also create more applications, which will give you a better understanding of the language and the tools involved.

Next, we'll drill down deeper into MacRuby basics and work with the other tools that you have at your disposal.

Using Macirb and the
Apple development tools

2

This chapter covers

- Loading external libraries
- Getting to know the MacRuby console
- Building a Pomodoro application

It'd be a shame if you couldn't use the many well-written Objective-C and Ruby libraries when writing MacRuby applications. In this chapter, you'll discover how to leverage these libraries to instantly add functionality to your applications. You have access not only to popular frameworks such as Cocoa but also to many Ruby libraries, which are known as *gems*. You'll learn how to load and take advantage of the Cocoa frameworks and MacRuby-compatible gems.

You'll also learn some ins and outs of using the MacRuby console, Macirb. Built on top of the Ruby console, Irb, Macirb allows you to experiment with any code you write, take advantage of the quick feedback of Ruby's console, and try out any of the more complicated API calls that you'll encounter along the way. With Macirb, you can experiment in a much simpler context than what you often find when doing the same in a full application.

Finally, you'll create your first useful MacRuby application using Xcode and Interface Builder. By the end of this chapter, you'll have a Pomodoro application that you can release to the world! If you're not familiar with the Pomodoro technique (www.pomodorotechnique.com), it's a simple way for people to efficiently manage their time.

Let's start by learning how external sources can extend MacRuby's reach.

2.1   *Using external libraries with MacRuby*

External libraries, such as Objective-C frameworks and Ruby gems, are tools that you'll use frequently when creating MacRuby applications. As you've already seen, the Cocoa framework gives you access to Cocoa classes and functions. What about other frameworks and Objective-C libraries? Ruby has a plethora of libraries, known as gems, and most of these will eventually be compatible with MacRuby. In this section, we'll discuss how to use frameworks, libraries, and gems in a MacRuby application.

2.1.1   *Loading frameworks*

Useful MacRuby Cocoa code generally requires the Cocoa standard libraries contained in the Foundation and AppKit frameworks. MacRuby wrapped both of these frameworks into one Cocoa framework that you can easily load to access Cocoa functions. To reference the Cocoa framework, call the following function:

```
framework 'cocoa'
```

If you reference the NSWindow class without first loading the Cocoa framework, you'll get an error letting you know that no constant named NSWindow is defined:

```
>> NSWindow
NameError: uninitialized constant NSWindow
```

To resolve the error, load the Cocoa framework by specifying it in the framework function:

```
>> framework 'cocoa'
=> true
>> NSWindow
=> NSWindow
```

You can now properly call NSWindow, because it's available by virtue of loading the Cocoa framework. The framework function gives you access to all the Mac development libraries. You can load any Cocoa framework that's available to a typical Cocoa application.

What about requiring a specific Cocoa framework? For example, suppose you want to call a WebView object, which is part of the Cocoa WebKit framework. You'll use this framework in-depth in chapter 4 to build a web browser. Watch what happens if you simply reference the class:

```
>> WebView
NameError: uninitialized constant WebView
```

Oops! As in the previous example, you must first load the framework associated with the WebView class:

```
>> framework 'webkit'
=> true
>> WebView
=> WebView
```

Only after explicitly loading the WebKit framework can you access the `WebView` class.

2.1.2 *Loading Objective-C libraries as bundles*

When you're working in the Xcode environment, using frameworks and Objective-C code is easy. Outside Xcode, you can require new frameworks if they're in your path.

If you want to include an Objective-C library outside Xcode (in a MacRuby script or HotCocoa application, for example), you must first create a bundle. This bundle will allow you to export custom functionality into other MacRuby applications.

Creating a bundle isn't too complicated; you create a dynamic library that has a bundle extension. Open Xcode, and let's walk through how to create a bundle.

CREATING A LIBRARY PROJECT AND ADDING FILES

Create a new project, and, from the Framework & Library template, click Cocoa Library as shown in figure 2.1.

Click Next, and then name the bundle. (We named the project Test Bundle.) After the project is created, select the Objective-C files you want to include and add them to the project.

To make sure the bundle works properly with MacRuby, you need to edit some build settings.

Figure 2.1 Creating a new Cocoa Library project in Xcode

EDITING BUILD SETTINGS

From the Project Navigator (at the left of the screen), click the Test Bundle project. Click the Test Bundle target, and make sure that the All tab is selected, not the Basic tab. This reveals all the settings that you need.

From the Architectures section, set Valid Architectures to at least i386 and x86_64. From the Compiler Version section, set the C/C++ Compiler Version to 4.0 or higher. Figure 2.2 shows these settings.

From the Packaging section, change Executable Extension from `dylib` to `bundle` and set the Product Name to something that's more idiomatic Ruby. For example, we named ours test_bundle. These settings are shown in figure 2.3.

Last, you need to modify any one of the implementation (.m) files that you added to the project. To add a constructor, you need at least one implementation file included in your bundle.

ADDING A CONSTRUCTOR

Because you named the product test_bundle, you need to add a constructor that Ruby recognizes to allow the bundle to behave like a C extension. Outside the implementation portion of the implementation file, add the following:

```
void Init_test_bundle(void) { }
```

Make sure to replace `test_bundle` in `Init_test_bundle` with the value you set as the Product Name. You can now build this project.

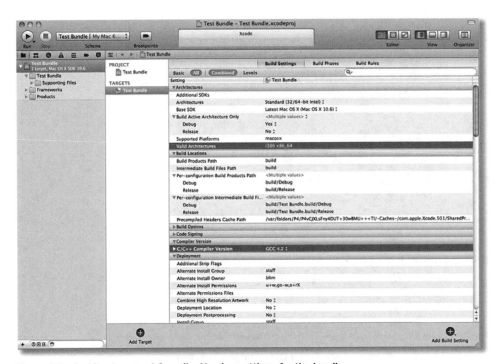

Figure 2.2   Architectures and Compiler Version settings for the bundle

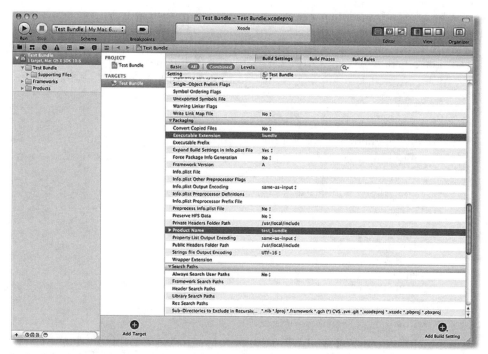

Figure 2.3 Executable Extension and Product Name settings for the bundle

To reveal the bundle, right-click the Products group in Xcode and choose Reveal in Finder. To use this bundle in a particular project, copy the bundle to the folder that contains the project. To include this bundle in any MacRuby script or HotCocoa app, specify the following:

```
require 'test_bundle'
```

You now have access to your Test Bundle. Let's now see how you can include Ruby gems in your MacRuby applications.

2.1.3 Loading Ruby gems

Gems are a standard for packaged and distributed programs and libraries for the Ruby language. Many gems are available that you could potentially use to add functionality to an application. To install a gem package, Ruby 1.9 comes with the RubyGems command-line tool, which is a library packaging system for gem management.

As of this writing, not all Ruby gems are compatible with MacGem, MacRuby's version of RubyGems. Over time, more gems will work properly with MacRuby. In the meantime, you can still try out MacRuby-compatible gems in Macirb. If you've installed Ruby gems before, the MacRuby process will look familiar. If you haven't done it before, it's simple.

To install a gem in Ruby, you type a command in the terminal. The following example installs a gem named HTTParty:

```
$ sudo gem install httparty
```

In MacRuby, installing a gem is just as simple. Instead of specifying gem, specify macgem:

```
$ sudo macgem install httparty
```

Let's load HTTParty (https://github.com/jnunemaker/httparty), a gem created by John Nunemaker that makes the consumption of RESTful APIs easier in Ruby:

```
>> HTTParty
NameError: uninitialized constant HTTParty
```

What happened? You loaded the HTTParty class, but you got an error because Macirb doesn't know what HTTParty is. To load a gem that you've installed, you must use the require function and pass in the library name.

This time, you'll use the require function to first require RubyGems and HTTParty:

```
>> require 'rubygems'
=> true
>> require 'httparty'
=> true
>> HTTParty
=> HTTParty
```

Now the gem is available for use.

Starting in chapter 1 and up to this point, you've used one of the tools MacRuby ships with: the MacRuby console, Macirb. Let's drill down and learn more about how to use it.

2.2   *Exploring Macirb*

Experimentation is a great way to learn a new technology, and an interactive console makes experimenting with a new language simple. Many interpreted languages have interactive console applications that let you run code in an interpreted environment to see how things work. Both Ruby and Python provide this type of application, and MacRuby is no exception.

In this section, we'll first discuss similarities between the Ruby console and Macirb, and then you'll get a chance to use Macirb. We'll round out the section with various Macirb tips and tricks that can simplify your life.

2.2.1   *Comparing the Ruby and MacRuby consoles*

Many Ruby developers are familiar with Interactive Ruby (Irb), Ruby's interactive console. If you're used to working with Irb, then you should be happy to know that MacRuby's console is pretty much identical.

Irb is a command-line shell that allows you to load libraries and run Ruby code in real time. Anything you can do in a Ruby script, you can do in Irb, including running network operations. It provides command history and gives you the opportunity to try out Ruby code on the fly. When you start Irb, you start a new session, and objects that you instantiate exist in memory for the life of that session.

Irb prints the output of every statement you type, as you've already seen in several of the code examples we've used. If you instantiate a new object, Irb echoes the value of the object back to you. It should come as no surprise that this type of behavior is the same in Macirb as well.

Macirb is MacRuby's implementation of the Ruby interactive console. More specifically, Macirb is built on top of DietRB (as of MacRuby 0.7), an open-source, slimmed-down version of Irb. Figure 2.4 shows first Irb and then Macirb in action. As you can see, they look similar.

If you're new to the concept of interactive consoles or shells, a good way to get familiar with the environment is to start the Macirb console and play around. To launch Macirb, type `macirb` at the console prompt.

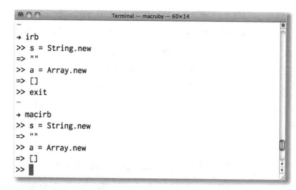

Figure 2.4   Starting Irb followed by starting Macirb shows how similar the tools are.

2.2.2 Working in the MacRuby console

From the MacRuby console, you can execute anything. After you press Enter, the line you typed is evaluated. If the line yields a valid result, you'll receive a response that returns the appropriate result. If what you typed contains an error, you'll be notified of that as well.

You can also type class definitions in Macirb, line by line, and then use that new class in your Macirb session. Neat, isn't it?

To get an idea of what's running under the hood of Macirb, enter the following commands in the console:

```
self.instance_eval("class<<self;self;end").ancestors
=> [TopLevel, NSObject, Kernel]
```

This strange-looking set of commands is a roundabout way of finding out which underlying objects power Macirb. The output is similar to what you'll see if you run the same commands in the Ruby console. The key difference is NSObject, which is the base object for the Cocoa libraries and for all objects in MacRuby.

Now that you've been introduced to Macirb, and you've seen how to use it, let's go over some ways to customize your Macirb experience.

2.2.3 Macirb tips and tricks

Irb users have a few tricks to make key tools and helpful methods available whenever they launch the console. As MacRuby matures, more of these tricks will become available to Macirb.

A custom Irb configuration comes in handy when you want to preset different shortcuts, predefine methods, initialize gems, and much more. You specify configuration settings in a text file named .irbrc. This file is automatically invoked every time you start the console. Luckily, because Macirb is built on top of Irb, most of the custom configuration you can specify for Irb in the custom initialization file can also be used for Macirb. Let's find out how to work with the .irbrc configuration file.

CREATING THE CONFIGURATION FILE

Unless you've previously modified Irb or Macirb, the .irbrc file doesn't exist. By default, Macirb doesn't create the file. Assuming you don't already have a custom initialization set up on your computer, go to the home directory of the Terminal application, create a file, and name it .irbrc. Open the file in your favorite text editor.

Sharing .irbrc with Macirb and Irb

Because Macirb and Irb both use the same configuration file, you need a way to specify which settings apply to MacRuby and which to Ruby. To determine which environment is in use, you can use DietRB as an identifier for Macirb, as shown in the following code

```
if IRB.version.include?('DietRB')
  # Macirb-specific customization
else
  # IRB-specific customization
end
```

Each time you modify the configuration file, the changes are available when you start a new Macirb session.

USING AUTOCOMPLETE AND HISTORY

Autocomplete, also called code completion, allows you to start typing a portion of a class or a function name and then press the tab key on your keyboard to have the name complete automatically. Imagine all the typing you'd have to do without this feature.

Without a command history feature, you can't hit the up arrow to populate the console with commands you executed previously. Imagine quitting a console session only to realize that you've lost everything you just typed.

Thankfully, because Macirb is built on top of DietRB, autocomplete and history are already implemented in Macirb as of version 0.7. With older versions of MacRuby, you have to modify your Irb configuration to enable this functionality.

LOADING GEMS AND FRAMEWORKS AUTOMATICALLY

Every time you want to load a gem into Macirb, you must first require RubyGems and then require every gem that you want to use during that session. Similarly, you must also require the Cocoa framework to use it in a Macirb session. To give your fingers a rest, you can configure Macirb to automatically load these tools.

Add the following require and framework function calls to your .irbrc file:

```
require 'rubygems'
framework 'cocoa'
```

In the configuration file, you can load any other framework or gem that you use frequently.

APPLYING CODE COLORIZATION

One of the popular gems for code colorization in Irb is Wirble. Sadly, Wirble doesn't work with Macirb. Fortunately, Macirb supports code colorization out of the box, thanks to its DietRB heritage. All you have to do is add the following to your initialization file:

```
require 'irb/ext/colorize'
```

If you use Macirb now, you'll see colorized output. Macirb provides the following three color schemes:

- `:dark_background`
- `:light_background`
- `:fresh`

The default color scheme is `:dark_background`. To modify colorization, type the following:

```
IRB.formatter.color_scheme = :light_background
```

Now, let's see how you can customize the default Macirb prompt.

CUSTOMIZING THE PROMPT

When you start Macirb, the command-line prompt contains text that might not make much sense. For example:

```
irb(main):001:0>
```

This default prompt displays the name of the current session (`main`); the current line number (`001`); and the indentation level (`0`). I (Brendan) consider this wasted space and never pay attention to what it says. You can get rid of this quite easily by adding the following line to your initialization file:

```
IRB.formatter.prompt = :simple
```

Now, when you run Macirb, you get a clean and unobtrusive prompt like this:

```
>>
```

This nice and simple change reduces the clutter in the MacRuby console.

USING ALIASING

If you know your way around UNIX, you might be familiar with custom aliases and aliasing, which allow you to substitute a long command with something much simpler and to your liking. For instance, when you want to load a new framework, you must type the full function name, `framework`. Wouldn't it be great if you could type `fw` instead? This is easy to specify:

```
alias fw framework
```

That's it! Make sure not to create aliases that could take over the execution of other important functions or classes that you may use in MacRuby. For instance, don't name an alias `NSString`.

ADDING HELPFUL PREDEFINED FUNCTIONS

You've added some nice customizations to your initialization file, and now you can add predefined functions to it. Imagine typing a class definition and helper methods in Macirb. You can use these functions in your session, but as soon as you close Macirb, you lose everything you defined. You must retype everything you did previously in subsequent sessions. Even with the command history feature, you still need to use the up arrow to execute each of those lines again each time you start a new session. This solution is definitely less than ideal. To save time (and the headache), add helpful predefined methods to your .irbrc file.

RETURNING OBJECT-SPECIFIC METHODS

By default, when you examine an object by calling `methods`, you get all the methods available on the object and all its ancestor classes. What you end up seeing repeatedly is a list of methods that are part of the base class, `NSObject`, each time you call `methods` on any object.

The base class methods make it difficult to find only the methods that belong to the specific class that you called the `methods` method on. The fix is simple: use the `superclass_methods` function. Type the following in your initialization file, and you'll have access to this function whenever you start a new session:

```
class Object
  def superclass_methods
    (self.methods - Object.instance_methods).sort
  end
end
```

The `superclass_methods` function doesn't return any methods on the base class, `NSObject`. Use this method to examine just the methods that are specific to the object you're executing it on.

EVALUATING LINES FROM FILE

How do you execute the code in a file from inside Macirb? You could copy and paste the code into the console. This isn't bad, but it isn't the best solution. A better solution is to add the `eval_file` function to your initialization file:

```
def eval_file(path_to_file)
  eval(File.readlines(path_to_file).join)
end
```

Now you can call the `eval_file` function and pass in the path to the file. This function will read in and execute all the files in the file specified.

Phew! You've absorbed quite a bit of information in a short amount of time. How about taking the knowledge you've gained and using it to build a tool that manages everyday productivity?

2.3   Building a Pomodoro application in Xcode

The Pomodoro application you build in this section will help users manage their time throughout the day.

> ### The Pomodoro Technique
>
> If you're not familiar with the Pomodoro Technique, it's a time-management system developed by Francesco Cirillo. Professional teams and individuals throughout the world now practice this technique. You manage your time by setting a timer for a 25-minute session during which you work on a specific task. After the timer goes off, you take a quick break, and then repeat the process. The technique got its name because the creator used a tomato-shaped timer. (In Italian, *pomodoro* means tomato.)

The application is simple enough to build, and you can use it to accomplish the tasks of your day-to-day life.

In this section, you'll use more of Xcode and Interface Builder. You'll walk through the entire development cycle from generating a new MacRuby project to creating a releasable version of your application. By the end of this section, you'll have done each of the following tasks:

- Create a MacRuby project.
- Design the application interface.
- Create and set up the controller.
- Connect the controller to the interface.
- Run the application.
- Release the application.

Let's get started creating our Pomodoro application by first opening Xcode.

2.3.1   Creating a new MacRuby project

Create a new MacRuby Application project in Xcode, and name it Pomodoro. You'll see the main project view in Xcode, which should be similar to what's shown in figure 2.5.

The project template automatically creates a few files for you. Open the main.m file in the Supporting Files group. The contents are shown here:

```
#import <MacRuby/MacRuby.h>

int main(int argc, char *argv[])
{
    return macruby_main("rb_main.rb", argc, argv);
}
```

This file is initially run by the application. The first line of the file imports the MacRuby framework. The third line calls the `macruby_main` function, which accepts a file to load and any given arguments.

NOTE   You'll rarely, if ever, need to modify main.m.

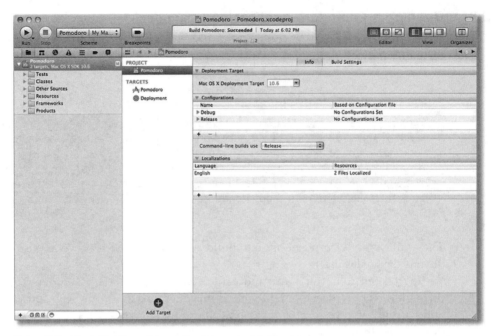

Figure 2.5   The initial Pomodoro application project in Xcode

The following listing shows the contents of rb_main.rb, the file that was specified in macruby_main.

Listing 2.1   Ruby-generated rb_main.rb file

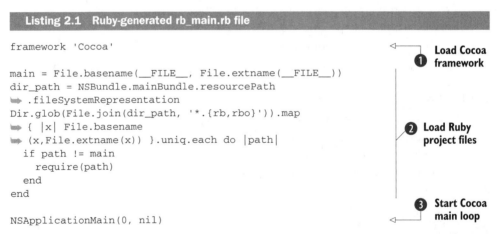

```
framework 'Cocoa'                                              ◁──┐ Load Cocoa
                                                               ❶   framework
main = File.basename(__FILE__, File.extname(__FILE__))
dir_path = NSBundle.mainBundle.resourcePath
⮡ .fileSystemRepresentation
Dir.glob(File.join(dir_path, '*.{rb,rbo}')).map
⮡ { |x| File.basename                              ❷ Load Ruby
⮡ (x,File.extname(x)) }.uniq.each do |path|            project files
  if path != main
    require(path)
  end
end
                                                               ❸ Start Cocoa
NSApplicationMain(0, nil)                              ◁────────  main loop
```

This code loads the Cocoa framework by using the Kernel#framework method ❶. You need to make sure to load the Cocoa framework so that you have access to all the Cocoa APIs for your application. If you need to load more frameworks, you can do that here, too.

Next, it locates and loads all the Ruby files in the project ❷. Last, it calls the NSApplicationMain function ❸ to launch the Cocoa run loop, which effectively launches your application.

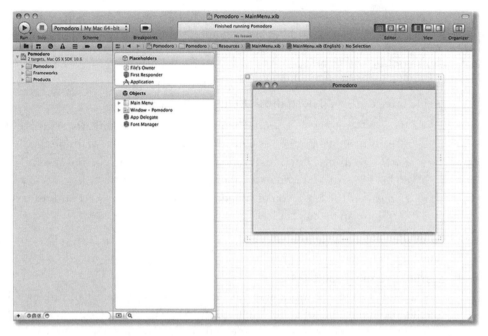

Figure 2.6   MainMenu.xib generates a user interface for you automatically. The Pomodoro application will need a few UI elements, such as a label and a button.

One more generated file we'll look at is MainMenu.xib, the main graphical interface that loads after you launch the application.

> **Pronounced *nibs*, not *zibs***
>
> Files such as MainMenu.xib are pronounced *nibs* even though they have an extension of .xib because prior to Xcode 3.0, these graphical user interface files had an extension of .nib, which stands for NeXT Interface Builder.

Click MainMenu.xib to load the interface editor in Xcode. A blank application window appears as shown in figure 2.6.

Let's run this application in its current state without modifying anything the MacRuby template generated. In Xcode, you can either click Run (the Play icon) at the top-left of the window or go to the Product menu and click Run. Alternatively, you can use the keyboard shortcut Command-R.

The application compiles and then launches a blank window, shown in figure 2.7.

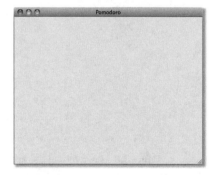

Figure 2.7   Running the base generated application

Not too exciting, is it? What you see is just about as basic as it gets for a Cocoa application. Next you'll add interface elements and functionality to this application.

2.3.2   Constructing the interface

You won't need too much visual pizzazz for the Pomodoro application. To have a usable interface, you'll need the following elements:

- *Window*—You need a window to contain the UI elements. This window has already been generated for you and is contained in the MainMenu.xib file.
- *Label*—To display how much time you have left in the current session, you'll use an NSTextField (shown as a Label in the Object library).
- *Button*—At the least, you also need a simple button to start and reset the timer. You'll use an NSButton.

From the project navigator, select MainMenu.xib so that you can build out the user interface.

CUSTOMIZING THE WINDOW

The default size of the window is too big for what you need it to display. Click and drag the bottom-right corner of the window to size it. Because the window will display only the label, which shows the time remaining, and a small button that starts or resets the Pomodoro timer, it can be as small as what's shown in figure 2.8.

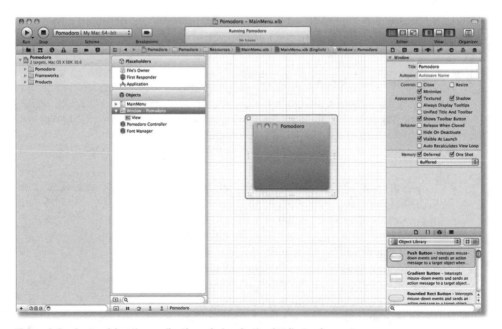

Figure 2.8   Customizing the application window in the Attributes inspector

Let's modify two window attributes. Click the window on the canvas and open the Attributes inspector (from the Xcode menu bar, choose View > Utilities > Attributes Inspector):

- *Resize*—Uncheck Resize to prevent people from resizing the application window and making it unnecessarily huge.
- *Textured*—For visual spice, make sure the Textured option is checked. This gives the window a slightly different shaded appearance. If you don't like the look, feel free to omit it.

The application window might look better now, but it's still in need of UI elements.

ADDING THE LABEL AND BUTTON

From the Object library at the bottom of the utility area, find a Push Button. To quickly find it, type `push button` in the search field at the bottom of the library pane. Drag the button to the bottom portion of the application window. A button is an `NSButton`, which is an element the user clicks. The push button is a type of `NSButton` with a different visual appearance than the other offerings you may find.

Next, search for a label, and drag it to the application window. A label is an `NSTextField`, which is an element used for displaying text.

Your interface should look similar to what's shown in figure 2.9.

Let's change the appearance of the button and label before we get started with the code. You could leave them as they are, but their default values of Label and Button aren't very informative to the user.

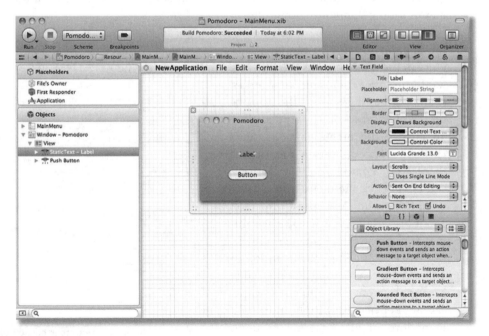

Figure 2.9 Adding a label and button to the Pomodoro application window

Click the button and, from the Attributes inspector, change its title to Start Pomodoro. Do the same with the label and change its title to 25, which represents the numbers of minutes left. It's this label that will be used to represent the timer as it counts down.

While you're in the Attributes inspector, change the justification of the label text to centered. To resize the label and add a little style to it, click the label and then find the button in the Font section of the Attributes inspector. Choose any font and size you like. Figure 2.10 shows the finished interface.

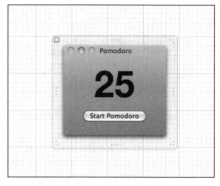

Figure 2.10　The finished appearance of the Pomodoro application window. A work session, called a Pomodoro, lasts 25 minutes.

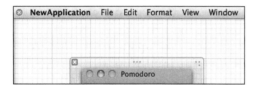

Figure 2.11　You'll customize the default menu bar for the Pomodoro application.

The last thing you should do is modify the menu bar of the Pomodoro application. The menu bar appears at the top of the screen for every Cocoa application you run. Some common menus are File, Edit, View, and so on as shown in figure 2.11. Right now, the application has a generic menu bar that was created by the template, and it doesn't have the correct menus for the Pomodoro application.

The menu should be visible above the application window. If it isn't, double-click the MainMenu entry in the Object library to bring it into view. By default, the first entry in the menu bar has the title NewApplication (see figure 2.11). You wouldn't want this title confusing your users. After all, they'll be using the application Pomodoro, not NewApplication. To change the menu name, double-click the NewApplication menu, and then type Pomodoro. Alternatively, you could click the menu and change its title in the Attributes inspector. You'll also notice that if you click this menu, it displays multiple menu items. The ones you need to pay attention to are About NewApplication, Hide NewApplication, and Quit NewApplication. Replace NewApplication with Pomodoro in all three menu items (see figure 2.12).

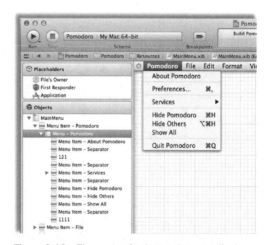

Figure 2.12　The customized menu bar now displays Pomodoro instead of NewApplication.

Now that you have your user interface in place, you can get started on the controller.

2.3.3 *Creating the controller*

The controller interacts with the interface elements that you created and houses the logic for this application. The controller also acts as a delegate for the window and the timer (which you've not yet set up). Let's start with the controller file.

SETTING UP THE CONTROLLER

From the project navigator, right-click the Pomodoro group and select New File. The Ruby File template should automatically be chosen for you. If not, look for it under the Ruby group. Click Next, and you'll be prompted to name the file. Name the controller PomodoroController.rb, and then click Finish.

You should have a blank template with nothing but a few comment lines at the top describing the name of the file, the project, and some copyright information. Add the following code to this file:

```
class PomodoroController
  attr_accessor :timer_label, :start_stop_button
  attr_accessor :pomodoro_timer, :min_left
end
```

You first declare the PomodoroController class. Next, you add outlets for the button and label using attr_accessor. This will allow you to hook up the user interface to the controller code later. You also add two other items that you're going to have access to in your controller: the timer and another object that calculates how many minutes are left on the timer.

> ### Customizing the Xcode environment
>
> To customize your environment, choose Xcode > Preferences. Click the tab of the area you want to customize. For example, from the Fonts & Colors tab, you can increase the font size in the editor or change the syntax coloring. From the Indentation tab, you can change the tab spacing.

Now you can start building out the functionality of the application.

ASSIGNING A DEFAULT MINUTES-REMAINING VALUE

You first define the awakeFromNib method. The awakeFromNib method is part of the NSNibAwaking protocol and is called right after the controller is instantiated from the nib, MainMenu.xib. In this method, you can set anything you need to initialize the application.

You're using it to set the default value of the min_left class instance variable, which calculates the minutes remaining on the timer. When you start the application, the timer is set for 25 minutes:

```
def awakeFromNib
  @min_left = 25
end
```

Next, you need an action, (also called an IBAction), that you can call when the button is clicked.

STARTING AND STOPPING THE TIMER

The action and the button serve two purposes. They start and stop the timer. You can accomplish both purposes in the same action:

```
def start_stop_timer(sender)
  if @pomodoro_timer.nil?
    @pomodoro_timer = NSTimer.scheduledTimerWithTimeInterval(60,
    ➥ target:self, selector:"min_passed:", userInfo:nil, repeats:true)
    @timer_label.textColor = NSColor.redColor
    @start_stop_button.title = "Stop Pomodoro"
  else
    reset_interface
  end
end
```

You first check the value of the class instance variable @pomodoro_timer:

- *not nil*—The timer is inactive, so you start the timer.
- *nil*—You call another method to reset the interface elements back to their default values and settings.

If the timer is indeed nil, the first thing you do is schedule a timer. You do this by creating an NSTimer with an interval of 60 seconds set to repeat. Every 60 seconds, you have it call a method (or a selector) named min_passed: (which you haven't yet implemented). This method accepts one parameter, which is an instance of the timer. You then set the color of the timer to red to indicate that the timer has started. You also change the text of the button to Stop, which cues users that clicking it will stop the timer.

Let's create the min_passed: method, which the timer calls.

COUNTING DOWN THE TIMER

This method must properly decrement the variable that stores how much longer is left on the timer and then change the label to reflect how much time is remaining.

If the timer has only 1 minute remaining and this method is triggered, that indicates that 0 minutes are left. You handle this by resetting the interface and then alerting the user that the Pomodoro has finished. Here's the code:

```
def min_passed(timer)
  if @min_left > 1
    @min_left -= 1
    @timer_label.stringValue = @min_left
  else
    reset_interface
    alert_user
  end
end
```

Next, you'll create the reset_interface method, which resets the interface.

RESETTING THE INTERFACE

This method is called when the timer is up or when the user clicks the button when it's in a state to stop the timer. The method code is shown here:

```
def reset_interface
  @min_left = 25
  @timer_label.stringValue = @min_left
  @timer_label.textColor = NSColor.blackColor
  @start_stop_button.title = "Start Pomodoro"
  @pomodoro_timer.invalidate
  @pomodoro_timer = nil
end
```

You reset the instance variable to the default time remaining, change the interface elements back to their default values, and then invalidate and declare the @pomodoro_timer instance variable nil.

The last method you need to implement alerts users that the Pomodoro session has finished.

ALERTING THE USER

Using the Objective-C class NSSpeechSynthesizer is a cool way to audibly alert users. Apple provides several voices. For now, let's use Victoria's voice. The method code looks like this:

```
def alert_user
  voice = NSSpeechSynthesizer.alloc.
  ➥ initWithVoice("com.apple.speech.synthesis.voice.Victoria")
  voice.startSpeakingString("Pomodoro complete. Time for a short break")
end
```

The following listing shows the controller in its entirety.

Listing 2.2 Pomodoro controller

```
class PomodoroController
  attr_accessor :start_stop_button, :timer_label
  attr_accessor :pomodoro_timer, :min_left

  def awakeFromNib
    @min_left = 25
  end

  def start_stop_pomodoro(sender)
    if @pomodoro_timer.nil?
      @pomodoro_timer = NSTimer.scheduledTimerWithTimeInterval(60,
      ➥ target:self, selector:"min_passed:", userInfo:nil, repeats:true)
      @timer_label.textColor = NSColor.redColor
      @start_stop_button.title = "Stop Pomodoro"
    else
      reset_interface
    end
  end
```

```
def min_passed(timer)
  if @min_left > 1
    @min_left -= 1
    @timer_label.stringValue = @min_left
  else
    reset_interface
    alert_user
  end
end

def reset_interface
  @min_left = 25
  @timer_label.stringValue = @min_left
  @timer_label.textColor = NSColor.blackColor
  @start_stop_button.title = "Start Pomodoro"
  @pomodoro_timer.invalidate
  @pomodoro_timer = nil
end

def alert_user
  voice = NSSpeechSynthesizer.alloc.
  ➥ initWithVoice("com.apple.speech.synthesis.voice.Victoria")
    voice.startSpeakingString("Pomodoro complete. Time for a short break.")
  end
end
```

You might have noticed that we used both Ruby- and Objective-C–specific methods in the controller. Nice to have that flexibility, isn't it?

Developer documentation

The Apple developer documentation contains a wealth of knowledge that you can always turn to for help. Apple's Cocoa API documentation is very readable. If you ever need to figure out what protocol methods to implement for a specific delegate or if you forgot what methods are available for a particular class, make sure to check the documentation first. One of the best things about the documentation is that it's easily accessible from the Xcode Help menu. You can even look up classes such as NS-SpeechSynthesizer to learn about the different voices you can use!

You're almost finished! The remaining task is to connect the actions and interface elements.

2.3.4   *Connecting the controller and the interface*

Let's hook up the controller to the nib file. From the interface, search the Object library for an NSObject. Drag this to the Objects section of the document outline pane (at the far-left of the window). From the Inspector selector bar (at the top of the utility area), click the third tab from the left, and then change the class property to PomodoroController (see figure 2.13).

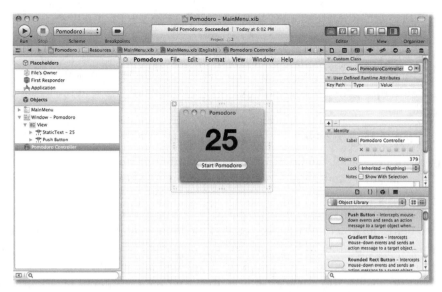

Figure 2.13 Adding the controller as an NSObject in the interface

From the Inspector selector bar, click the third tab from the right (look for the arrow icon) to start connecting the user interface with the controller's outlets and actions. This tab lists the outlets and actions you have access to from the controller:

- Connect the timer_label outlet to the label that represents time remaining in the application window.
- Connect the start_stop_button outlet to the push button (see figure 2.14).

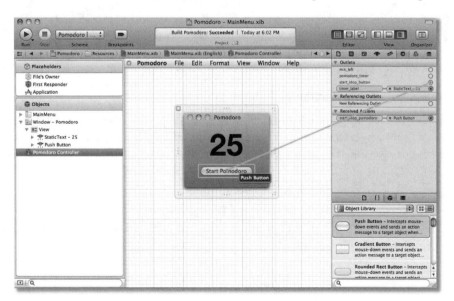

Figure 2.14 Connecting the controller's start_stop_button outlet to the button

- Connect the `start_stop_pomodoro` action to the push button. When the button is clicked, it executes this action.

Make sure you save the Interface Builder file.

The interface is in place, you've created the controller, and both items can talk to each other properly. You're finally ready to put your hard work to the test and run the application.

2.3.5 *Running the application*

To run the application, click Run (the Play icon) at the top-left of the Xcode window. The application should begin compiling, and the window you created should pop up in its own application.

If you have everything set up properly, you won't get any compile errors. When you click Start, the timer should turn red and the button should say Stop Pomodoro. You could wait 25 minutes to hear the alert when the timer finishes, or you could change the `NSTimer` interval to speed things up. If you feel like speeding things up for testing purposes, change the interval from `60` to `1`, and then relaunch the application. You should hear Victoria's voice alerting you that the Pomodoro has completed.

> **Viewing errors and logging in the debug console**
>
> If your application crashes while it's running, you can view the errors in the Xcode debug console. To view errors or logging output in the console, choose View > Show Debug Area or use the keyboard shortcut Command-Shift-Y.

Congratulations! You've developed a simple but useful Cocoa application using MacRuby. In no time, you'll be making amazing Cocoa applications that millions of people might end up using every day. You most likely want to know how to make a version that you can unleash into the world.

2.3.6 *Releasing the application*

Luckily, by using the MacRuby application template to create your project you get an extra build target that helps you package your application for mass consumption.

Before we walk through how to create a releasable version, let's make some quick changes to the application.

EDITING APPLICATION PROPERTIES

From Xcode, expand the Supporting Files group to reveal Pomodoro-Info.plist. In Cocoa development, you'll encounter many .plist files. The Pomodoro-Info.plist file stores the application properties.

Property lists

Property lists are XML files that contain a list of key/value pairs. The values for these keys can be strings, numbers, dictionaries, arrays, Booleans, dates, and data. Property lists are often used to store application properties and other configuration data that can be used in an application.

You need to update these properties to get your application ready for distribution:

- *Bundle Identifier*—The Bundle Identifier property represents the CFBundle-Identifier configuration property. By default, the value is com.yourcompany.[application name]. Change this to something unique to properly identify the application. You might have done this already when you created your Mac-Ruby project, but if not, it's important that you make this change. This unique bundle identifier will be necessary if you plan on submitting your application to the Mac App store.

- *Icon File*—The Icon File (CFBundleIconFile) property adds an application icon to your project. If you have an icon file, right-click your project entry (or any one of the subgroups you want to add the file to) and choose Add > Existing File. This adds the file to your Xcode project and allows you to use it in your application.

    If you want to add an icon to the Icon File property, you don't need to specify the full path; if you've added the file to your project, you can specify just the full name of the file (for example, icon.ico).

    If you want to create your own icon, Xcode provides the Icon Composer, which you can find in /Developer/Applications/Utilities.

- *Bundle Version*—The Bundle Version (CFBundleVersion) property specifies the current version of the application. If you make subsequent versions of an application, increase the version number so that each version of the application is identifiable. Because this is the first release of the Pomodoro application, leave this property at version 1.0.

You also need to change the copyright text, which involves editing a different file.

CUSTOMIZING THE COPYRIGHT TEXT

If you run the application in its current state and choose Pomodoro > About Pomodoro from the menu bar, you'll see that an About window has been generated for you. To edit the copyright text displayed at the bottom of this window, open the file called InfoPlist.strings.

This file contains different strings that an application uses when localization is a factor. If you expand this file, you'll see that, by default, it has an entry for English.

The default localization is English, and the application looks in this file for human-readable versions of certain properties. In this file, you should see the NSHuman-ReadableCopyright property. Change the value of the string to your copyright information (for example, Copyright 2011 Brendan Lim). If this property isn't in InfoPlist.strings, type the following to add it:

```
NSHumanReadableCopyright = @"My Company, 2011";
```

VIEWING THE BUILD CONFIGURATION

To view the build configuration settings for the application, expand the Targets group in Xcode, right-click the application name, and then click Get Info. This exposes the build settings for each build configuration that you have. By default, you have two build configurations, Debug and Release. You can make changes to an individual build configuration or all of them at once. You can change the base SDK, architectures, and many other build settings. For this application, leave the settings as they are. You don't need any special build configuration settings.

To create a releasable version of the application, you need to modify the Deployment scheme.

BUILDING THE APPLICATION

So far, you've used the default scheme to run the application, which is named after the Pomodoro application. But, in its current state, the application in the Product folder will fail to run if you send it to somebody who doesn't have MacRuby installed.

Instead, you'll use the Deployment scheme, which runs a script that packages both the MacRuby framework and the application so that it can run on machines that don't have MacRuby installed.

Click the bar at the right of the Stop button and select Deployment from the menu that appears (see figure 2.15).

From the same menu, choose Edit Scheme. Click Build from the list at the left, and then click the plus sign (+) at the bottom of the window as shown in figure 2.16. From here, you can add a new target to the build phase.

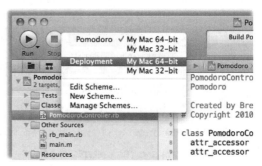

Figure 2.15   Selecting the Deployment scheme

From the Targets list, click and drag Pomodoro until it's above Deployment. This ensures that the application is built before the script in the Deployment target executes. Figure 2.17 shows the finished build phase.

Now that the Deployment scheme is set up, make sure it's selected. You need to make sure the supported architecture is set up properly before you can proceed.

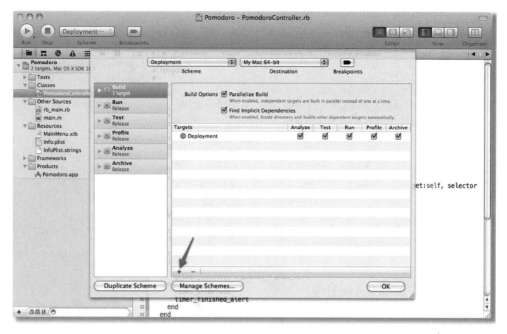

Figure 2.16   Adding a new target to the build phase

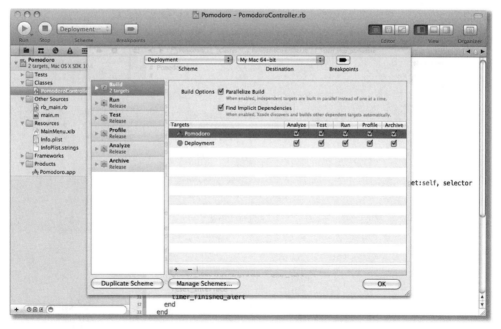

Figure 2.17   The finished build phase of the Deployment scheme

SUPPORTED ARCHITECTURE SETTINGS

At the time of writing, the template you used to create the MacRuby Pomodoro application sets the supported architecture in your build settings to x86_64 and i386. There's one small problem though: MacRuby doesn't support i386. To build the project, you need to modify this setting. Complete the following steps:

1 From the project navigator at the left of the screen, click the project name (Pomodoro), and then click the Deployment target.

2 Click the Build Settings tab. You should see a setting labeled ARCHS. The value should be set to x64_86 i386. You need to make sure that you support only x64_86 architectures.

3 Double click the ARCHS entry for the Deployment target. You should see $(ARCHS_STANDARD_32_64_BIT) as the specified value.

4 Change the value to $(ARCHS_STANDARD_64_BIT) as shown in figure 2.18.

Now that you have the supported architecture set up, you can move on to archiving the application.

ARCHIVING THE APPLICATION

From the Xcode menu bar, choose Product > Archive to archive the app and launch the Xcode Organizer window.

> **TIP** If the Organizer window doesn't automatically appear, choose Window > Organizer to launch it.

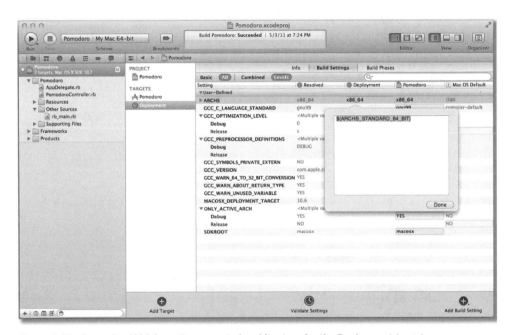

Figure 2.18   Removing i386 from the supported architecture for the Deployment target

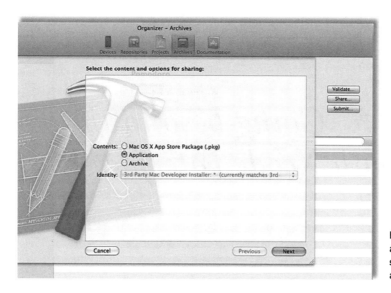

Figure 2.19 Use the archives organizer to share an archived application.

From the Organizer, click Archives. The Pomodoro application appears in the application list of the archives organizer.

From the archives list, click the latest application archive, and then click Share. This will allow you to choose an option to distribute your application, as shown in figure 2.19. For now, click Application, which allows you to save the archived application anywhere you want.

You've successfully created a releasable version of the Pomodoro application! From the folder where you saved the application, you can now zip/archive and send the app to anybody you wish. In Chapter 11, you'll learn how to distribute applications to the Mac App Store.

2.4 Summary

In this chapter, you accomplished quite a bit and, in the process, became more familiar with MacRuby and its toolset. You learned how to utilize external libraries in your application by loading frameworks and gems. You played with the MacRuby console, Macirb, and learned how to use it more effectively. You also got deeper into Xcode to create a releasable Pomodoro application.

In the next chapter, you'll create a task-management application to explore advanced user interface development in Xcode.

Going beyond the basics
with Xcode Interface Builder

This chapter covers

- Mastering Interface Builder in Xcode 4
- Using outlets and actions
- Creating an application interface

One feature that many Mac applications have in common is a beautiful user interface (UI). The best UIs are strikingly beautiful, and, at the same time, they enhance the usability of the application. Crafting a unique and intuitive UI is no easy task, but expert developers understand that the UI can make the difference between a mediocre and a great application. The UI is one of the features that people have come to love about using a Mac. We should strive for the same excellence when building Cocoa applications with MacRuby.

What do most developers use to create these UIs for Mac applications? Kudos if you answered Interface Builder or Xcode (Interface Builder has been integrated into Xcode 4). Some people prefer to write their interfaces programmatically, but most prefer using the Xcode tools. We're firm believers in using the tools available to us. They're provided for a reason. Interface Builder is an important tool for Mac OS X development that provides powerful shortcuts to create innovative UIs.

Instead of painstakingly hand-coding the visual elements in an application, you use your mouse to drag, drop, and resize items. More importantly, Interface Builder bridges the gap between an application's code and its UI. The functionality and logic in the code can be connected to the interface with a few mouse clicks.

In this chapter, you'll get an in-depth look at Interface Builder and its tools. You'll create a task-management application that uses these tools more extensively than in previous chapters. You'll learn your way around the environment, understand the connection process, and experiment with more advanced MacRuby along the way.

You briefly used Interface Builder in chapters 1 and 2, but let's step back and formally introduce you to Xcode's visual user interface editor.

3.1 About Interface Builder

Interface Builder is exactly what its name suggests: a tool in Xcode to build Mac application interfaces. That only scratches the surface, though. With Interface Builder, you can manipulate many aspects of a UI and connect its elements to code. Compared to hand-coding, creating interfaces with Interface Builder is easy.

Before we dive into Xcode's Interface Builder and take a tour of its environment, we'll give you a brief history of how it came to be. It's a quick story that reveals how we ended up with the tool that most Mac developers use today.

3.1.1 History of Interface Builder

When Steve Jobs founded NeXT, after being forced to leave Apple in the 1980s, he saw a need for a tool that made creating application interfaces easier. Before Interface Builder, developers had to create interfaces programmatically or contend with counter-intuitive tools.

Created in 1988, Interface Builder initially appeared as part of the NeXTSTEP software. Interface Builder was one of the first commercial applications that allowed developers to visually arrange interface elements using a mouse. Another interesting fact is that the creators of the first web browser application, WorldWideWeb, used Interface Builder to design the interface.

After Apple acquired NeXTSTEP, not only did its key executives adopt Objective-C and Project Builder (Xcode), but they also chose to add Interface Builder to Apple's suite of application development tools. Today, the interfaces of almost all Mac applications are built with Interface Builder. As of Xcode 4, Interface Builder is fully integrated into Xcode and is no longer a separate application.

Launch Xcode, and we'll get started by showing you around the Interface Builder environment.

3.1.2 Getting around Interface Builder

To create a new interface file, create a new project and save it with a name of your choosing. Your new project is already provided with an interface file (MainMenu.xib), but for the same reason you might separate different models into separate classes, you might want to create separate interface files for separate windows.

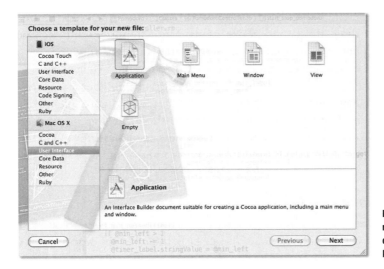

Figure 3.1 Adding a new Interface Builder document to an existing MacRuby project

After your new project loads in Xcode, choose File > New > New File. From the window that appears, choose User Interface from the template categories. Depending on the installed SDKs, what you see may be different from what's shown in figure 3.1.

You're building a MacRuby Cocoa application, so let's get familiar with the files the Application template (under Mac OS X) generates.

After clicking next, you'll be prompted to specify a name for the new interface file. For now, though, let's use what was generated for you in the project you just created.

Click MainMenu.xib to open Interface Builder in Xcode. As we mentioned, your new project already has an interface, based on the Application template, and is in the MainMenu.xib file. You've used some of the inspectors and libraries that appear in the utility area, but we haven't explained what they do and how to use them to build graphical interfaces.

USING THE DOCK

The document window (which has been renamed the dock in Xcode 4) at the left of the Interface Builder pane shows all the objects and elements associated with the UI. Initially, you may be presented with the document view as a list of icons. To switch to outline view, which shows the interface objects hierarchically, click the dock mode button at the bottom of the dock (see figure 3.2).

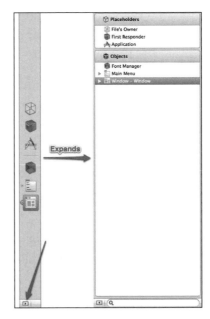

Figure 3.2 Click the dock mode button to toggle between the icon view (shown at left) and the outline view (shown at right) of the interface objects and placeholders.

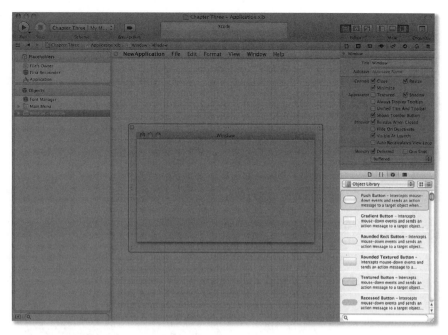

Figure 3.3 Use the library pane to search for objects and resources to add to the UI.

An interface is made up of objects such as windows, views, buttons, and so on. It might also include controllers or other objects that hook into it.

You can think of the document window as the place to see which elements directly interact with or are part of your UI.

FINDING OBJECTS IN THE LIBRARY PANE

Use the library pane to add objects or resources to your interface. If you're looking for a button, label, table view, and so on, you'll find it in the library. After you locate the item you want to use, drag it to the document window or directly to the view you want to place it in. Figure 3.3 shows the library pane.

If you don't see the library pane, choose View > Utilities > Object Library from Xcode's application menu.

MODIFYING OBJECTS IN THE INSPECTOR PANE

To adjust the attributes or settings of any object in the UI, use the inspector pane. You can change an element's title value, colors, fonts, positioning, and much more. The inspector pane is shown in figure 3.4.

From the inspector pane, you can also adjust static and dynamic positioning of a specific UI element. For instance, suppose you want to fix the position of a text label so that it remains centered in your application. You can make it stretch with its parent window, vertically or horizontally, using the Size tab of the inspector pane. Making the same adjustment programmatically takes more time. In addition to changing attributes and positioning, the inspector also allows you to add effects, view bindings and connections, and edit the identity of an object.

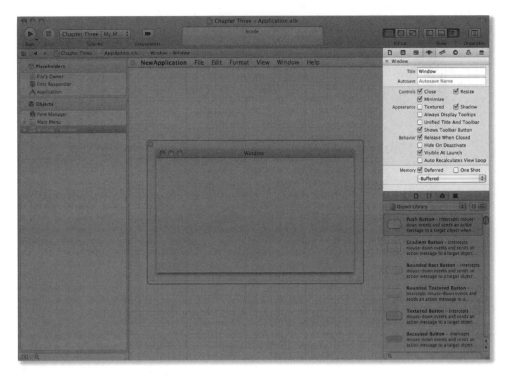

Figure 3.4   The inspector pane

To view the tabs in the inspector that open tools such as the File Inspector, Quick Help, Effects Inspector, Size Inspector, Binding Inspector, and so on, choose View >Utilities from Xcode's application menu. Table 3.1 lists the inspector pane tabs.

Table 3.1   Inspector pane tabs

Tab	Description
Attributes	Displays many different object-specific attributes and allows you to change these individual attributes
View Effects	Allows you to add Core Animation or Core Graphics effects to specific objects
Size	Displays size information for a specific object and allows you to change autosizing and alignment attributes
Bindings	Displays specific bindings for an object and allows you to set bindings for one or more controllers
Connections	Displays the outlets and actions available for creating and removing bindings on objects
Quick Help	Displays snippets of documentation related to the view or object you're working with
Identity	Displays information that allows you to view or change the identity of an object

You'll be spending a good deal of time with the inspector throughout the rest of this chapter.

When building an interface, you might not always have the code in place for the UI. For these situations, Interface Builder provides a feature to simulate the interface.

SIMULATING AN INTERFACE

Simulation mode is a handy way to view and interact with your interface and get instant feedback on how your changes affect it. For example, if you set up autosizing for multiple UI elements, you can use the simulator to test whether they behave as expected when you resize a window. It's good practice to get a feel for how the interface behaves after modifications.

To launch the simulator, choose Editor > Simulate Document from Xcode's application menu. The interface launches in its own base application. From here, you can play around with the interface and see if things work the way you expect. To exit simulation mode, quit the application that the interface launched or use the keyboard shortcut Command-Q.

Now that you've had a tour of the Interface Builder tools, let's turn our attention to how to make connections between MacRuby code and the interface.

3.2 *Creating connections*

When you build a UI, parts of it interact directly with MacRuby code. Without this interaction, the UI remains static. An application can't be too useful if it doesn't do anything when you click its buttons.

In this section, you'll learn how to create connections between code and interface elements. *Outlets* and *actions*, which you worked with when you built the Pomodoro application in chapter 2, expose the UI elements to controller or model objects. You can then manipulate the UI elements programmatically and respond to certain events.

3.2.1 *Understanding outlets*

Interface Builder outlets, commonly referred to as IBOutlets, are special types of instance variables of an object that communicate with the interface, the controller, and other objects. Outlets create connections between object instances in code and UI elements.

CREATING OUTLETS

To create an outlet in an Objective-C application, you write code in the interface portion of the source file. The following example is just one way to declare an instance variable of an NSButton as an interface builder outlet:

```
IBOutlet NSButton *start_button;
```

It's much simpler to create an outlet in MacRuby. Any instance variable you set up using attr_accessor is instantly an outlet in Interface Builder. Here's the same example in MacRuby:

```
attr_accessor :start_button
```

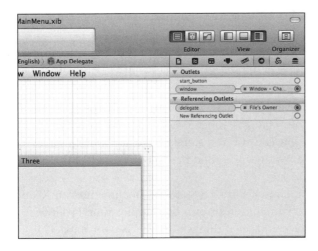

Figure 3.5   Interface Builder lists available outlets in the Connections tab of the inspector pane.

You don't have to specify that it's an outlet, what type of object it is, and so on. You set it up as you would any other variable in the controller. Simple, isn't it? As soon as you hook the controller into the interface, the start_button outlet is visible from Interface Builder. To view the outlets in the Connections tab of the inspector pane, as shown in figure 3.5, click the controller object in the document window.

So how do you connect these outlets to the interface? You may already know from the previous example, but let's walk through the process.

CONNECTING OUTLETS

Without connections between the outlets and the interface objects, you're stuck in a situation where the code can't talk to the interface and vice versa.

To quickly demonstrate how to connect an outlet to an element in the interface, you'll add an NSButton to the window and connect the start_button outlet to it:

1 From the library pane, locate an NSButton and drag it to the view.
2 From the Connections tab in the inspector pane, click the circle icon at the right of the start_button outlet and drag a line to the NSButton (see figure 3.6).

That's it, the connection is made. Now, the controller knows that manipulating the start_button instance variable alters the NSButton interface object.

Alternatively, you could start from the push button to connect to the start_button outlet:

1 Right-click the NSButton in the window to display the floating Connections menu.
2 At the bottom of this menu, you'll see something labeled New Referencing Outlet. Make a connection from here to the controller in the document window, which then lists the available outlets in the controller.
3 From here, choose the appropriate outlet, start_button.

Let's move on to actions and how to work with them.

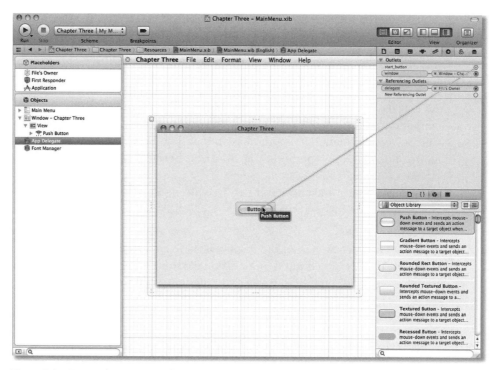

Figure 3.6 Connecting the `start_button` outlet to the `NSButton` requires only a few mouse clicks.

3.2.2 *Understanding actions*

An action, also called a target, is code that executes after an event occurs. In Interface Builder, actions are commonly referred to as IBActions. Actions respond to certain events that are triggered by user interaction. For instance, if you click a button, you expect it to execute some code that performs an action. Interface Builder gives you the ability to connect controls, such as the button, to the code you want to execute after an event occurs.

CREATING ACTIONS

In traditional Objective-C-based Cocoa development, there's a specific way to declare a method as an IBAction. For example, if you create a method that prints out a log statement every time a button is clicked, you would write the following:

```
-(IBAction) pressedButton:(id)sender {
    ...
}
```

Instead of a return type, you specify `IBAction`, which is defined as void. Also, actions always take one parameter of type `id`. This allows the parameter to be dynamic. The `sender` parameter in this example is the object that called the event. In this case, it's the `NSButton` being clicked. Using the `sender` parameter gives you access to all the `NSButton` methods.

With MacRuby, as expected, it's much easier to declare a method as an IBAction. The following code is the MacRuby equivalent of the Objective-C IBAction example:

```
def pressed_button(sender)
  ...
end
```

You may have noticed that the method name follows standard Ruby practice and uses an underscore instead of camel casing. You don't need to specify a return type in Ruby code, so you can't label the method as an IBAction. Fortunately, Interface Builder recognizes this MacRuby method as an IBAction because the method accepts only one parameter named `sender`.

After you create an action in the source file, you can return to Interface Builder to connect the action to a control.

CONNECTING ACTIONS

From the Connections tab of the inspector pane, you should see the `pressed_button` action listed under Received Actions. To make the button aware that it should invoke the `pressed_button` method, you'll make a connection the same way you did with the `start_button` outlet.

Drag a connection from the `pressed_button` action to the `NSButton` as shown in figure 3.7.

With the key components of Interface Builder under your belt, we can now connect the dots and create a more in-depth MacRuby application.

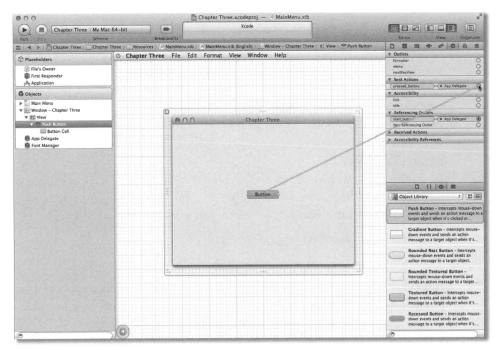

Figure 3.7 Connecting the `pressed_button` action to the button

> **Breaking a connection**
>
> To remove a connection you no longer need or created in error, open the Connections tab in the inspector pane, and then click the x next to the outlet or action that you want to remove.

3.3 Creating the Todo List application

You'll be building a useful application that manages daily tasks. This application is more advanced than our previous attempts in chapters 1 and 2. Named Todo List, the application has a complex UI and showcases some of the many features that make Interface Builder an outstanding tool. You'll also dive into some advanced MacRuby.

The development process should look familiar to you by now:

- Build the UI.
- Create the model and controller.
- Connect outlets and actions.
- Run and package the application.

Fire up Xcode, and create a new project named Todo.

3.3.1 Constructing the user interface

From your new project, locate and open MainMenu.xib. Table 3.2 summarizes the elements you'll include in the UI based on the tasks you want to accomplish.

Table 3.2 UI elements in the Todo List application

Task	UI element
View a list of all upcoming tasks	Table view
Create a new task	Button
Mark a task as completed	Button
Add descriptive text about a newly created task	Text field

Let's get started!

ADDING A TABLE VIEW

Bring the main application window into view. From the Object library, search for the table view. Drag it to the application window and then size it to fit the layout. When sizing interface elements, Interface Builder helps you guide and snap them into place. Feel free to size the table view similar to what's shown in figure 3.8. Leave enough space at the bottom for a text field and two buttons.

Now that the table view is in place, make sure it's configured properly. Open the document window (you may need to click the dock mode button to switch to outline

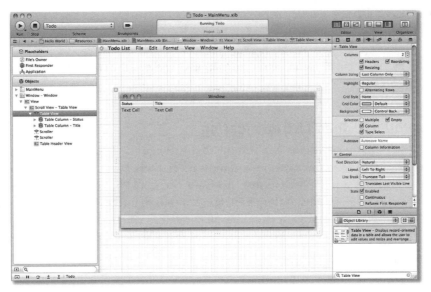

Figure 3.8   The resized table view. The space at the bottom of the window is for the text field and two push buttons.

view) and expand the window object to expose its subviews (see figure 3.8). Find the two NSTableColumn objects for the table view (see figure 3.8). Click the first one to view the attributes in the inspector pane. From here, change the title to Status and the identifier to status (see figure 3.9). Do the same for the other NSTableColumn object, but give it the title Title with an identifier of title.

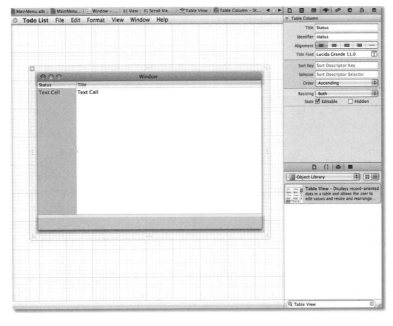

Figure 3.9
Changing
attributes
of the first
NSTableColumn

Next, you'll need two push buttons: one to create a new task and another to mark it as completed.

ADDING BUTTONS AND A TEXT FIELD

Locate a push button (NSButton) and a text field (NSTextField) in the library pane. Drag two buttons and the text field to the application window. You may resize and position them to your liking.

Click the first button to view its attributes in the inspector pane. Rename the button title from Button to Create. Rename the title of the second button Complete.

Let's move on to the text field and modify two of its attributes to improve its appearance. Click the text field to view its attributes in the inspector pane:

- To add flair, change the Border attribute option to the one with rounded corners.
- To provide users with helper text in the text field when it's not focused, enter some text in the Placeholder attribute.

Figure 3.10 shows the application in its current state with the buttons in place and the styled text field.

Next, you'll customize the application window.

LABELING THE APPLICATION WINDOW AND MANAGING ITS SIZE

Right now, the application title bar is labeled Window. You wouldn't want to ship an application with this generic title. Select the Window in the document window and change the Title attribute to Todo List in the inspector pane.

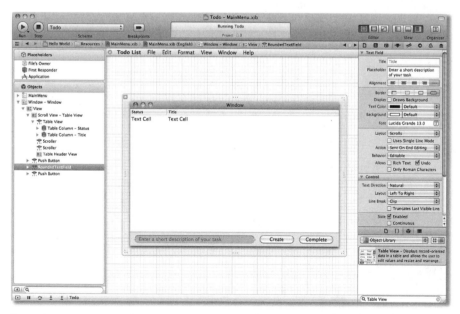

Figure 3.10 To change the appearance of the buttons and text field, use the Attributes tab in the inspector pane.

If you run the application now, the current window size looks good, but if you maximize or resize it, the elements don't resize with the window. Here's where you can take advantage of the autosizing tools that Interface Builder provides for free. But even with autosizing configured for the elements, if a user resizes the window so that it's extremely small, it can result in a poor user experience. To fix this potential sizing issue, you'll first set a minimum width and height for the window.

From the document window, select the NSWindow, and then click the Size tab in the inspector pane (look for the ruler icon). Scroll down and check the Minimum Size box. This setting prevents users from resizing the window smaller than its current size.

Next, you'll apply autosizing to each interface element. You'll start with the table view.

AUTOSIZING THE UI ELEMENTS

The table view lists all tasks. You'll notice that this table view is housed in an NSScrollView if you look in the document window. With the parent NSScrollView selected, click the Size tab in the inspector pane, and locate the Autosizing section.

What exactly do the lines in the autosizing box do?

The lines outside the inner gray box determine positioning and spacing. Activating the lines in the inner gray box tells Interface Builder in which direction(s) the view is permitted to stretch or shrink when its parent window is resized.

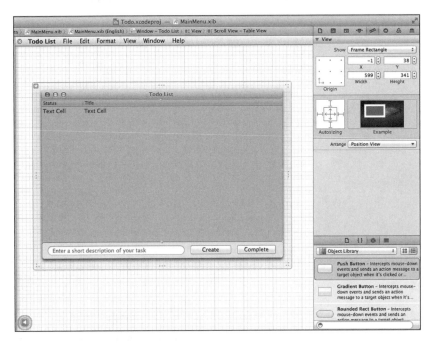

Figure 3.11   Setting autosizing for the NSScrollView, which contains the child NSTableView

In the autosizing box, you'll enable autosizing for all directions. This view is already anchored to the top-left of the window. You want it to stretch proportionally in all directions when the parent window is resized. Figure 3.11 shows the autosizing settings for the NSScrollView.

Next, you'll set up autosizing for the text field.

When the main window is resized, you don't want the text field to stretch vertically, but you do want it to stretch horizontally. Outside the inner gray box, enable the left, right, and bottom directions. Inside the inner gray box, enable the arrows that point to the left and right because you want it to stretch only horizontally.

You don't want the buttons to get any bigger in any direction, but you want them to retain their position when the main window is resized. Outside the inner gray box, enable the bottom and right directions. This will ensure that the buttons remain at the bottom-right of the window at all times. You can see the autosizing for these buttons in figure 3.12.

The main application window is now ready to go. Launch the simulator in Interface Builder to test out your autosizing changes. The interface elements should now resize properly when you resize the main window. Pretty slick that it does this automatically for you, right? The best part is that you've written zero lines of code!

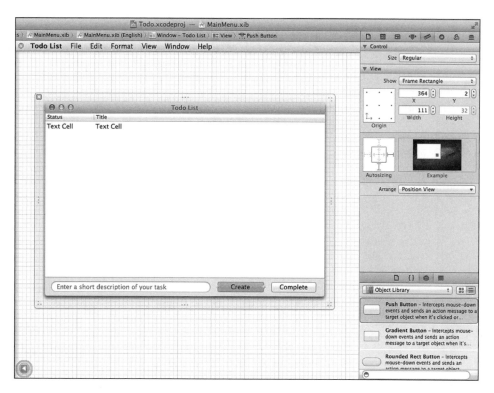

Figure 3.12   With autosizing, the position and size of the buttons remains fixed when the window is resized.

The last piece of the UI you need to modify is the menu bar.

CUSTOMIZING THE MENUS

A menu bar appears at the top of the screen in every Cocoa application you run. Some common menus are File, Edit, View, and so on. Right now, the Todo List application has a generic menu titled NewApplication that was created by the template. If you created the Pomodoro application in chapter 2, you already know how to customize the menu title and its items.

Click NewApplication, and change the title to Todo List in the inspector pane. Replace NewApplication with Todo List in the following menu items: About, Hide, and Quit. Rename the menu item in the Help menu as well.

Figure 3.13 shows the customized Todo List menu.

TIP   You can also double-click menus and menu items to rename them.

That completes the interface. Using Interface Builder, you created a nice UI without writing a single line of code! Give yourself a well-deserved pat on the back! Interface Builder makes this all so easy for you.

Next, we're going to dive into some MacRuby to finish off the application. What good is a nice interface if you can't put it to use? Let's add some real functionality to the Todo List application.

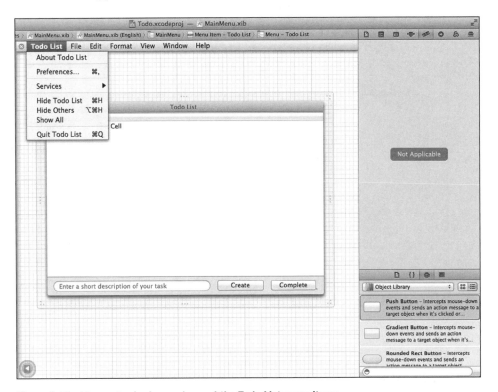

Figure 3.13   The customized menu bar and the Todo List menu items

3.3.2 Creating the model

Let's get started on building the model. The model represents each new task that users create.

With the project open in Xcode, right-click the Classes group and choose Add > New File. From the Ruby template, select Ruby File and name the new file Task.rb. (You're creating a MacRuby file, but it's labeled as a Ruby file in Xcode.) The model represents each individual task in the table view. Each `Task` object has a `status` and a `title` attribute. To set up the getters and setters for these two attributes, you use the `attr_accessor` method. The following listing shows the Task model in its entirety.

Listing 3.1 Task model

```ruby
class Task
  attr_accessor :status, :title

  def initialize
    @status = "Open"
  end

  def complete
    @status = "Completed"
  end
end
```

You set the instance variable `status` to `Open` because when you create a new task, the default status is `Open`. You also create an instance method to change `status` to `Completed` when a user marks an item as complete.

Now that you have the model in place, let's work on the controller.

3.3.3 Creating the controller

The controller interacts with the Task model and the view. As you did for the model, add a new Ruby file to the Classes group and name it TasksController.rb. You'll set up the foundation first so that you can interact with the elements in the view.

CREATING VARIABLES

To hook into the table view, you'll add a variable. You do the same for the text field because you need to access it to retrieve the text that it contains:

```ruby
class TasksController
  attr_accessor :tasks_table_view, :task_text_field
end
```

After you create these variables, you can focus on the protocol methods for the table view.

SPECIFYING INITIALIZATION TASKS

You first define the `awakeFromNib` method, which is part of the `NSNibAwaking` protocol. This method is called right after the controller is instantiated from the nib, Main-Menu.xib:

```ruby
def awakeFromNib
  @tasks = []
```

```
  @tasks_table_view.dataSource = self
  @tasks_table_view.delegate = self
end
```

You set up a task array to store all the tasks currently in memory, and you specify the controller (self) as the data source for the table view. The NSTableView class has a data source attribute for which you can specify any object. For now, you'll specify the array, whose job is to store all the tasks that a user creates.

The data source stores data and feeds it to the table view when the table view calls for it. To do this, the data source needs to conform to the NSTableDataSource protocol. This protocol requires implementing at least two methods that tell the table view how to handle and display the data. (You haven't yet created these methods.)

You also set the controller (self) as the delegate for the table view. The table view must conform to the NSTableViewDelegate protocol. You'll learn more about delegates in chapter 4.

HANDLING AND DISPLAYING DATA

The data source feeds data to the table view, but the table view must determine the number of rows to display and what data to display. You have to set up a few required methods to pass this information to the table view.

You'll define the numberOfRowsInTableView: method to tell the table view how many rows to display:

```
def numberOfRowsInTableView(view)
  @tasks.size
end
```

This method simply returns the size of the task array.

You'll define the tableView:objectValueForTableColumn:row: method to tell the table view what data to display based on the column identifier and row number:

```
def tableView(view, objectValueForTableColumn:column, row:index)
  task = @tasks[index]
  case column.identifier
    when 'status'
      task.status
    when 'title'
      task.title
  end
end
```

You'll use the row index to retrieve a specific task from the task array. Then depending on the column's identifier attribute, which you specified previously, you return the task information to display.

Next, let's set up the action that will be invoked when the Create button is clicked.

CREATING A NEW TASK

To create a new task, define the create_task action:

```
def create_task(sender)
  if @task_text_field.stringValue != ""
```

```
    task = Task.new
    task.title = @task_text_field.stringValue
    @tasks << task
    @task_text_field.stringValue = ""
    @tasks_table_view.reloadData
  end
end
```

To make sure that the text field contains text, you check the `stringValue` method on the `task_text_field` object. You don't want to list any blank tasks without titles.

If the string is not blank, you instantiate a new task, set its title to the text in the text field, and add it to the `task` array. You then reset the text field by setting `stringValue` to a blank string.

To reload the data, you invoke the `reloadData` method on the table view. This also invokes the two protocol methods you previously set up, which determine the number of rows to display and populate the table view.

The final method you'll implement is another action, which you'll hook up to the Complete button.

MARKING A TASK AS COMPLETED

To identify the task and mark it completed, create the `complete_task` action:

```
def complete_task(sender)
  if @tasks_table_view.selectedRow != -1
    @tasks[@tasks_table_view.selectedRow].complete
    @tasks_table_view.reloadData
  end
end
```

You call the `selectedRow` method on the table view to return the index of the currently selected row. If no row is selected, the method returns the value -1.

If a row is selected, you retrieve the corresponding task. You use the index of the selected row to find the task in the `task` array.

Next, you call the `complete` instance method that you created, and then call `reloadData` to refresh the table view.

The following listing shows the completed controller, TasksController.rb.

Listing 3.2 Tasks controller

```
class TasksController
  attr_accessor :tasks_table_view, :task_text_field, :create_button    ◁─┐
                                                                         │  Sets variables
  def awakeFromNib                                         ◁──────┐      │
    @tasks = []                                                   │ Specifies
    @tasks_table_view.dataSource = self                          │ initialization tasks
    @tasks_table_view.delegate = self
  end

  def numberOfRowsInTableView(view)                       ◁──────┐ Returns number of
    @tasks.size                                                  │ rows to display
  end
```

```
def tableView(view, objectValueForTableColumn:column, row:index) start
  task = @tasks[index]
  case column.identifier
    when 'status'
      task.status
    when 'title'
      task.title
  end
end

def create_task(sender)
  if @task_text_field.stringValue != ""
    task = Task.new
    task.title = @task_text_field.stringValue
    @tasks << task
    @task_text_field.stringValue = ""
    @tasks_table_view.reloadData
  end
end

def complete_task(sender)
  if @tasks_table_view.selectedRow != -1
    @tasks[@tasks_table_view.selectedRow].complete
    @tasks_table_view.reloadData
  end
end
end
```

Displays tasks

Creates new task

Modifies task status

Feeling good about what you put together? You're almost there!

Before you run the application, you need to hook up the controller and its outlets and actions in Interface Builder.

3.3.4 *Connecting outlets and actions*

Now that the controller is ready to go, you can connect the code and the view.

Open MainMenu.xib file again. From the Object library, search for an NSObject, which is represented by a blue cube, and drag it to the document window. This NSObject represents the controller, TasksController.rb.

As you know, all objects are subclasses of NSObject in MacRuby. Click the NSObject you added, and then click the third tab from the left in the inspector pane. Change the Class property to TasksController as shown in figure 3.14.

If you set this up correctly, the Connections tab of the inspector pane lists the outlets and actions that you created previously.

> **TIP** If you don't see any outlets or actions, make sure that the class name for the NSObject doesn't contain a typo.

From the Connections tab, make connections from the outlets to their respective controls:

- Drag the task_text_field outlet to the NSTextField.
- Drag the tasks_table_view outlet to the table view.

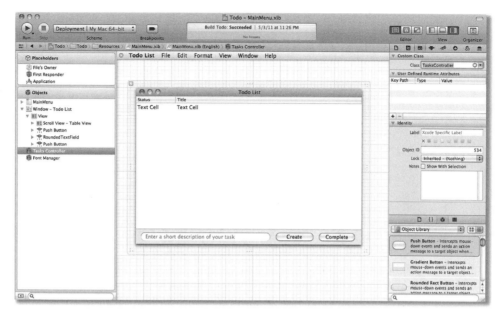

Figure 3.14 Adding the controller in Interface Builder

From the Received Actions section in the Connections tab, connect the actions to the two buttons. The actions will execute when users create a task or mark it complete:

- Drag the `create_task:` action to the Create button.
- Drag the `complete_task:` action to the Complete button.

The Connections tab may look similar to figure 3.15.

With the outlet and action connections in place, the UI and the code can now talk to each other. Time to run the application!

3.3.5 Running and packaging the application

Return to Xcode and click Run (the Play icon) to compile and run the application. The finished product in shown in figure 3.16.

You successfully built a functional, easy-to-use task management application. You can create a new task, highlight it, and then mark it as completed. As an exercise, you should try on your own to create a way to unmark a task as completed.

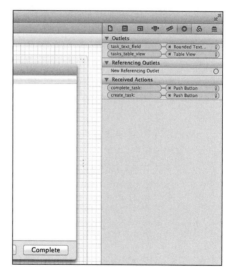

Figure 3.15 With TasksController selected, you can see that the outlets and actions are now connected to UI elements.

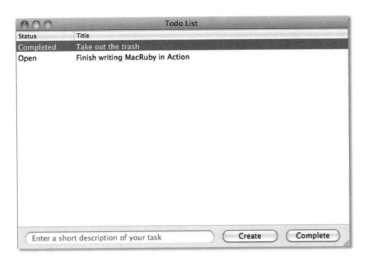

Figure 3.16   The finished Todo List application

The application does need an enhancement or two. For example, if you quit the application, you lose all your previously entered tasks the next time you run it. In chapter 7, we'll return to the Todo List application, and you'll learn how to alleviate this issue using the Core Data framework.

You can now package the application using the Deployment scheme, which we discussed in chapter 2, and send it to your friends.

3.4   *Summary*

In this chapter, you explored UI development using Xcode Interface Builder. You learned how to navigate within the environment, how to work with IB actions and outlets and connect them to your codebase, and how to simulate an interface without compiling your application.

You created the Todo List application, which employs more advanced MacRuby and Cocoa features, such as data sources, working with table views, and delegate methods, which we haven't formally introduced yet. You'll learn more about delegates in chapter 4.

There are countless ways to create an interface for any kind of application. You're now able to explore more of Xcode's Interface Builder to create something great for your next application. In the next chapter, you'll learn about delegates and how to use the delegate design pattern in a new MacRuby application.

Part 2

Take it for a spin

This part of the book focuses on MacRuby and Cocoa. Cocoa provides the real power when you're developing for the Mac platform. We'll take a tour of the core concepts of Cocoa from the MacRuby perspective using examples with the MacRuby language.

Using the delegate pattern

If you've done any Cocoa development, chances are you've already used the delegate pattern. If you haven't, this chapter will explain the important role delegation plays in MacRuby Cocoa application development. Delegation is a common design pattern for object-oriented programming languages. The Cocoa framework makes heavy use of delegation, which makes it a vital concept to understand if you plan to write MacRuby Cocoa applications.

In this chapter, you'll get a good understanding of delegates, including how to use them, how to create your own, and how to use them in your applications. You'll even get a chance to build a MacRuby web browser using the knowledge you've gained about delegates.

4.1 What are delegates?

A *delegate* is an object that responds to or acts upon a certain event or action that another object called. The object that triggers the call to a delegate is referred to as the *delegating* or *responder* object. Full responsibility is given to the delegate to decide how to respond to a certain event.

You typically use delegates to deal with actions that involve the user interface. If you feel confused, don't worry; in this section, we're going to explain where you've used delegates before and how they work, and then we'll walk you through some delegate method examples.

To understand how delegates work, we'll first look at a few delegate methods that exist in Cocoa classes, such as the `NSWindow` class.

4.1.1 How do delegate methods work?

The `NSWindow` class is a good example of a simple class that you use in most MacRuby Cocoa applications. `NSWindow` has a protocol called `NSWindowDelegate`, which defines all the delegate methods that an `NSWindow` can implement.

Protocols allow you to define interfaces that contain methods that are independent of the class hierarchy. Protocols allow you to follow a convention through an API. What's great is that if two separate classes implement the same protocol, they can potentially communicate with each other without having the same super class. Delegates implement many, if not all, of the methods defined in a protocol. Formal protocols require that you implement all methods defined, whereas informal protocols don't have such requirements. For this discussion, we selected three methods defined in the `NSWindowDelegate` informal protocol:

- `windowShouldClose:`
- `windowWillClose:`
- `windowDidResize:`

There are three key words in this group of methods: `should`, `will`, and `did`. It's these types of key words that should trigger in your mind that you're dealing with a delegate method. These methods ask the delegate object what they should do or how they should respond to these events. Table 4.1 summarizes the expected response to these key words. Of the many keywords that delegate methods can include, these three are the most popular.

Table 4.1 Key words you'll often see in a delegate method name

Key word	Meaning	Expected response
Should	Should an event happen?	Yes or No
Will	Event about to happen; how would you like to prepare?	The code to execute before the event occurs.
Did	Event has happened; how would you like to react?	The code to execute after the event occurs.

Figure 4.1 Safari implements the `windowShouldClose:` delegate method.

Protocols such as `NSWindowDelegate` define these methods as optional. This means the delegating object may already have default behavior predefined, but it lets you override and provide your own functionality or action based on an event.

Let's take a closer look at the `windowShouldClose:` delegate method. This method is called when you click the close button in a Cocoa window, and it expects a Boolean response. If the response is `yes`, the window should close, if `no`, it shouldn't.

To see this method in action, launch the Safari web browser, open more than one tab, and then click the close button. A prompt appears, similar to that shown in figure 4.1.

By providing a dialog for the user to choose the appropriate action, Safari lets the user decide whether it returns `yes` or `no` to this delegate method.

Let's experiment with the `windowShouldClose:` delegate and replicate the Safari functionality in a simple script.

4.1.2 Implementing the delegate pattern

Let's create a quick MacRuby Cocoa script that creates an `NSWindow`, sets itself as the delegate, and implements the `windowShouldClose:` delegate method, which gets called when the close button is clicked.

Create a new .rb file (feel free to use any text editor), and then add the following code to load the Cocoa framework, set up an NSApplication instance, and create a window:

```
framework 'cocoa'

@app = NSApplication.sharedApplication

def setup_window
  win = NSWindow.alloc.initWithContentRect([300,300,300,100],
  ➡ styleMask:NSTitledWindowMask | NSClosableWindowMask |
  ➡ NSMiniaturizableWindowMask | NSResizableWindowMask,
  ➡ backing:NSBackingStoreBuffered, defer:false)

  win.delegate = self
  win.title = "Delegate Test"
  win.display
  win.orderFrontRegardless
end
```

You first create a new NSWindow in the setup_window method. Next, you set the window's delegate to this class (self). The remaining lines in the method specify the title of the window and ensure that the window displays properly.

Since you set the script as the delegate for the NSWindow, you can now implement a protocol method.

ALERTING THE USER

To emulate what was shown in the Safari example, you'll implement windowShould-Close: to bring up an NSAlert that allows the user to decide whether the window should be closed. Add the following code to the script:

```
def windowShouldClose(sender)
  alert = NSAlert.alertWithMessageText("You clicked the close button",
  ➡ defaultButton:"Okay",
  ➡ alternateButton:"Cancel",
  ➡ otherButton:nil,
  ➡ informativeTextWithFormat:"Are you sure you want to exit this
  ➡ application?")
  return (alert.runModal == NSAlertDefaultReturn ? true : false)
end
```

In this delegate method, you first create an NSAlert to ask users if they want to quit the application. Next, you run the NSAlert and listen for the response. If the default button (Okay) is clicked, the method returns true, which tells the NSWindowDelegate to close the window. If the alternate button (Cancel) is clicked, it tells the NSWindow-Delegate not to close the window.

To make sure that the setup_window method is called and the application starts, add the following lines to the script:

```
setup_window
@app.run
```

From the Terminal application, navigate to the directory where you saved the script, and run it using the `macruby` command.

Figure 4.2   The NSAlert appears when the windowShouldClose: method is triggered.

You'll see a blank window, but no need to worry; this is intended. The magic happens when you click the red close button at the top-left of the window. The alert you're presented with is what you created in the `windowShouldClose:` method (see figure 4.2).

But you're not finished yet. After you click Okay, the alert window closes, but the application is still running. If you quit the application in the `windowShouldClose:` method, the NSAlert can't display, and the user isn't given the choice to either keep the window open or close it. Also, the method wouldn't return anything to the NSWindowDelegate, which expects either a `true` or `false` response. You need to implement another delegate method that lets you know that the window is closing. At that point, you can end the application.

STOPPING THE APPLICATION

Luckily, there's a delegate method named `windowWillClose:` that's called when the window will close. Add the following to the script:

```
def windowWillClose(notification)
  @app.stop(self)
end
```

The `windowWillClose:` method takes an NSNotification as its only parameter. You don't need to use this parameter since all you want to do is tell the application to stop. You pass the sender when you call the `stop` method on the NSApplication instance.

The next listing shows the script in its entirety.

Listing 4.1   NSWindow delegation script

```
framework 'cocoa'

@app = NSApplication.sharedApplication

def setup_window
  win = NSWindow.alloc.initWithContentRect([300,300,300,100],
  ➥ styleMask:NSTitledWindowMask | NSClosableWindowMask |
  ➥ NSMiniaturizableWindowMask | NSResizableWindowMask,
  ➥ backing:NSBackingStoreBuffered, defer:false)

  win.delegate = self
  win.title = "Delegate Test"
  win.display
  win.orderFrontRegardless
end

def windowShouldClose(sender)
```

Display alert window ←⎯⎯

```
alert = NSAlert.alertWithMessageText("You clicked the close button",
➥ defaultButton:"Okay",
➥ alternateButton:"Cancel",
➥ otherButton:nil,
➥ informativeTextWithFormat:"Are you sure you want to exit this
➥ application?")
return (alert.runModal == NSAlertDefaultReturn ? true : false)
end

def windowWillClose(notification)                          ⟵─┐  Stop
  @app.stop(self)                                            │  application
end

setup_window
@app.run
```

Run the application again and click the red close button. When you click Okay in the alert window, the application now quits.

Delegate vs. data source

Data sources are nearly identical to delegates. The biggest differentiator between the two is where they're used. Delegates are primarily used to respond to events that occur in the user interface. Data sources are used to manage the data that may belong to a certain view. To use either object, you implement specific delegate methods.

Usually, objects that act as a host's data sources, also act as the host's delegates. You used data sources in the Todo List application in chapter 2. You specified the controller as the data source for the `NSTableView`—the object that displays all tasks in memory. As you may recall, you specified the data source in the `awakeFromNib` method:

```
def awakeFromNib
  ...
  @tasks_table_view.dataSource = self
end
```

To successfully use the controller as a data source for the `NSTableView`, you implemented two of the delegate methods defined in the `NStableViewDataSource` protocol. The first method, `numberOfRowsInTableView:`, specifies the number of rows the `NSTableView` should expect. The second method, `tableView:objectValueForTableColumn:row:`, specifies what data to display for each individual row.

Now that you've had a chance to work with delegates, we'll show you how to define your own in MacRuby. The ability to use delegates to extend an application is one of the benefits of this design pattern.

4.2   *Delegation as an extension technique*

Creating your own delegate methods in MacRuby is a little different from creating them in Objective-C. There are various ways to implement your own version of the delegate pattern with MacRuby. In this section, we'll show you two ways to implement the delegate pattern in your own applications.

4.2.1 Delegation the Cocoa way

Let's create a class named HostClass and an instance variable named delegate. The class acts as the host and uses a delegate to implement some of its methods:

```
class HostClass
  attr_accessor :delegate
end
```

The delegate instance variable represents the object you can delegate specific tasks to. Suppose you have a method named someActionWillOccur. In Objective-C, you might write the following code to determine whether you can call this method on the delegate:

```
-(void) someActionWillOccur {
  if(delegate && [delegate respondsToSelector:
    @selector(someActionWillOccur:)]) {
    [delegate someActionWillOccur];
  } else {
    // Perform default behavior
  }
}
```

In MacRuby, you can do the same for the HostClass with the following code. (To conform to Ruby standards, and because it's a method we made up, we chose not to use camel casing in the method name.)

```
def some_action_will_occur
  if @delegate && @delegate.respond_to?("some_action_will_occur")
    @delegate.some_action_will_occur
  else
    # Perform default behavior
  end
end
```

You can then create an instance of the HostClass in a new class, set that class as the delegate, and implement the delegate method some_action_will_occur.

One downside is that you can't create formal or informal protocols in MacRuby, so there's nothing "automagically" built in to ensure that delegate objects implement required methods.

Another way you can use delegates in MacRuby is through the Forwardable module, which is included in Ruby's standard library.

4.2.2 Delegation using Forwardable

Using the Forwardable module, you explicitly set the class, and then set the methods you want to delegate using the def_delegators method. You first need to require Forwardable and extend it:

```
require 'forwardable'
class HostClass
  extend Forwardable
  attr_accessor :delegate
```

```
      def_delegators :@delegate, :some_action_will_occur
end
```

To test out how this works, create a delegate class and implement the some_action_will_occur method in the same file:

```
class DelegateClass
  def initialize
    @host = HostClass.new
    @host.delegate = self
    @host.some_action_will_occur
  end

  def some_action_will_occur
    puts "This is from DelegateClass"
  end
end
```

You first require the HostClass. Next, upon initialization, you create a new HostClass instance, set self as the delegate, and call the some_action_will_occur method on that instance.

If you run this code and call DelegateClass.new, it returns the message This is from DelegateClass. The HostClass knows that its delegate is set to DelegateClass and forwards the method request.

You've been briefed on how to use delegates and how to implement your own. Next, you'll create a MacRuby application using a framework that relies on delegation.

4.3   *Using delegation in a custom MacRuby web browser*

Creating a web browser gives you the opportunity to dive into the world of delegates. You'll use WebKit, an Objective-C framework that heavily relies on the WebKit-Delegate protocol, and WebKit's open-source browser engine. You won't create the next Safari or Firefox, but your web browser will be worthy of showing off to your friends, nevertheless.

Here's the development plan:

1 Create the interface.
2 Write the controller code.
3 Define delegate methods.
4 Connect outlets and actions.
5 Run the application.

WebKit provides so much functionality out of the box that you'll be surprised at how easy this project will be to accomplish.

4.3.1   *Creating the browser interface*

Create a new project in Xcode called MacRuby Browser. We're fans of building the user interface first, so open MainWindow.xib in Interface Builder. To keep this simple, you'll use only two UI items: an NSTextField and a WebView. The WebView is the portion of the screen that displays the web page that the user is currently viewing. The `NSTextField` serves as the input method for users to enter a URL, and this field also displays the URL of the web page they're currently viewing.

CUSTOMIZING THE MAIN WINDOW

Stretch out the main window to the size you prefer. For styling purposes, we enabled the textured option in the inspector pane. While you're still in the inspector pane, set the title of the window to MacRuby Browser. If you like, feel free to change the titles of the MainMenu section of the interface. By default, the menu items include NewApplication in their titles instead of MacRuby Browser.

ADDING THE URL ADDRESS BAR AND WEB-PAGE VIEW

To represent the address bar, grab an `NSTextField` from the Library, and drag it to the top of the window. In the Attributes tab of the inspector pane, set the placeholder to Enter URL to indicate that this field is for entering a web address. Also, under the Action drop-down list, choose Sent on Enter Only. This causes the `NSTextField` to send you an action when a user presses Enter. This is an appropriate solution for you, since you won't provide an explicit button that navigates to the specified URL. You can add a button if you prefer; we covered how to do this in chapter 3.

From the library pane, find the `WebView` object and drag that into the window, underneath the `NSTextField`. Adjust its size so that it takes up the rest of the interface window.

> **TIP** Feel free to go into the Size tab of the inspector pane to make sure that these elements adjust their size correctly when the window is resized.

ADDING A LOADING INDICATOR

When the browser is actually loading something, it's nice to indicate that to users in the interface. You'll use the `NSProgessIndicator`, which displays as a spinner. From the library pane, drag this into the window and place it to the right of the `NSText-Field`. In the inspector, make sure to uncheck Display When Stopped because you want the spinner to appear only when there's activity.

The finished browser window is shown in figure 4.3.

Now that you've set up a basic (and we mean really basic) interface for the browser, you can start digging into the delegates for the `WebView` object.

4.3.2 *Setting up the controller*

Before you create a controller file, you need to add the WebKit framework to the Xcode project. Without the framework, the

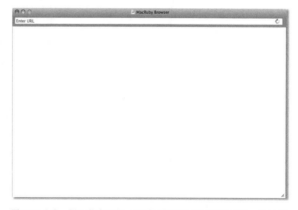

Figure 4.3 The finished, albeit simple, MacRuby Browser UI

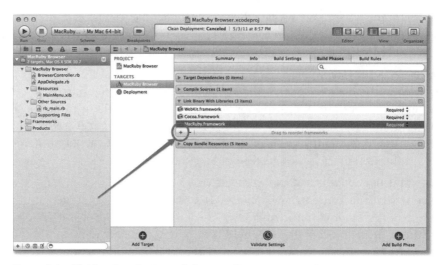

Figure 4.4   Clicking the + button to link a new library to your project

project would throw many errors because it wouldn't have access to any of the WebKit classes, such as the `WebView` and the `WebFrameLoadDelegate`.

ADDING THE WEBKIT FRAMEWORK

To add the WebKit framework, click the project name in the project navigator. This should show you your project settings.

Click the Build Phases tab, and expand Link Binary With Libraries. Next, click the + button as shown in figure 4.4.

From the dialog box that appears (see figure 4.5), enter `Webkit` in the search field. Click WebKit.framework, and then click Add.

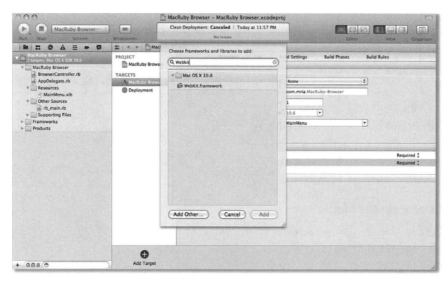

Figure 4.5   Searching for and then adding WebKit.framework

You're now ready to get started on the application's main controller. From Xcode, create a new class called BrowserController.rb.

SPECIFYING INITIALIZATION TASKS AND THE DELEGATE

You start by initializing the NSWindow, NSTextField, WebView, and NSProgress-Indicator with the attr_accessor function:

```
class BrowserController
  attr_accessor :window, :url_field, :web_view, :indicator
end
```

You then implement the awakeFromNib method to set the controller as the delegate for the WebFrameLoadDelegate protocol:

```
def awakeFromNib
  @web_view.frameLoadDelegate = self
end
```

> **NOTE** Alternatively, you could have specified the delegate in Interface Builder by dragging the frameLoadDelegate outlet to the Browser-Controller object.

Next, you'll create an IBAction, which you'll later connect to the NSTextField.

LOADING AND FORMATTING URL REQUESTS

After a user types in a URL and presses Enter, you want the following code to execute. Let's name this method url_entered:

```
def url_entered(sender)
  url = NSURL.URLWithString(format_url(@url_field.stringValue))
  request = NSURLRequest.requestWithURL(url)
  @web_view.mainFrame.loadRequest(request)
end
```

You call the URLWithString method to create an NSURL object. You'll notice that there's a call to a method called format_url:, which you haven't yet implemented. (You'll define this method next.) After you have the URL, you make an NSURLRequest object and then take that object and use it to perform the loadRequest: method on the current frame in the WebView.

Now you can create that format_url: method. How often do you include http:// when you type a URL into your web browser? Probably not very often. When you create an NSURL, it expects the protocol, http or otherwise, to be specified. The format_url: method is a convenience method that prepends http:// to all requests that don't include it. Here's what it looks like:

```
def format_url(url)
  url = "http://#{url}" unless url.include?("http://") ||
  ➥ url.include?("https://")
  url
end
```

You conditionally prepend http:// to the incoming URL, and return the newly formed URL.

You're almost finished with the controller. You haven't yet implemented the delegate methods, though.

4.3.3 *Implementing delegate methods in the controller*

Some features in the browser depend on the implementation of delegate protocol methods. You'll make use of the `WebFrameLoadDelegate` protocol, which is notified when the URL in the `WebFrame` changes. The `WebFrame` contains the `WebView`, which displays the web page. The `WebView` will be calling these methods on your `Browser-Controller` delegate.

Specifically, you'll implement the following four methods:

- `webView:didStartProvisionalLoadForFrame:`
- `webView:didFinishLoadForFrame:`
- `webView:didReceiveTitle:forFrame:`
- `webView:didFailProvisionalLoadWithError:forFrame:`

SETTING UP THE LOADING INDICATOR

Let's first get the `NSProgressIndicator` to spin when the `WebView` is actively loading a page and update the `NSTextField` with the URL address currently loaded. You'll grab the URL that's been loaded and set that as the value for the `NSTextField`. These tasks are easily accomplished by implementing the `webView:didStartProvisionalLoad-ForFrame:` method defined in the `WebFrameLoadDelegate` protocol:

```
def webView(sender, didStartProvisionalLoadForFrame:frame)
  @indicator.startAnimation(self)
  if frame == sender.mainFrame
    @url_field.stringValue = frame.provisionalDataSource.request.URL
    ➥ .absoluteString
  end
end
```

You first tell the `NSProgressIndicator` to start its spinning animation. You pass in `self` to specify the controller as the sender. Next, you ensure that the URL request occurred in the main frame of the `WebView`. You then set the value of the `NSTextField` to the string value of the URL that's being loaded for that frame.

To stop the animation after the page loads, you'll implement the `webView:didFinishLoadForFrame:` method. Otherwise, the `NSProgressIndicator` would be stuck spinning forever. This delegate method lets you know when the frame is finished loading:

```
def webView(sender, didFinishLoadForFrame:frame)
  @indicator.stopAnimation(self)
end
```

TIP Remember to check the spelling of these delegate methods. If they're spelled incorrectly, they won't get executed.

Let's change the title of the `NSWindow` to match the title of the page that was loaded.

MAKING THE WINDOW TITLE AND THE WEB PAGE TITLE MATCH

You'll implement the `webView:didReceiveTitle:forFrame:` method to sync the window and web page titles. Other frames may be loading other elements, which could result in an incorrect page title being displayed. To ensure that the URL request came from the main frame of the `WebView`, you'll set a condition in the method:

```
def webView(sender, didReceiveTitle:title, forFrame:frame)
  @window.setTitle(title) if frame == sender.mainFrame
end
```

If the frame passed to this method is the main frame (the `WebView`) of the sender, you set the title of the window to the title of the web page that you're viewing.

Let's make sure the browser is capable of responding to an error.

HANDLING INVALID REQUESTS

In the case of a problem loading the specified URL, you'll implement one more delegate method. Using the `webView:didFailProvisionalLoadWithError:forFrame:` method, you can display an error message to the user describing the problem. Without an appropriate response to an error, the `NSProgressIndicator` continues spinning, and the user isn't aware of the problem.

The following code displays an alert and stops animating the `NSProgressIndicator`:

```
def webView(sender, didFailProvisionalLoadWithError:error, forFrame:frame)
  if frame == sender.mainFrame
    alert = NSAlert.alloc.init
    alert.setMessageText("There was a problem loading URL:")
    alert.setInformativeText(@url_field.stringValue)
    alert.beginSheetModalForWindow(@window, modalDelegate:self,
    ➥ didEndSelector:nil, contextInfo:nil)
    @indicator.stopAnimation(self)
  end
end
```

Great job! That's all you need for the controller. The following listing shows the controller code in its entirety. Amazing that less than 50 lines of code is all you need to build a web browser. That's the beauty of using a framework such as WebKit.

Listing 4.2 Completed browser controller

```
class BrowserController
  attr_accessor :window, :url_field, :web_view, :indicator

  def awakeFromNib
    @web_view.frameLoadDelegate = self          ⟵  Set delegate
  end

  def url_entered(sender)                        ⟵  Load request
    url = NSURL.URLWithString(format_url(@url_field.stringValue))
    request = NSURLRequest.requestWithURL(url)
    @web_view.mainFrame.loadRequest(request)
  end
```

```
def format_url(url)
  url = "http://#{url}" unless url.include?("http://") ||
  ➥ url.include?("https://")
  url
end
```
— Format URL

```
def webView(sender, didStartProvisionalLoadForFrame:frame)
  @indicator.startAnimation(self)
  if frame == sender.mainFrame
    @url_field.stringValue =
    ➥ frame.provisionalDataSource.request.URL.absoluteString
  end
end
```
— Start animating

```
def webView(sender, didFinishLoadForFrame:frame)
  @indicator.stopAnimation(self)
end
```
— Stop animating

```
def webView(sender, didReceiveTitle:title, forFrame:frame)
  @window.setTitle(title) if frame == sender.mainFrame
end
```
— Set window title

```
def webView(sender, didFailProvisionalLoadWithError:error,
➥ forFrame:frame)
  if frame == sender.mainFrame
    alert = NSAlert.alloc.init
    alert.setMessageText("There was a problem loading URL:")
    alert.setInformativeText(@url_field.stringValue)
    alert.beginSheetModalForWindow(@window, modalDelegate:self,
    ➥ didEndSelector:nil, contextInfo:nil)
    @indicator.stopAnimation(self)
  end
end
end
```
— Display alert

You're now ready to connect a few outlets and actions in Interface Builder.

4.3.4 *Connecting outlets and actions*

To get the interface and the controller to communicate, you'll first add the controller to the interface and then connect the outlets and actions. In Interface Builder, add an NSObject from the library pane and set its class to BrowserController in the inspector pane. Right-click Browser Controller in the document window (the dock at the far-left side of the screen). You should see available outlets and actions similar to what's shown in figure 4.6.

Drag connections from each outlet to its respective object in the interface. Then drag the url_entered: action to the NSTextField to set it as the action that NSTextField will call. The connections are shown in figure 4.7.

Phew! It's taken a little time to get this far, but if everything has been connected properly, you can now run the MacRuby Browser application.

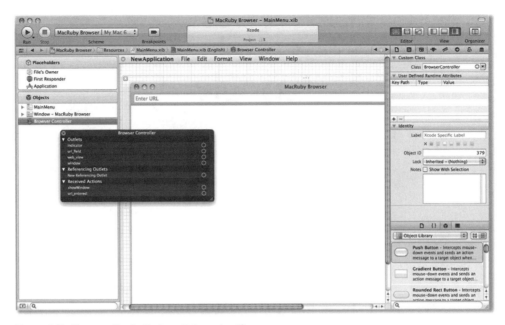

Figure 4.6   Browser Controller's outlets and actions

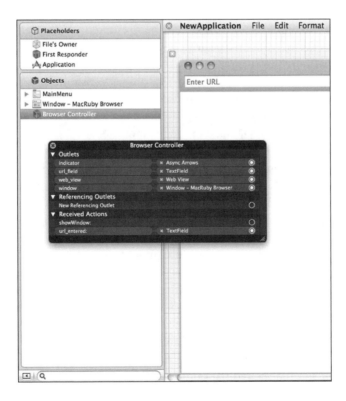

Figure 4.7   Browser Controller's outlets and actions connected

Figure 4.8   Loading the Google website in MacRuby Browser

4.3.5   *Taking MacRuby Browser for a spin*

Let's jump in and run the application. You should be presented with a blank screen and a blank NSTextField for you to type in a web address. Go ahead and type in google.com, with or without the http:// prefix—it shouldn't be an issue since you made sure to take care of this in the code. Figure 4.8 shows the running application. The full URL, http://google.com, displays in the address bar (NSTextField), Google's website displays in the WebView, and Google is the title of the window, as implemented in the webView:didStartProvisionalLoadForFrame: method.

If you click a link or navigate to a different URL, you'll notice that the NSProgress-Indicator spins whenever something is being loaded, as implemented in the webViewdidStartProvisionalLoadForFrame: method. The NSProgressIndicator should disappear when the website is done loading, as implemented in the web-View:didFinishLoadForFrame: method.

Now, go to a web address that doesn't exist. Type a random URL and see what happens. As of this writing, the web address shown in figure 4.9 doesn't exist.

As expected, the NSAlert displays, as implemented in the webView:didFail-ProvisionalLoadWithError:forFrame: method.

The browser application is functional, but it's missing a few features. You didn't create buttons to go back or forward, stop, reload, and so on. As a practice exercise, feel free to add these features if you like. You created a functioning web browser using MacRuby and Cocoa in a short amount of time by using the WebKit framework and its delegates. Give yourself a well-deserved pat on the back!

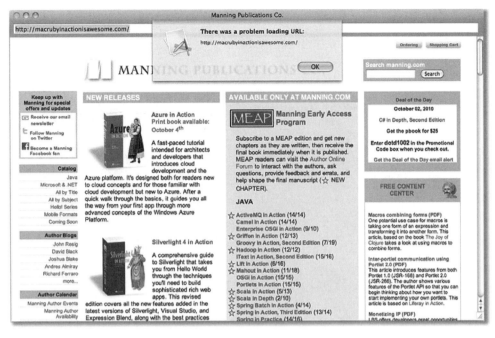

Figure 4.9   Attempting to go to a website that doesn't exist causes an alert message to appear.

4.4   Summary

In this chapter, you learned how to use the delegate pattern, which is a significant design pattern in Cocoa development. You learned what delegates are, how to implement them, and you learned two techniques for creating your own delegates. To top it off, you even created your own web browser with the WebKit framework. Creating the MacRuby Browser application gave you a chance to experiment with delegate methods and learn more about how they work, firsthand. And best of all, you wrote the application in under 50 lines of code!

In the next chapter, you'll continue to learn development techniques for advanced MacRuby applications. We'll be going over Cocoa's notification system, which we can take advantage of in MacRuby to write applications that are more event-driven.

Notifications and implementing the observer pattern

This chapter covers

- Notifying multiple objects
- Posting and queuing notifications
- Observing notifications
- Building an iTunes-notification observer

In chapter 4, you learned a core fundamental of Cocoa development: delegation. But sometimes creating your own delegates won't work. This is where notifications come in. Delegates are important and are used throughout Cocoa, but delegates assign *one* object as the delegate object—this single object is responsible for responding to an event. What if you need multiple objects to respond to the same event? That's when you want to use notifications.

By the end of this chapter, you'll be a notification ninja. We'll explore what makes up notifications, how to register with and use observers, and how to send information with a notification. With a good understanding of notifications you'll be well equipped to create a notification observer tool that displays the iTunes tracks that are playing, paused, and so on.

Before we dive into some code, let's discuss why you might need notifications in a MacRuby application.

5.1 *Notifying multiple objects*

When we talk about notifications, we're actually talking about using the observer pattern. This is a software design pattern where an object notifies its observers automatically for specific events. You'll soon see that it's an easy-to-understand pattern that you can use to your advantage. We'll first go over when and why you would need to use notifications instead of delegates. We'll then introduce notification centers and queues, which take care of delivering notifications.

5.1.1 *When to use notifications*

As you learned in chapter 4, you typically assign one delegate per host when you implement the delegation pattern. Suppose you want to assign multiple delegates per host when you create your own delegates. Let's try that in an example.

Create a generic host object called `HostClass` and then create an instance variable called `delegates` to store an array of delegates:

```
class HostClass
  attr_accessor :delegates
end
```

Now add a delegate method for the delegate objects to respond to:

```
def event_foo_occurred
  responded = false
  @delegates.each do |delegate|
    if delegate.respond_to?("event_foo_occurred")
      delegate.event_foo_occurred
      responded = true
    end
  end
  unless responded
    # Perform default behavior
  end
end
```

You first set the variable `responded` to `false`. Then you iterate through the array of delegates and check each `delegate` to see if it responds to the `event_foo_occurred` method. If it does, you call the `event_foo_occurred` method on `delegate` and set `responded` to `true`. If none of the delegates implemented this method, you perform the default behavior.

This implementation has at least two problems:

- *It's not clean or simple.* The host needs to explicitly know every one of the delegate objects. The host needs to check each of its delegates to ensure they conform to the protocol.
- *The problem is addressed incorrectly.* Hosts are supposed to allow the delegate objects to respond to a specific event by allowing them to modify or reject the

default behavior—having multiple objects determine the outcome of an event isn't good design. Delegates should be used for "to-one" or bidirectional communication.

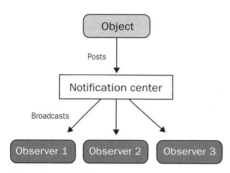

Figure 5.1 **An object posts notifications to multiple objects (observers).**

A notification, on the other hand, is designed for "to-many" communication. As shown in figure 5.1, one object *posts* a notification, which is then *broadcast* to many observers.

Unlike delegation, the object that posts the notification doesn't need to know anything about the observers that respond to the event. The observers don't determine the outcome of a certain event. Objects that use delegation are tightly coupled—the event occurs and they're allowed to respond.

In chapter 3 you created a Pomodoro application. When the timer goes off, you can send an application-wide notification. Any object in the application can observe and listen for this specific notification and respond accordingly.

Notifications are part of the Foundation framework and are a much cleaner and more powerful way to notify multiple objects (observers) of an event. Notifications are Cocoa's implementation of the observer pattern, which allows objects to automatically notify many observers of any event.

In figure 5.1 we explained that an object posts a notification, but we didn't tell you where it posts the notification. We'll tell you about the options Cocoa provides next.

5.1.2 *Managing notifications*

In the delegation pattern the host object is in charge of maintaining all the delegate objects and making sure that the appropriate messages are being sent to them. When using notifications in Cocoa, you don't need to define a custom host, and you don't need to maintain the list of objects that you want to notify. Cocoa uses notification centers which handle this for you.

NOTIFICATION CENTER

To send and receive notifications you use the NSNotificationCenter class. NSNotificationCenter instances manage notifications, which are NSNotification objects. You'll learn more about these objects in section 5.2.

You could create your own NSNotificationCenter instance, but for most purposes you won't need to. A default NSNotificationCenter instance is available throughout your application, which is more than sufficient for handling all your needs. To access the default notification center call the defaultCenter class method on NSNotificationCenter:

```
NSNotificationCenter.defaultCenter
```

The `defaultCenter` method returns the singleton instance of `NSNotificationCenter`. It's this singleton instance that you use throughout an application to manage all the notifications that you want to broadcast and listen to. You'll learn how to broadcast and observe notifications in section 5.2.

DISTRIBUTED NOTIFICATION CENTER

Every application also has a default *distributed* notification center, which is represented by the `NSDistributedNotificationCenter` class. Use this to send and retrieve notifications between different processes on a single machine. Distributed notifications are delivered only to the run loop of a process. To receive the notification the run loop must be in the correct mode, such as `NSDefaultRunLoopMode`. You can't depend on the notification being sent to the main thread of an application.

You'll use the `NSDistributedNotificationCenter` to listen to notifications from other applications in section 5.4.

Because notification centers deliver notifications to observers synchronously you have to wait until all observers have received and processed each notification. You can get around this by using a notification queue.

> ### Run loops and distributed notifications
>
> Remember that distributed notifications are delivered only to a process's run loop. If you're not receiving distributed notifications you probably don't have your MacRuby script set up in a run loop. You can start the run loop with `NSApplication.shared-Application.run`. Knowing this can potentially save you hours of troubleshooting.

NOTIFICATION QUEUE

By queuing the notifications that the `NSNotificationCenter` will deliver, the `NSNotificationQueue` allows you to broadcast many different notifications asynchronously. Not only that, but you can also have multiple notification queues per thread. Just as an application has a default `NSNotificationCenter` and `NSDistributed-NotificationCenter`, it also has a default `NSNotificationQueue` for each thread.

Notifications in the queue are delivered in the order in which they're added. This is known as first in, first out (FIFO) order. Keep this in mind for MacRuby applications that are dependent on notifications being received in a certain order. We'll discuss how to use a queue in more detail in section 5.3.

Now that you know how the `NSNotificationCenter` and the `NSNotification-Queue` work, let's find out how to work with notifications in an application.

5.2 *Setting up notifications*

In this section you'll learn how to set up notifications. You'll see a few ways you can do this by passing in different types of information to potential observers. Also we'll look at how you can post notifications to the notification center.

We'll first show you how easy it is to create your own notification.

5.2.1   *Creating notifications*

As mentioned previously, the NSNotification class represents a notification. NSNotification defines a few methods to create notifications.

THE BASICS

You can quickly create a notification using the notificationWithName:object: method:

```
notification = NSNotification.notificationWithName("foo", object:nil)
```

This is a notification in its most basic form. You create a notification with the name foo, and you set the object parameter. In this case, you specify nothing (nil) because you don't want to send any particular object with the notification. The object parameter is used to pass in any object that the poster wants to send with the notification. Observers that receive this notification will know that the foo notification has been sent and that there was no object attached.

You could also attach information to a notification.

PASSING IN ADDITIONAL DATA

It's most common to send over a dictionary or hash object that contains additional data that the observer uses. To pass in information with a notification, you use the noticationWithName:object:userInfo: method. You'll now create a notification and pass in a hash object:

```
data = {:first => "John", :last => "Doe"}
notification = NSNotification.notificationWithName("foo", object:nil,
➥ userInfo:data)
```

You first create a hash that contains information about John Doe, specifically his first and last name. You then pass in this data variable as the userInfo parameter.

Watch what happens when you inspect the name and the object values of this notification:

```
notification.name        #=> "foo"
notification.userInfo    #=> {:first => "John", :last => "Doe"}
```

You're returned back just what you created by calling the instance methods, name and userInfo.

You can now pass this notification to the NSNotificationCenter to be broadcast.

5.2.2   *Posting notifications to the notification center*

To post a notification you could use the postNotification: method:

```
NSNotificationCenter.defaultCenter.postNotification(notification)
```

As we discussed previously, you call the class method, defaultCenter, on the NSNotificationCenter to return the singleton instance for the class. You also pass in the notification that you created previously (notification).

Rather than creating the NSNotification object separately and storing it in its own variable, you can do this when you post a notification to the NSNotification-

Center. This is easier and saves you a few lines of code. The following code uses the postNotificationName:object:userInfo: method:

```
NSNotificationCenter.defaultCenter.postNotificationName("foo", object:nil,
➥ userInfo:{:first => "John", :last => "Doe"})
```

In one line you can post the notification to the NSNotificationCenter.

Let's take a closer look at the notification queue and find out how to queue multiple notifications.

5.3 *Queuing notifications*

Suppose you want to send multiple notifications at one time, but you don't want to wait for each notification to finish. In this case, use the NSNotificationQueue to post the notifications in the order in which they're added to the queue. The queue can also send notifications to the notification center asynchronously.

5.3.1 *Using posting styles*

The NSNotificationQueue gives you a good amount of control over when and how it delivers notifications by providing posting styles (NSPostingStyle). Table 5.1 lists the three posting styles.

Table 5.1 `NSPostingStyle` options for `NSNotificationQueue`

Constant	Description
NSPostASAP	Notifications posted after the current notification callout or timer
NSPostWhenIdle	Notifications posted when the run loop is in an idle state
NSPostNow	Notifications posted immediately after coalescing, synchronously

We'll first look at the most basic way of queuing a notification. To grab the singleton instance of the NSOperationQueue for an application, you can use the defaultQueue class method. This looks similar to what you used to grab the singleton instance of the NSNotificationCenter:

```
NSNotificationQueue.defaultQueue
```

Now, to queue a notification, you first need to create an NSNotification object. Let's use the notification that you created previously, which specifies object as nil:

```
notif = NSNotification.notificationWithName("my_notification", object:nil)
```

You can now take this notification and queue it with the enqueueNotification :postingStyle: method:

```
framework "foundation"
NSNotificationQueue.defaultQueue.enqueueNotification(notif,
➥ postingStyle:NSPostNow);
```

You take the singleton instance of NSNotificationQueue, add the notification to the queue, and specify the NSPostNow option to post the notification immediately.

Posting synchronously

Adding a notification to the NSNotificationQueue with a posting style of NSPostNow is exactly the same as adding a notification directly to the NSNotificationCenter. This notification posted as NSPostNow is processed immediately and synchronously.

Next we'll look at ways to combine multiple notifications into one.

5.3.2 Coalescing notifications

Suppose you want to post a notification only once in a queue. You could set a Boolean flag to determine whether a specific notification has already been sent, but sometimes situations beyond your control prohibit use of this technique.

Specifying a coalesce option when you add a specific notification to a queue removes similar previously posted notifications. You can specify matching criteria based on the notification type, the sender, or a combination of the two. Table 5.2 summarizes the coalesce options.

Table 5.2 NSNotificationCoalescing options for NSNotificationQueue

Constant	Description
NSNotificationNoCoalescing	Don't coalesce any notifications in the queue.
NSNotificationCoalescingOnName	Coalesce notifications with the same name.
NSNotificationCoalescingOnSender	Coalesce notifications with the same object specified in object.

You can specify an individual coalesce option or combine them. To coalesce on both name (NSNotificationCoalescingOnName) and sender (NSNotification-CoalescingOnSender), use a bitwise OR operator (|). You can also specify an array of run modes as a condition when queuing notifications.

MATCHING NAME

Suppose you want your application to send a notification when the main window loses focus. You wouldn't want multiple notifications queued up at one time—in this case, you'd want only one notification for this event. Luckily, you can handle a situation like this with NSNotificationQueue.

To be notified of changes to an NSWindow, you can use one of the predefined notification names that the NSWindow class posts for certain events. Table 5.3 lists the predefined notification names that are frequently used. The NSWindow class documentation lists many more.

Table 5.3 `NSWindow` **predefined notifications**

Notification	Posted When...
`NSWindowDidBecomeKeyNotification`	`NSWindow` becomes key window.
`NSWindowDidBecomeMainNotification`	`NSWindow` becomes the main window.
`NSWindowDidChangeScreenNotification`	Portion of `NSWindow` moves off or onto another screen.
`NSWindowDidMiniaturizeNotification`	`NSWindow` is miniaturized.
`NSWindowDidEndSheetNotification`	`NSWindow` closes an attached sheet.
`NSWindowDidResignMainNotification`	`NSWindow` resigns as the main window.
`NSWindowWillCloseNotification`	`NSWindow` will close.

To be notified when the main window loses focus you'll use `NSWindowDidResign-MainNotification`.

To see this window resize notification in action you'll use the `enqueue-Notification:postingStyle:coalesceMask:forModes:` method:

```
framework "cocoa"
notif = NSNotification.notificationWithName(
➡ NSWindowDidResignMainNotification,
➡ object:nil)
NSNotificationQueue.defaultQueue.enqueueNotification(
➡ notif,
➡ postingStyle:NSPostASAP,
➡ coalesceMask:NSNotificationCoalescingOnName,
➡ forModes:nil)
```

You first add the `NSWindowDidResignMainNotification` notification to the `NSNotificationQueue`. To post it as soon as possible you specify a posting style of `NSPostASAP`. You set one coalesce mask, `NSNotificationOnName`, to prevent this notification from being posted multiple times. If a notification with the same name (`NSWindowDidResignMainNotification`) has already been added to the queue, this one won't be posted because it matches on the name. Lastly you set `forModes` to `nil`, meaning that it'll use the default run loop.

What if you wanted to coalesce on both the name of the notification and the object that sends the notification?

MATCHING NAME AND SENDER

Suppose you want to post a notification whenever the user selects a certain column in a table view. You can pass in the column identifier as the object in your notification:

```
notif = NSNotification.notificationWithName("column_selected",
➡ object: column.identifier)

NSNotificationQueue.defaultQueue.enqueueNotification(notif,
➡ postingStyle:NSPostASAP,
```

```
➥ coalesceMask:
➥ NSNotificationCoalescingOnName|NSNotificationCoalescingOnSender,
➥ forModes:nil)
```

You specify a `coalesceMask` of `NSNotificationCoalescingOnName` and `NSNotifica-tionCoalescingOnSender`, using a bitwise OR condition (`|`) to separate the masks. This prevents multiple instances of notifications with the same name (`column_selected`) and object (`column.identifier`) from being queued at the same time.

Now that you know how to queue notifications using different posting styles and coalescing options, let's dig into how the queue handles multiple notifications.

5.3.3   *Queuing multiple notifications*

As we explained previously, the notification queue handles notifications in FIFO order. To illustrate how notifications are ordered, taking coalescing into consideration, let's create three notifications:

```
notifOne = NSNotification.notificationWithName("action_one",
➥ object:"some string")
notifTwo = NSNotification.notificationWithName("action_two",
➥ object:nil)
notifThree = NSNotification.notificationWithName("action_three",
➥ object:nil)
```

Now you'll add the notifications to the notification queue as shown in the following listing.

Listing 5.1   Queuing multiple notifications

```
NSNotificationQueue.defaultQueue.enqueueNotification        ◁─┐ Add notifOne,
➥ (notifOne,                                                   │ no coalescing
➥ postingStyle:NSPostASAP,
➥ coalesceMask:NSNotificationNoCoalescing,
➥ forModes:nil)

NSNotificationQueue.defaultQueue.enqueueNotification        ◁─┐ Add notifThree,
➥ (notifThree,                                                 │ no coalescing
➥ postingStyle:NSPostASAP,
➥ coalesceMask:NSNotificationNoCoalescing,
➥ forModes:nil)

NSNotificationQueue.defaultQueue.enqueueNotification        ◁─┐ Add notifOne, coalescing
➥ (notifOne,                                                   │ on name and sender
➥ postingStyle:NSPostASAP,
➥ coalesceMask:NSNotificationCoalescingOnName|
➥ NSNotificationCoalescingOnSender,
➥ forModes:nil)

NSNotificationQueue.defaultQueue.enqueueNotification        ◁─┐ Add notifTwo,
➥ (notifTwo,                                                   │ no coalescing
➥ postingStyle:NSPostASAP,
➥ coalesceMask: NSNotificationNoCoalescing,
➥ forModes:nil)
```

```
NSNotificationQueue.defaultQueue.enqueueNotification
➥ (notifOne,
➥ postingStyle:NSPostASAP,
➥ coalesceMask:NSNotificationNoCoalescing,
➥ forModes:nil)
```
◁── **Add notifOne, no coalescing**

Let's determine which notifications will be posted and the order in which they'll be processed. Based on FIFO, you can see that they'll be processed in the same order in which they were added: notifOne, notifThree, notifOne, notifTwo, and notifOne. That's fairly straightforward. But which ones will be broadcast and in which order? Table 5.4 lists the broadcast order.

Table 5.4   Notification broadcast order

Notification	Broadcast?
notifOne	Yes.
notifThree	Yes.
[notifOne]	No. This instance was merged with previous notifOne as per coalescing on name and sender.
notifTwo	Yes.
notifOne	Yes.

The second instance of notifOne was omitted from the broadcast because it was coalesced when the mask you specified matched on the name and sender object of the notification.

Now you know how to post notifications with coalescing, but did you know that you can also use coalescing to manually remove notifications you've already added to the queue?

5.3.4   *Removing notifications*

Depending on the posting style specified, notifications might not be posted immediately. If it hasn't been posted yet, it's possible to remove the notification from the queue. You can do this by passing in the notification you want to remove as well as the coalescing mask to match upon using the dequeueNotificationsMatching:coalesceMask: method. Let's walk through a few examples to demonstrate.

MATCHING NAME

Imagine that you've created a notification with the name foo and added it to the queue. Because it hasn't yet been posted, you can remove it with the following code:

```
notif = NSNotification.notificationWithName("foo", object:nil)
NSNotificationQueue.defaultQueue.dequeueNotificationsMatching(notif,
➥ coalesceMask:NSNotificationCoalescingOnName)
```

You create a new notification with the same name as the notification you want to remove. Then you call dequeueNotificationsMatching:coalesceMask: on the singleton instance of the notification queue using the NSNotificationCoalescingOn-Name mask.

Suppose you don't want to dequeue a notification based on the name; instead you want to dequeue based on the sender object only.

MATCHING SENDER

The following code removes a notification from the queue that contains an object called my_object:

```
notif = NSNotification.notificationWithName("foo", object:my_object)
NSNotificationQueue.defaultQueue.dequeueNotificationsMatching(notif,
➡ coalesceMask:NSNotificationCoalescingOnSender)
```

You create a notification with the same object as the notification you want to remove. You then dequeue it using a coalesce mask of NSNotificationCoalesceOnSender.

You can also dequeue notifications based on both name and sender.

MATCHING NAME AND SENDER

Combining coalesce masks allows you to remove notifications based on the name and object attached. The following code removes a notification that matches the name update_downloaded and contains the generic object my_object:

```
notif = NSNotification.notificationWithName("update_downloaded",
➡ object:my_object)
NSNotificationQueue.defaultQueue.dequeueNotificationsMatching(notif,
➡ coalesceMask: NSNotificationCoalescingOnName|
➡ NSNotificationCoalescingOnSender)
```

Note that you use the bitwise OR (|) operator to add both masks.

With posting, queuing, and removing notifications under your belt, we'll show you how to receive and respond to them next.

5.4   *Responding to notifications*

To receive notifications you must register observers. You can then respond to notifications sent from your application as well as notifications sent from processes outside of your own application. To stop receiving notifications you must unregister observers. In this section, we'll explain how to add and remove observers from an application's notification center.

Let's start with adding observers.

5.4.1   *Adding notification observers*

To add an observer you'll need to invoke the addObserver:selector:name:object: method on the application's notification center. You pass in the following parameters:

- Selector—The method that will be called when the observer is notified
- Name—The name of the notification
- Object—The object to observe

If you don't pass in anything in the `object` parameter the observer will receive all notifications that match the specified notification name.

For instance, you'll now add an observer to a notification named `column_selected`. The method that you use as the selector can be named whatever you want; for this example, call it `respond_to_selected_column:`. You want to listen only for the notification named `column_selected`, regardless of which object sent it, so you'll leave the `object` parameter as `nil`:

```
NSNotificationCenter.defaultCenter.addObserver(self,
➡ selector:"respond_to_selected_column:",
➡ name:"column_selected", object:nil)
```

Whenever the notification named `column_selected` is broadcast from the application, the `respond_to_selected_column:` method is called.

If you noticed, the `respond_to_selected_column:` method expects one parameter, which represents the notification object. The following code implements this method:

```
def respond_to_selected_column(notification)
  ...
end
```

This method could check the `notification` parameter to see if a `userInfo` or `object` has been passed in. You could then use this information to properly respond to the notification in any way you please.

When you use the default notification center you listen only for notifications that are broadcast within the scope of your application. To listen for notifications from applications outside of yours, call the same `addObserver:selector:name:object:` method on the default *distributed* notification center. For example, the iTunes application sends a notification when you play a specific track. The following code adds an observer to respond to the notification:

```
NSDistributedNotificationCenter.defaultCenter.addObserver(self,
➡ selector:"track_changed:",
➡ name:"com.apple.iTunes.playerInfo", object:nil)
```

To receive distributed notifications your process must be running in a run loop. You can still add yourself as an observer, but unless you're in the run loop you won't receive anything.

In a MacRuby script you call `NSApplication.sharedApplication.run` when you start your application to make sure your process is running in a run loop.

In an Xcode application you may have to add the following line:

```
NSRunLoop.currentRunLoop.runUntilDate(NSDate.distantFuture)
```

This code gets the current run loop and forces it to run until a later date, specified by `NSDate.distantFuture`.

You'll see this same distributed notification in section 5.5 when you write a script that listens for iTunes notifications. But first you'll learn how to remove observers from the notification center.

5.4.2   Removing notification observers

You may want to stop receiving notifications for a specific object. It's important to do so if the object you're using to respond to a *distributed* notification no longer exists. If the notification center tries to deliver a notification to an object that doesn't exist your application may crash. The following code shows how to stop an object from receiving notifications (`self` being the object this line is executed from):

```
NSNotificationCenter.defaultCenter.removeObserver(self)
```

To remove all observers from the distributed notification center, call the same `removeObserver:` method on the singleton instance of the `NSDistributed-NotificationCenter`.

If you want to remove an observer for a specific notification, you can do that as well by using the `removeObserver:name:object:` method. This method expects you to specify the observer, the name of the notification, and the sender object. If no sender object is specified it will match only on the name of the notification. The following code removes the notification named `column_selected`:

```
NSNotificationCenter.defaultCenter.removeObserver(self,
➥ name:"column_selected", object:nil)
```

Now that we've explained how to post and observe notifications you should have a solid grasp of how to use them properly. Let's stretch your skills and show you how to put your notification knowledge to use.

5.5   Building an iTunes-notification observer

To illustrate the observer pattern you'll build a script that uses the `NSDistributed-NotificationCenter` to listen for notifications sent by iTunes. Based on the `userInfo` object sent with the notifications the script will display the current state of iTunes and information about the track currently playing.

Although you'll build a simple script in this section you can reuse most of it if you choose to develop a full-fledged notification application with its own graphical user interface.

Start by opening Xcode or your favorite editor—you're writing a script, so you can work in a tool other than Xcode if you prefer.

5.5.1   Creating the script

Create a new file named track_notify.rb and include the Cocoa and Foundation frameworks:

```
framework "cocoa"
framework "foundation"
```

Next, declare a class called `TrackNotify`:

```
class TrackNotify
end
```

You'll define one method in `TrackNotify` to display iTunes and track information.

ADDING A METHOD

Create a method called `display_itunes_info:` that takes one parameter, `notification`. You'll grab the `userInfo` from the notification object and use that as the information source:

```
def display_itunes_info(notification)
  info = notification.userInfo
  puts "\nStatus:\t #{info["Player State"]}"
  puts "Track:\t #{info["Artist"]} - #{info["Name"]}"
  puts "Album:\t #{info["Album"]}"
  puts "Genre:\t #{info["Genre"]}"
end
```

This method takes an `NSNotification` object and displays iTunes and track information that has been passed to it. The information this method displays is fairly self-explanatory. You grab the `userInfo` `NSDictionary` and use it to display iTunes' status, the name of the artist and track currently playing, the album title, and the track's genre. You use Ruby's `puts` function to print each line.

Next you'll register the observer.

REGISTERING AN OBSERVER

Because iTunes notifications originate in a process outside the track_notify.rb script, you'll register an observer on the `NSDistributedNotificationCenter`, not the regular `NSNotificationCenter`.

Outside the `TrackNotify` class, implement the `addObserver:selector:name:object:` method:

```
NSDistributedNotificationCenter.defaultCenter.addObserver(TrackNotify.new,
➥ selector:"display_itunes_info:",
➥ name:"com.apple.iTunes.playerInfo", object:nil)
```

In this method you first register a new instance of `TrackNotify` as the observer object. You then specify the `display_itunes_info:` method, which you defined previously, as the `selector`. Next you specify com.apple.iTunes.playerInfo as the name of the notification to listen for. iTunes broadcasts this notification to the `NSDistributed-NotificationCenter` whenever the state of the iTunes player changes. Because you don't need to listen for any particular object associated with the notification you set `object` as `nil`.

Before you can try out the script you need to make sure the main run loop starts.

STARTING THE MAIN RUN LOOP

Add the following line at the bottom of the script:

```
NSApplication.sharedApplication.run
```

This tells the script to start running and kicks off the main run loop, which is necessary for an NSDistributedNotificationCenter to receive incoming notifications.

The entire script is shown in the following listing.

Listing 5.2   iTunes-notification observer script

```
framework "cocoa"
framework "foundation"

class TrackNotify
  def display_itunes_info(notification)
    info = notification.userInfo
    puts "\nStatus:\t #{info["Player State"]}"
    puts "Track:\t #{info["Artist"]} - #{info["Name"]}"
    puts "Album:\t #{info["Album"]}"
    puts "Genre:\t #{info["Genre"]}"
  end
end

NSDistributedNotificationCenter.defaultCenter.addObserver(TrackNotify.new,
➥ selector:"display_itunes_info:",
➥ name:"com.apple.iTunes.playerInfo", object:nil)

NSApplication.sharedApplication.run
```

You can now start listening.

5.5.2 *Running the script*

From the Terminal application type macruby track_notify.rb. The script should do nothing and should keep running without any output.

Now open iTunes and play a song of your choice. The script should display output similar to the following:

```
Status:        Playing
Track:         Best Song Ever Made - Brendan G. Lim & Paul Crawford
Album:         MacRuby in Action's Greatest Hits
Genre:         Mind-blowing
```

You may not see the exact same output as above. (That song is banned in all fifty states, mainly because most individuals can't comprehend how amazing it is. Don't ask us how you got it.) You should, though, see something similar. Go ahead and pause, stop, and play another track in iTunes. The script should pick up notifications for your actions and display them.

5.6   *Summary*

In this chapter you learned when to use notifications rather than delegates to notify multiple objects when an event or action occurs.

We discussed notification centers, which broadcast notifications to registered observers. You learned how to post notifications to the notification center and add notification observers to listen for incoming notifications. You also worked with the distributed notification center which allows you to listen to notifications outside your own processes.

We completed our survey of the observer pattern by discussing how to create a script that listens for notifications sent by iTunes.

In the next chapter we'll introduce key-value coding and show you how to leverage this important Cocoa concept.

Using key-value coding
and key-value observing

6

This chapter covers

- Learning key-value coding (KVC)
- Tying KVC to the UI
- Using key-value observing (KVO)

Throughout this book you've called getter and setter methods to retrieve or modify attributes of object instance variables. Using a mechanism called key-value coding (KVC), you can manipulate object properties indirectly. With KVC comes the ability to observe changes to a particular key value, which is known as key-value observing (KVO). These two concepts go hand-in-hand and are the building blocks of other Cocoa frameworks, such as Core Data, which we'll cover in chapter 7.

In this chapter we'll introduce KVC and KVO and walk you through the process of building a MacRuby application that utilizes these mechanisms. By the end of this chapter you'll have a good understanding of both concepts, and you'll be increasing the dynamic functionality of your MacRuby Cocoa applications in no time.

6.1 Simplifying code with key-value coding

KVC isn't an Objective-C language feature. It's the Cocoa framework that gives you the ability to use KVC with MacRuby. KVC is a mechanism that allows you to access properties without directly invoking accessor methods or instance variables. KVC uses a string, referred to as the *key*, to identify an attribute or property for a given object. Ruby developers may find KVC similar to the send method and other metaprogramming techniques. In some ways it's similar, but as you dive deeper into Cocoa development you'll understand the value of knowing how to use KVC in your applications.

In this section you'll learn what key paths are and how to use them, some special ways you can use dictionaries and arrays with KVC, and how to know when an object is key-value compliant. First we'll show you how to properly get and set variables using KVC.

6.1.1 Accessing object properties with KVC

Before we go deeper into KVC we'll cover the basics, and that's why we're starting with getting and setting properties. To get hands-on practice working with keys, imagine that a company called Brent's Super Store has hired you to develop a desktop application to help employees manage the store's product inventory. We'll compare how you retrieve and store property values first without KVC, and then with KVC.

GETTING PROPERTIES

To keep track of all the products at Brent's Super Store you'll create a Product class. Each product can have many different properties, but for the sake of simplicity we've outfitted this class with the bare necessities you'll need for this example:

```ruby
class Product
  attr_accessor :name, :sku, :manufacturer, :price, :quantity
end
```

If you remember, the attr_accessor function sets up the getter and setter methods for the properties and attributes that you specify in a KVC-compliant way. By now it should be second nature for you to use dot-notation to access properties of objects. To retrieve the name of a product, for example, you normally do the following:

```ruby
product.name
```

To use KVC you need to determine the key of the property that you want to retrieve. In this case it's name.

> **NOTE** Keys use only ASCII characters, must start with a lowercase character, and must not contain any spaces.

To retrieve the name of a product using KVC you pass in the key (name) as a string to the valueForKey: method:

```ruby
product.valueForKey("name")
```

You might be wondering, "Why would I want to do this instead of using the shorter, straightforward version that I'm familiar with?" Suppose you have a key dynamically

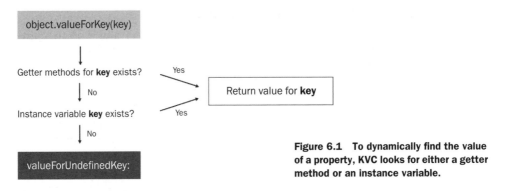

Figure 6.1   To dynamically find the value of a property, KVC looks for either a getter method or an instance variable.

returned at runtime, and you want to retrieve its value on a given object. You could hardcode `product.name` in the application, but you'd be stuck always having to manually retrieve the name of a product. KVC gives you the flexibility to dynamically retrieve any property on the object.

Imagine that in the Product Inventory application for Brent's Super Store you've decided to provide users with a blank text field that brings up the value of any property. To return the SKU for a product, the user enters `sku` in the text field and presses Enter. The user could also type `name` to return the name of the product. Using KVC you can create a method that dynamically returns the value of any property:

```
def display_property(property_name)
  self.valueForKey(property_name)
end
```

How does KVC retrieve the correct value for the specified key? Figure 6.1 shows the flow for the `valueForKey:` method.

Upon being called the `valueForKey:` method immediately checks to see if you've defined a getter for the specified key. If a method doesn't exist it looks for the instance variable of that key. If it finds either it retrieves and returns the value. If neither is found, it calls the `valueForUndefinedKey:` method. We'll talk more about handling unknown keys in section 6.1.2, but before we get to that, we'll show you how to set properties with KVC.

SETTING PROPERTIES

Just as you can dynamically retrieve a value with the `valueForKey:` method, KVC provides a method to dynamically set the value for any particular key.

You don't need to worry about creating setter methods in the `Product` class because you used `attr_accessor`. With setter methods readily available you can dynamically set properties. Normally, you set the value of a property like this:

```
product.price = 999.95
```

Using KVC you set the value of the `price` property using the `setValue:forKey:` method:

```
product.setValue(999.95, forKey:"price")
```

You use a string value to represent the key and an object to represent the value to store. You can use this method to set any value you want for any key. KVC is straightforward and gives your code a great deal of flexibility out of the box. KVC also provides methods that allow you to work specifically with arrays and dictionaries.

SETTING AND GETTING WITH DICTIONARIES AND ARRAYS

Using KVC you can set or retrieve the values of multiple properties at once. To illustrate how to set multiple values, let's add more properties to the Product instance. Without using KVC there are a few ways to set properties. You could add a custom initialize method to the Product class, or you could set each property value manually, as shown:

```
prod = Product.new
prod.name = "Headphones"
prod.quantity = 37
prod.sku = 6637782
prod.price = 129.99
```

To set properties using KVC you use the setValuesForKeysWithDictionary: method, which you get for free with KVC. You pass the method a dictionary (hash) of the keys and objects you want to store:

```
dict = {"name" => "Headphones", "quantity" => 37, "sku" => 6637782,
➥ "price" => "129.99"}
prod = Product.new.setValuesForKeysWithDictionary(dict)
```

Using KVC is a quicker, less tedious way to set the values for any object.

Now that you've set these values we can show you how to retrieve them at one time using the dictionaryWithValuesForKeys: method:

```
keys = ["name", "quantity", "sku", "price"]
prod.dictionaryWithValuesForKeys(keys)
=> {"name" => "Headphones", "quantity" => 37, "sku" => 6637782,
  "price" => "129.99"}
```

You specify an array that contains the keys you want to retrieve values for. You then pass the array into the dictionaryWithValuesForKeys: method and it returns a dictionary of the keys that you specified and their values.

Now that you're familiar with getting and setting object properties, let's find out how KVC handles cases in which a particular key doesn't exist.

6.1.2 *Handling unknown keys*

Because you're using strings to represent the keys you want to access you won't catch any errors when you compile the application for Brent's Super Store. You might misspell a property key or specify a key that doesn't exist. Referring back to figure 6.1, you can see that if you try to retrieve the value of a key that doesn't have a getter or an instance variable it calls the valueForUndefinedKey: method. If you don't overload this method and provide a way to properly handle unknown keys the application throws a runtime exception.

For example, suppose a user wants to look up a product name in the application for Brent's Super Store. The user accidentally enters `title` in the text field instead of `name` and gets the error shown in the following code:

```
product.valueForKey("title")
RuntimeError: NSUnknownKeyException: [<Product 0x200051a60>
valueForUndefinedKey:]: this class is not key value coding-compliant
for the key title.
```

The application threw a runtime error, specifically `NSUnknownKeyException`. You should either catch this error or provide a default value for unknown keys. In this case, let's return the value of `name` when a user enters `title`. Add the following to the Product class:

```
def valueForUndefinedKey(key)
  case key.to_sym
    when :title then self.name
    else super
  end
end
```

If you were to repeat `product.valueForKey("title")` with this new method in place you'd get the value of the `name` property instead of an error. If none of the cases is executed you call `super` to execute the default action. Now you know how to handle unknown keys when you retrieve values, but what about when you set them?

If you call `setValue:forKey:` for a key that doesn't exist, you need to overload the `setValue:forUndefinedKey:` method. By default this method throws the following error if you set a value for an undefined key:

```
product.setValue("Toy Car", forKey:"title")
RuntimeError: NSUnknownKeyException: [<Product 0x200243e20>
setValue:forUndefinedKey:]: this class is not key value coding-
compliant for the key title.
```

You might want this method to throw an error when something like this occurs; alternatively, you could customize it to always store and return values. One way that you can deal with undefined keys is to add a dictionary (or a hash) to your `Product` class to capture and retrieve unknown values and keys. To demonstrate this technique let's add a new property named `meta` to the `Product` class. What you name it is entirely up to you:

```
class Product
  attr_accessor :name, :sku, :manufacturer, :price, :quantity, :meta
end
```

With the property in place you can customize the `setValue:forUndefinedKey:` method:

```
def setValue(value, forUndefinedKey:key)
  self.meta = {} if self.meta.nil?
  meta[key] = value
end
```

You first initialize the dictionary/hash that you're using if it's `nil`. Next you store the information passed in the hash by the provided key. You can now modify the `value-ForUndefinedKey:` method you defined previously:

```
def valueForUndefinedKey(key)
  return self.meta[key] if self.meta.has_key?(key)
  case key.to_sym
    when :title then self.name
    else super
  end
end
```

Whether you want to keep that case statement in the method is up to you, but we wanted to show you how to take advantage of these methods in a way that lets you store and retrieve anything for any key, defined or undefined.

With all of this in place you can do the following:

```
product.setValue("foo", forKey:"randomKey")
product.valueForKey("randomKey")
=> "foo"
```

Everything continues to work as expected for keys that exist because the code you added is executed only when a key doesn't exist.

Let's explore another part of KVC—key paths and collection operators.

6.1.3 *Understanding key paths and collection operators*

You've learned that a key is a string representation of a specific object's attribute or property. A key path is also represented by a string, but is composed of dot-separated keys that specify a sequence of object properties. Each key added to the sequence is related to the previous key.

> **TIP** Rails developers might find the key path concept familiar; it's easy to think of it in terms of how you'd describe a one-to-one or a one-to-many relationship.

For instance, the `Product` class has a `manufacturer` property. This attribute/property references a `Manufacturer` object. The `Manufacturer` class also contains a property named `products`, which contains an array of `Product` objects. This design allows folks at Brent's Super Store to track down who made a certain product or view all the products by a single manufacturer. These relationships are shown in figure 6.2.

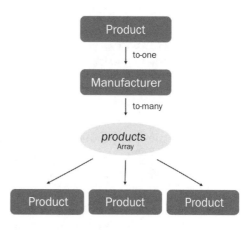

Figure 6.2 The application for Brent's Super Store includes both to-one and to-many relationships.

The Product-to-Manufacturer relationship is a to-one relationship. The Manufacturer-to-*products* is a to-many relationship (see figure 6.2). You can describe these relationships using key paths.

USING KEY PATHS

To illustrate how to use a key path, let's walk through fleshing out a simple Manufacturer class:

```
class Manufacturer
  attr_accessor :name, :products
end
```

Set up the relationship between the Product and Manufacturer:

```
prod = Product.new
prod.name = "Game Sphere 9000"

manu = Manufacturer.new
manu.name = "Happy Fun Games, Inc."

prod.manufacturer = manu
```

The newly created manufacturer, Happy Fun Games, Inc., is the manufacturer of Game Sphere 9000.

To retrieve this manufacturer name you can use a key path and the instance of the Product:

```
prod.valueForKeyPath("manufacturer.name")
=> "Happy Fun Games, Inc."
```

The key path manufacturer.name allows us to access a property (name) of another object (manufacturer) by utilizing the to-one relationship between a Product and a Manufacturer.

What about to-many relationships? As you saw in figure 6.2 a manufacturer can have many products. You'll now take the existing manufacturer and give it an array that contains five products:

```
manu.products = []
(1..5).each do |x|
  new_prod = Product.new
  new_prod.name = "Toy #{x}"
  manu.products << new_prod
end
```

To retrieve all products that relate to a specific manufacturer, use a key path:

```
prod.valueForKeyPath("manufacturer.products")
=> [#<Product:0x2000b9380 @name="Toy 1">,
 #<Product:0x2000b9be0 @name="Toy 2">,
 #<Product:0x2000c8c80 @name="Toy 3">,
 #<Product:0x2000c3e00 @name="Toy 4">,
 #<Product:0x2000c9080 @name="Toy 5">]
```

That's pretty neat, given that you only need one quick line to retrieve an array of products using this to-many relationship.

What if you want to retrieve an array of only the product names? Key paths make this a simple task:

```
prod.valueForKeyPath("manufacturer.products.name")
=> ["Toy 1", "Toy 2", "Toy 3", "Toy 4", "Toy 5"]
```

You retrieved, from a single product instance, the names of each product in the `prod-ucts` array based on its related manufacturer. Using key paths you did this in one quick and simple line. Key paths are good not only for retrieving values based on relationships, but also for performing computations on the results.

USING COLLECTION OPERATORS

Collection operators allow you to perform operations on collections using KVC. You insert them into key paths that you pass to the `valueForKeyPath:` method. You can use collection operators to calculate the sum of all collection items, the average value of all items, and so on. Cocoa provides a variety of built-in collection operators out of the box. Most of them are listed in table 6.1.

Table 6.1   Collection operators for key paths

Operator	Description
@avg	Average value of all properties specified by key path collection
@count	Count of all properties specified by key path collection
@max	Maximum value of all properties in key path collection
@min	Minimum value of all properties in key path collection
@sum	Summation of all properties in key path collection
@distinctUnionOfObjects	Array of all unique values in key path collection
@unionOfObjects	Array of all values in key path collection (not unique)

NOTE   Custom collection operators are not currently supported.

Suppose you want to calculate the total number of products that belong to the product's manufacturer. Here's how to use the `@count` collection operator:

```
prod.valueForKeyPath("manufacturer.products.@count")
```

You'll now break this key path into three pieces to better understand the structure:

- `manufacturer.products`—The left key path
- `@count`—The collection operator

Let's see the output of this key path:

```
prod.valueForKeyPath("manufacturer.products.@count")
=> 5
```

You could also do this directly from the manufacturer instance that you set up:

```
manu.valueForKeyPath("products.@count")
=> 5
```

Next you'll experiment with another operator, `@distinctUnionOfObjects`, to see what kind of output it returns:

```
manu.valueForKeyPath("products.@distinctUnionOfObjects.name")
=> ["Toy 1", "Toy 2", "Toy 3", "Toy 4", "Toy 5"]
```

The operator returns all the existing products because all their names are unique.

Next change the last product name to make it match an existing entry:

```
manu.products.last.name = "Toy 1"
manu.valueForKeyPath("products.name")
=> ["Toy 1", "Toy 2", "Toy 3", "Toy 4", "Toy 1"]
```

Now use the `@distinctUnionOfObjects` operator again:

```
manu.valueForKeyPath("products.@distinctUnionOfObjects.name")
=> ["Toy 1", "Toy 4", "Toy 3", "Toy 2"]
```

The array now has four strings because it returns only unique titles.

If you're interested in some extra credit, experiment with other operators on your own.

We're not finished with the Product Inventory application just yet, but before we get back to it we'll introduce the other side of the KVC coin: key-value observing.

6.2   *Using KVO to implement observers*

KVO allows you to observe a particular property on an object and be notified when it changes.

In chapter 5 you learned how to use notifications. KVO uses the same observer pattern, which allows many objects to act as observers. As you know, this pattern allows a single object to notify many observers without knowing anything about those observers. One key difference between notifications and KVO is that, unlike notifications, KVO doesn't provide a centralized notification center that broadcasts notifications. All KVO-based communication occurs directly between the observer and the observed object.

In this section you'll learn how to register and unregister observers, notify observers of changes, and respond to changes.

6.2.1   *Adding and removing observers*

With KVO you can observe to-one and to-many relationships. This means that you can observe properties on related objects. To add an observer you call the `add-Observer:forKeyPath:options:context:` method on the object that you want to observe.

When you create an observer you can specify many different options; table 6.2 lists four of them.

Table 6.2   Options when registering a new observer

Operator	Description
NSKeyValueObservingOptionNew	Return new property value, if possible
NSKeyValueObservingOptionOld	Return old property value, if possible
NSKeyValueObservingOptionInitial	Send notification to observer immediately before observer registration method returns
NSKeyValueObservingOptionPrior	Send notification to observer before and after the value of the property changes

Let's look at a quick example of how to add an observer:

```
framework "cocoa"
product.addObserver(self, forKeyPath:"quantity",
➥ options:(NSKeyValueObservingOptionNew|NSKeyValueObservingOptionOld),
➥ context:nil)
```

You specify `self` to set the calling object as the observer. The key path you want to observe is the `quantity` property. To include the old and the new value for `quantity` in the notification that you receive you pass in the `NSKeyValueObservingOptionNew` and `NSKeyValueObservingOptionOld` options.

In this example you didn't specify a context object, but you have the option to specify anything you want to help you identify the change being observed.

To remove an observer you call the `removeObserver:forKeyPath` method:

```
product.removeObserver(self, forKeyPath:"quantity")
```

Let's look at one more example of adding an observer. This time you'll observe both a to-one and a to-many relationship.

```
product.addObserver(self, forKeyPath:"manufacturer.name",
➥ options:(NSKeyValueObservingOptionNew|NSKeyValueObservingOptionOld),
➥ context:nil)
```

Assuming the product has a manufacturer specified, this observer is notified automatically when the manufacturer's name changes (utilizing the to-one relationship). We say automatically because by default, when an observed property changes, that information is broadcast to its observers. At times, however, you may want to disable automatic observing and notifying of an object's property.

6.2.2   *Manually notifying observers of changes*

By default the `automaticallyNotifiesObserversForKey:` method returns true. You can override this functionality and have it perform a different action based on what key is passed in. This change needs to be done to the object that's *being* observed. Manual observing requires a little more work but can come in handy.

Suppose you don't want anything to be broadcast automatically when the name property for a Product changes:

```
def automaticallyNotifiesObserversForKey(key)
  key != "name"
end
```

You use a tertiary operator to determine whether to return `true` or `false`. If the key is name then you return `false`; otherwise, you return `true` and observers are notified automatically.

So how exactly would you *manually* notify observers of a change to the name property? You override the setter for the property that you want to notify. Because you used `attr_accessor` you don't manually define setters and getters. The setter for the name property looks like this:

```
def name=(value)
  @name = value
end
```

You add two method calls to the setter before and after you define the property. Adding the `willChangeValueForKey:` and `didChangeValueForKey:` methods results in a setter that looks like the following:

```
def name=(value)
  willChangeValueForKey("name")
  @name = value
  didChangeValueForKey("name")
end
```

It's important that you add both the `willChangeValueForKey:` and the `didChange-ValueForKey:` method calls because some observers may rely on knowing when a property is *about* to change and when it has *already* changed.

If you register to observe a property on an object you want to be able to respond when its value changes.

6.2.3   *Responding to observed objects*

To respond to changes you implement the `observeValueForKeyPath:ofObject:change:context:` method. Any notifications that you receive from any object pass through this method. You'll need to do some checking to make sure that you're working with the correct object type and the correct key path.

To respond to the first observation example in which you were observing the name property of a Product you could do the following:

```
def observeValueForKeyPath(keyPath, ofObject:object, change:change,
    context:context)
  if object.is_a?(Product)
    case keyPath
      when "name"
        puts "Old Value: " + change[NSKeyValueChangeOldKey]
        puts "New Value: " +change[NSKeyValueChangeNewKey]
    end
```

```
    end
end
```

You first check if the object is of the correct type that you're expecting. If so, you check if the `keyPath` parameter matches name. If so, you print the old value and the new value of name.

You might have noticed that the change object is a dictionary. You can retrieve different values using predefined keys. Table 6.3 describes some of these keys.

Table 6.3 Observer change keys

Operator	Description
NSKeyValueChangeOldKey	Returns old value when NSKeyValueObservingOptionOld specified as an option on observer registration.
NSKeyValueChangeNewKey	Returns new value when NSKeyValueObservingOptionNew specified as an option on observer registration.
NSValueChangeKindKey	Enumerates value related to the option that triggered the broadcast.
NSKeyValueChange-NotificationIsPriorKey	If NSKeyValueObservingOptionPrior is set, this value is available in the changes dictionary.

In this example, suppose the value of `product.name` is Happy Fun Ball. If you change the name to Happy Fun Ball Extreme Edition, the `observeValueForKeyPath:of-Object:change:context:` method prints the following results:

```
Old Value: Happy Fun Ball
New Value: Happy Fun Ball Extreme Edition
```

With a solid understanding of KVC and KVO let's return to Brent's Super Store so you can apply your knowledge to the Product Inventory application.

6.3 *Building out the Product Inventory application*

You're ready to create the Product Inventory application for Brent's Super Store. To track product inventory the application will consist of a table view that displays all products and their property values. Users can edit properties in the table view, and the application notifies them when a product is out of stock. Although a barebones application it'll be just what the employees of Brent's Super Store need at the moment, and you'll get to practice using KVC and KVO.

6.3.1 *Creating the user interface*

Let's get started. Open Xcode and create a new MacRuby application named Product Inventory. Then follow these steps:

1 Open MainMenu.xib, and create a table view with four columns. To increase the number of columns in an `NSTableView`, use the Attributes tab in the inspector pane as shown in figure 6.3.

2 Set the following column titles: Name, SKU, Price, and Quantity (see figure 6.4).

3 It's critical that you don't miss this step. Select the Name column of the table view, and then open the Attributes tab in the inspector pane. Set the Identifier field to the same value as the Title field, except use lowercase for the identifier. Matching these fields allows you to dynamically refer to the value of one of the Product properties. Do the same for the other columns, as shown in figure 6.5.

That should be enough for the user interface. Now you can start writing some code.

Figure 6.3   Set the number of columns in the `NSTableView` in the Attributes tab of the inspector pane.

6.3.2   *Using KVC to retrieve product information*

Create a new Ruby file named Product.rb to represent the `Product` class. You'll be using the same `Product` class that you've used throughout this chapter, except it won't have the `manufacturer` attribute. Add the following to the Product class:

```ruby
class Product
  attr_accessor :name, :sku, :price, :quantity
end
```

Next, create another Ruby file named InventoryController.rb, which will represent the controller.

SETTING UP THE CONTROLLER

The controller class has three instance variables: one to access the window, one for an array of products, and another to serve as an outlet for the table view:

```ruby
class InventoryController
  attr_accessor :window, :products, :products_table
end
```

You've already used an `NSTableView` in previous chapters, so you might remember that you need to implement its delegate methods. These include the

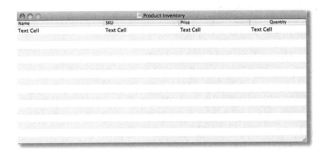

**Figure 6.4
The Product Inventory application interface consists of a four-column table view.**

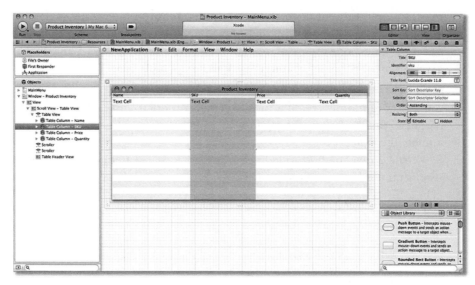

Figure 6.5 **To dynamically reference the SKU property the identifier and the title of the SKU table column must match.**

`numberOfRowsInTableView:` and `tableView:objectValueForTableColumn:row:` methods. Let's start with the `numberOfRowsInTableView:` method:

```
def numberOfRowsInTableView(view)
  @products.size
end
```

This method represents how many products are in the products array.

Next you'll implement `tableView:objectValueForTableColumn:row:` to display the appropriate information in each column of the `NSTableView`. This is where your understanding of KVC makes a difference.

Without using KVC you'd have to do something like the following:

```
def tableView(view, objectValueForTableColumn:column, row:index)
  product = @products[index]
  case column.identifier.to_sym
    when :name
      product.name
    when :sku
      product.sku
    when :price
      product.price
    when :quantity
      product.quantity
  end
end
```

Using KVC you can simplify this method down to a much smaller size:

```
def tableView(view, objectValueForTableColumn:column, row:index)
  @products[index].valueForKey(column.identifier)
end
```

Your method just went from 13 lines to only 3! (Your fingers and your keyboard can thank KVC later.) Because the identifiers match the properties on the Product class you can create a one-to-one mapping with each column identifier and a product key.

Now you need some products to populate the table view.

POPULATING THE TABLE VIEW

You'll now randomly create a variety of new products and add them to the array of products. You'll take advantage of the setValuesForKeysWithDictionary: method to simplify the code.

Create a new method called seed_products that generates 20 new products and assigns random values to the properties:

```
def seed_products
  20.times do |x|
    product = Product.new
    values = {
      "name" => "Item #{x}",
      "price" => rand(500),
      "sku" => 123*rand(500),
      "quantity" => rand(50)
    }
    @products << product.setValuesForKeysWithDictionary(values)
  end
end
```

Feel free to change the property values. The setValuesForKeysWithDictionary: method populates the newly created product objects and adds them the products array.

One other thing you need to do is make sure to initialize the products array. You can do this in the awakeFromNib method. From here, you can also call the seed_products method that you just created:

```
def awakeFromNib
  @products = []
  seed_products
end
```

The Inventory Controller class is complete for now. You can see it in its entirety in the following listing.

Listing 6.1   Inventory Controller class

```
class InventoryController
  attr_accessor :window, :products, :products_table

  def awakeFromNib
    @products = []
    seed_products
  end

  def seed_products
    20.times do |x|
```

```
      product = Product.new
      values = {
        "name" => "Item #{x}",
        "price" => rand(500),
        "sku" => 123*rand(300)*3,
        "quantity" => rand(30)
      }
      @products << product.setValuesForKeysWithDictionary(values)
    end
  end

  def numberOfRowsInTableView(view)
    @products.size
  end

  def tableView(view, objectValueForTableColumn:column, row:index)
    @products[index].valueForKey(column.identifier)
  end
end
```

Next, you'll hook up the controller to the interface and connect its outlets.

ADDING THE CONTROLLER AND CONNECTING OUTLETS

Head back to your interface, grab an `NSObject` from the Object library, and drag it into the Objects pane in the Dock.

From the inspector pane set the class to `InventoryController` as shown in figure 6.6.

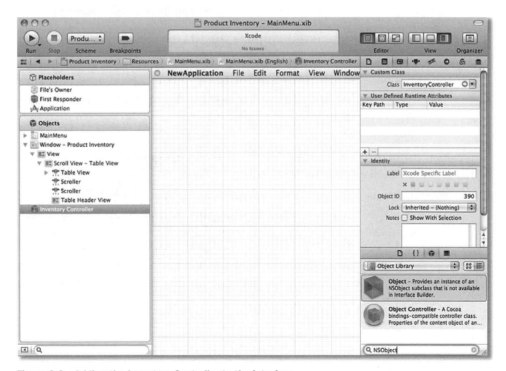

Figure 6.6   Adding the Inventory Controller to the interface

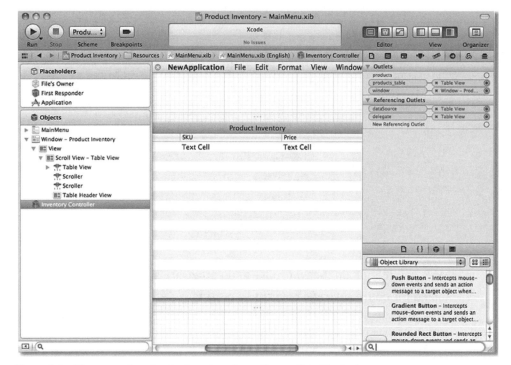

Figure 6.7   The connections for the Inventory Controller are listed in the inspector pane.

After you add the Inventory Controller connect the outlets:

- Connect the `window` instance in Inventory Controller to the main `NSWindow`.
- Connect the `products_table` instance to the `NSTableView`.
- To set the Inventory Controller as the delegate and data source, right-click the `NSTableView` and then drag the `dataSource` and `delegate` outlets to the Inventory Controller.

Your connections should look like those shown in figure 6.7.

Next you'll run the application.

RUNNING THE APP

To launch the application click the Run button. If all went well, you should see 20 rows populated with product information. Figure 6.8 shows the application in action.

Your values will be different from ours, but they should all be populated. Using KVC you were able to create this application quickly. KVC also makes it easy to add application functionality. In addition you'll incorporate KVO to alert users when a certain attribute or property has been updated.

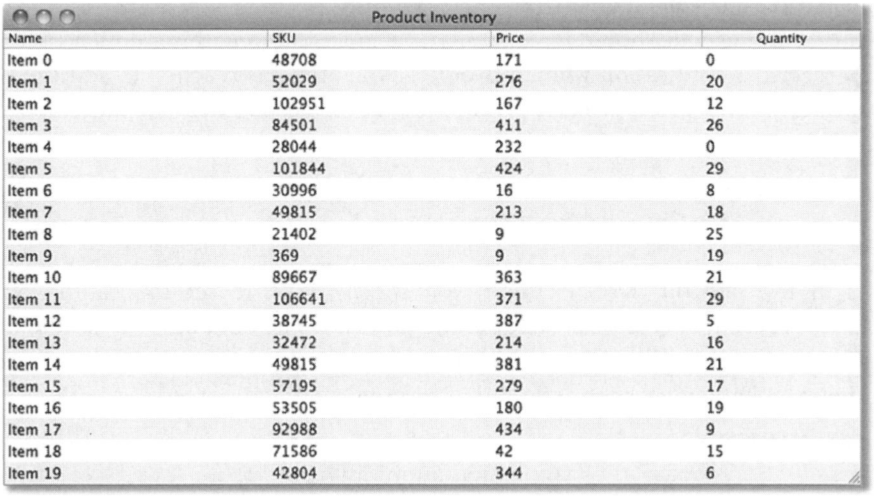

Name	SKU	Price	Quantity
Item 0	48708	171	0
Item 1	52029	276	20
Item 2	102951	167	12
Item 3	84501	411	26
Item 4	28044	232	0
Item 5	101844	424	29
Item 6	30996	16	8
Item 7	49815	213	18
Item 8	21402	9	25
Item 9	369	9	19
Item 10	89667	363	21
Item 11	106641	371	29
Item 12	38745	387	5
Item 13	32472	214	16
Item 14	49815	381	21
Item 15	57195	279	17
Item 16	53505	180	19
Item 17	92988	434	9
Item 18	71586	42	15
Item 19	42804	344	6

Figure 6.8   The Product Inventory application displays the 20 seeded products.

6.3.3   Adding features with KVC and KVO

The ability to view all products is nice, but Brent's Super Store employees also need the ability to complete the following tasks:

- Keep product information up to date.
- Manage product quantities.
- Take action when a product is out of stock.

If you double-click a cell in the table view you can edit the value, but as is, it doesn't actually modify the product. Let's enable users to edit product information.

UPDATING THE PRODUCT ARRAY

To make the table view editable, you'll use the `tableView:setObjectValue:for-TableColumn:row:` method. This method is triggered when a column value is edited in an `NSTableView`.

Using KVC you can have this method update a product in the array:

```
def tableView(view, setObjectValue:object, forTableColumn:column,
➥ row:index)
  @products[index].setValue(object, forKey:column.identifier)
end
```

Without this method implemented you'll notice that when you edit a column, it reverts back to its previous value when you're done. This is because the table view reloads its data from its data source, which, in this case, is the array of products. What you're doing in the code is updating the value for a key, which is specified by the column identifier.

To monitor the quantity of each product, you'll add an observer to the product instances that you created in the `seed_products` method.

ADDING KVO ON PRODUCT QUANTITY

The following code should look familiar; we looked at something similar in section 6.2. To receive a notification when a product's quantity has reached 0, add the following line right after you add each product to the products array in the seed_products method:

```
product.addObserver(self, forKeyPath:"quantity",
➡ options:NSKeyValueObservingOptionNew,
➡ context:nil)
```

As in the previous KVO example you specify self to set the calling object (an InventoryController instance) as the observer. The key path you want to observe is the quantity property. You also return the new quantity value, which you'll need when you implement the method that responds to the observed key path.

RESPONDING TO A CHANGE

Listing 6.2 shows the implementation of the observeValueForKeyPath:of-Object:change:context method. You check to make sure the object being passed is a Product. If so, you check if the key path matches quantity, which is what you're specifically observing.

Listing 6.2   Responding to observed key path changes

```
def observeValueForKeyPath(keyPath, ofObject:object, change:change,
➡ context:context)
  if object.is_a?(Product)
    case keyPath
      when "quantity"
        new_value = change[NSKeyValueChangeNewKey]
        if new_value.to_i == 0
          alert = NSAlert.alloc.init
          alert.setMessageText("Product is currently out of stock.")
          alert.beginSheetModalForWindow(@window,
            ➡ modalDelegate:self,
            ➡ didEndSelector:nil,
            ➡ contextInfo:nil)
        end
    end
  end
end
```

You grab the new value by retrieving the value of the NSKeyValueChangeNewKey key from the change object. If the new value is 0 you display an alert as a modal sheet to notify the user that the product is currently out of stock.

The following listing shows the finished Inventory Controller.

Listing 6.3   Finalized Inventory Controller

```
class InventoryController
  attr_accessor :window, :products, :products_table

  def awakeFromNib
```

```ruby
    @products = []
    seed_products
  end

  def seed_products
    20.times do |x|
      product = Product.new
      values = {
        "name" => "Item #{x}",
        "price" => rand(500),
        "sku" => 123*rand(300)*3,
        "quantity" => rand(30)
      }
      @products << product.setValuesForKeysWithDictionary(values)
      product.addObserver(self, forKeyPath:"quantity",
      ➥ options:NSKeyValueObservingOptionNew,
      ➥ context:nil)
    end
  end

  def numberOfRowsInTableView(view)
    @products.size
  end

  def tableView(view, objectValueForTableColumn:column, row:index)
    @products[index].valueForKey(column.identifier)
  end

  def tableView(view, setObjectValue:object, forTableColumn:column,
  ➥ row:index)
    @products[index].setValue(object, forKey:column.identifier)
  end

  def observeValueForKeyPath(keyPath, ofObject:object, change:change,
  ➥ context:context)
    if object.is_a?(Product)
      case keyPath
        when "quantity"
          new_value = change[NSKeyValueChangeNewKey]
          if new_value.to_i == 0
            alert = NSAlert.alloc.init
            alert.setMessageText("Product is currently out of stock.")
            alert.beginSheetModalForWindow(@window,
            ➥ modalDelegate:self,
            ➥ didEndSelector:nil,
            ➥ contextInfo:nil)
          end
      end
    end
  end
end
```

You can now run the application again and try out the KVO functionality.

Name			Quantity
Item 0			0
Item 1			4
Item 2			2
Item 3			0
Item 4			1
Item 5			0
Item 6	18081	416	16
Item 7	4059	411	5
Item 8	72693	132	5
Item 9	33948	499	27
Item 10	26568	105	8
Item 11	51660	491	22
Item 12	10701	321	19
Item 13	85608	210	5
Item 14	60885	448	22
Item 15	71217	363	2
Item 16	108117	33	10
Item 17	83025	437	28
Item 18	80073	451	13
Item 19	45387	132	22

Figure 6.9 When a product's quantity changes to 0 an alert message appears, indicating that the product is out of stock.

KVO IN ACTION

From the table view change any of the column values, and you'll notice that the changes now persist. Change the Quantity column to 0 for any product. You should see an alert message similar to what's shown in figure 6.9.

If the modal sheet displays only when the `quantity` property has changed to 0 your observer was registered properly and your application is responding correctly. The folks at Brent's Super Store are sure going to be pleased with your work! We wouldn't be surprised if they hired you again to add more functionality to the application.

6.4   *Summary*

This chapter included challenging material, and we're glad you stuck it out. The knowledge you've gained will serve you well when you create your own MacRuby applications.

We started with an introduction to key-value coding (KVC) and showed you how to retrieve and set properties dynamically. This gave you a chance to experiment with the basics and provided a behind-the–scenes look at how KVC works. You also learned about key paths and discovered that using collection operators can save you quite a bit of time. For example, you saw how you can use the `@count` operator to quickly retrieve a sum of specific items.

You learned how to use key-value observing (KVO) to observe changes to a property and to properly respond when you're notified of a change.

To apply this knowledge you created the Product Inventory application for Brent's Super Store.

In the next chapter you'll learn all about Core Data, which is the abstract data layer for dealing with modeling and storing application data.

Implementing persistence with Core Data

7

This chapter covers

- Learning Core Data basics
- Using the `NSManagedObject` and `NSManagedObjectContext` classes
- Creating a MacRuby application that uses Core Data

When you create your own MacRuby applications, take into account that almost every application persists some amount of information. When your application depends on user-created content it's important that this information be available each time the application is used.

In chapter 3 you created a Todo List application that stores individual tasks in memory. When you relaunch the application, none of the previously created items appear. Core Data provides a way to persist this data. In this chapter we'll investigate Core Data and you'll also create a new version of the Todo List application to remedy the lost-data issue.

7.1   Introducing Core Data

Core Data is a framework that you can use with Cocoa in your MacRuby applications. In this section you'll get a brief introduction to Core Data, learn why you'd want to use it, and get insight into what makes it different from other data storage solutions. You'll also see how Xcode makes it simple to work with Core Data.

7.1.1   Core Data concepts

The Core Data framework allows you to provide a great deal of functionality in your application before you write a single line of code. Its main purpose is to provide object-graph management and persistence out of the box. When you need to save application data Core Data archives and persists your objects in a persistent store.

Core Data's object-graph management is much more than data persistence. Object-graph management is what allows you to keep the relationships between different objects in sync. A common misconception about Core Data is that it's only a database API. Although it does allow you to store data in a database, you'll learn throughout this chapter that it's much more than that. Core Data helps you manage your application's model layer in the same way that Interface Builder helps you with your view layer. By managing the model layer Core Data allows you to focus on the business logic in the controller layer.

Before you get hands-on with Core Data, let's look at what makes Core Data different from a traditional relational database.

> **This chapter only scratches the surface of Core Data**
>
> You can find many books that are dedicated to Core Data alone. This chapter covers only the basics of using Core Data effectively in a MacRuby application.

7.1.2   Differences between Core Data and traditional databases

You're probably wondering what makes Core Data different from other database solutions. After all, many Cocoa applications out there rely on traditional database solutions, such as SQLite, and completely ignore Core Data. Let's compare Core Data with these databases.

WHAT CORE DATA DOES WELL

As we already mentioned, object-graph management is one of the main features of Core Data. But we haven't discussed what this feature entails. Imagine you have `Employee` and `Manager` objects. Managers likely have many employees, but each employee has only one manager.

Using a SQLite database, you have to use foreign keys and manage this relationship manually. If you modify one of these objects you must manually make changes to the other. For instance, if you delete the `Manager` of an `Employee` but change nothing else, you could end up with an orphaned relationship. If you don't manually fix this the employee record may still be related to the non-existent manager record. SQLite by itself doesn't know about the relationship between two objects that are represented as rows in tables.

A benefit of Core Data's object-graph solution is that it automatically syncs the relationship between objects. Using Core Data, if you change the connection between either object in the previous example, the other is updated, which also triggers notifications. Deleting the `Manager` of an `Employee` object could also trigger a notification or even allow for cascading deletion if you wanted it to.

Another great benefit Core Data provides is that after you instantiate a single object you can retrieve all its connected objects by following its relationships. This is possible because every object and its relationships are stored in memory. To do this in SQLite you have to perform separate queries.

On the flip side, the fact that Core Data keeps everything in memory could be limiting depending on the persistence store you use.

WHAT CORE DATA DOESN'T DO WELL

When you need to update a large number of objects at one time performance is an area in which Core Data is limited. Suppose you're creating a newsreader and you need a "mark all as read" feature.

With a traditional database this isn't of much concern. You could write one simple update statement to mark all unread items as read without having to worry about performance issues. Databases like SQLite don't need to load large amounts of data into RAM to update a large amount of data.

With Core Data each object you need to update has to be stored in memory when fetched. There are ways of reducing the amount of memory used when doing this, but it's an issue of concern if you're dealing with large amounts of data.

Data constraints are another limitation. Traditional SQL databases offer data constraints, such as unique keys, out of the box. Data constraints don't exist in Core Data because Core Data expects you to deal with them on the business-logic side of an application.

There are other pros and cons, but ultimately it's up to you to decide whether Core Data is the right solution for your application.

Let's lay the groundwork of the application you'll build out in this chapter.

7.1.3 *Creating a base Core Data project*

Before we drill down into code examples of Core Data, we'll show you how to create an application using the built-in Core Data application template. This base application will provide a point of reference throughout this chapter.

After we examine Core Data more closely, you'll put your knowledge to use to create a new version of the Todo List application that you built in chapter 3. You'll start by creating a brand-new project:

1 Open Xcode and choose File > New Project.
2 Select the Application templates and choose MacRuby Application.

Figure 7.1   Selecting the MacRuby Core Data Application template

3   On the next screen, select Use Core Data to make this a Core Data application (see figure 7.1).

4   Name the project Todo Core Data (feel free to name it something else if you want).

    We chose this particular name so that you don't confuse it with the previous non-Core-Data-version of the Todo application.

After your base application project is created you can examine exactly what the Core Data template provided for you. Take a look at the generated files, and you'll notice a few differences between this application and previous applications you've created:

- The Core Data framework is included.

- A file called AppDelegate.rb has been created. This file contains Core-Data-related methods that handle persistent stores and managed-object contexts. Don't worry if you don't know what these are yet. You'll learn about them soon.

- A file called Todo_Core_Data.xcdatamodel has been created. This may be called MacRubyApp.xcdatamodel, depending on which version of MacRuby you have installed. This file represents the Core-Data-managed object model, which you'll use to set up your entities, their properties, and their relationships.

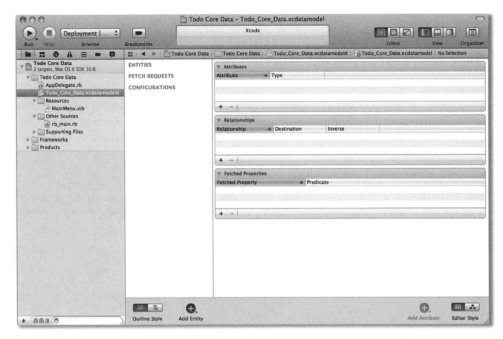

Figure 7.2   Editing the Core Data model in Xcode

Click this file, and it opens in its own editor—the Core Data model editor—in Xcode (see figure 7.2).

The Core Data model editor provides a few tools for working with an application's managed object model:

- *Add Entity*—To add a new entity click the button at lower left in the editor.
- *Add Attribute*—To add an attribute to an entity use this button at lower right in the editor.
- *Attributes pane*—You view, add attributes to, and edit entities in the top pane.
- *Relationships pane*—The middle pane displays a description of the relationships between different entities.
- *Fetched Properties pane*—This pane displays properties that are fetched through relationships.
- *Editor Style*—To toggle between graph and table mode click the button at lower right in the editor. Use graph mode to display a visual representation of entities and their relationships.

Let's take a closer look at the managed object model of this base application.

7.2   Understanding the persistent store and managed objects

A managed object model defines the data that you want to persist in an application. Core Data provides different ways of persisting your data using persistent stores. In this section you'll learn how to work with a persistent store and managed object model.

7.2.1   *Anatomy of a persistent store*

Core Data gives you several choices of persistent store for an application. If you create your MacRuby Core Data application using the predefined template as you did, the store is XML. You'll now find out where this is specified in an application.

Open the AppDelegate.rb class which was generated for you in the project and find the method named persistentStoreCoordinator.

This method should look similar to what's shown in the following listing.

Listing 7.1   The persistentStoreCoordinator method in AppDelegate.rb

```
def persistentStoreCoordinator
  unless @persistentStoreCoordinator
    error = Pointer.new_with_type('@')

    fileManager = NSFileManager.defaultManager          ◀──┐  ❶ Find folder
    applicationSupportFolder = self.applicationSupportFolder

    unless fileManager.fileExistsAtPath(applicationSupportFolder,
      isDirectory:nil)
      fileManager.createDirectoryAtPath(applicationSupportFolder,
        attributes:nil)
    end                                                      Initialize
                                                             coordinator
    url = NSURL.fileURLWithPath(applicationSupportFolder.      ❷
      stringByAppendingPathComponent("Todo Core Data.xml"))
    @persistentStoreCoordinator = NSPersistentStoreCoordinator.alloc.
      initWithManagedObjectModel(self.managedObjectModel)   ◀──┘
    unless
      @persistentStoreCoordinator.addPersistentStoreWithType(NSXMLStoreType,
        configuration:nil, URL:url, options:nil, error:error)
      NSApplication.sharedApplication.presentError(error[0])
    end
  end

  @persistentStoreCoordinator
end
```

This method retrieves an instance of the persistence store coordinator for the application delegate. It first uses the NSFileManager to see if an application support folder exists ❶. Typically this folder is in the ~/Library/Application Support/*<App Name>* folder. If the folder doesn't exist it creates it. The method then looks for Todo Core Data.xml in this directory. After this it initializes the persistent store coordinator using the application delegate's managed object model ❷ (we'll discuss the managed object model in the next section). If this file doesn't exist it's created when the persistent store is added to the coordinator.

Core Data provides four different types of persistent store: Atomic, In-Memory, SQLite, and XML. Table 7.1 lists advantages and disadvantages of each.

Table 7.1　Advantages and disadvantages of different persistent store types

Persistent Store	Advantages	Disadvantages
Atomic	Fast, full object-graph capabilities	Less secure than SQLite.
In-Memory	Fast, full object-graph capabilities	Does not scale well.
SQLite	Fast, possible to import existing SQLite databases into Core Data	Partial object-graph solution. Most secure solution.
XML	Easy to debug, supports external parsing, full object-graph capabilities	Slow. Less secure than SQLite.

It's up to you to decide which persistent store is best for you. For the sake of simplicity you'll use the XML store for easier debugging.

SQLite persistent store and Core Data

Even though you can use SQLite as a way of persisting data you can't create a native SQLite database and use it directly with Core Data. Also, you shouldn't manipulate or inspect your Core Data store, even if you're using SQLite, because Core Data works with SQLite in a different manner. If you have an existing SQLite database it's possible to import it into Core Data, although you need to take special steps to make it compatible.

Now that you understand the persistent store we'll discuss the managed object model, how to create entities, and how to work with managed objects and managed object contexts.

7.2.2　*Working with the managed object model*

The Core Data managed object model defines the schema of the data that you want to persist. A managed object model is an instance of the NSManagedObjectModel class. Every Core Data application has at least one managed object model. Figure 7.3 provides a bird's-eye view of a managed object model.

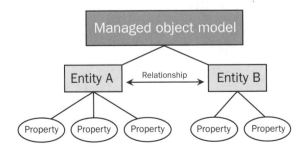

Figure 7.3　Overview of the managed object model

The managed object model is made up of entities, properties, and relationships (although only one relationship is shown in figure 7.3). The Todo_Core_Data .xcdatamodel file that you viewed in the previous section is the managed object model that you'll use for the Todo application. Let's discuss the entity's role.

ADDING ENTITIES

An entity is a description of something that you want to store in Core Data. For the Todo List application you want to store *tasks*. To relate this to a typical SQL-style database, an entity is like the table that you'd use to store the data in your model. In Core Data the `NSEntityDescription` class represents entities in a managed object model. An `NSEntityDescription` stores the metadata of an entity—its name, properties, and relationships.

You'll now add a Task entity to the Todo application's managed object model:

1 From Xcode, make sure the managed object model is selected.
2 Click Add Entity at the bottom of the screen and name the entity Task as shown in figure 7.4.

Now that you've created the Task entity we'll show you how managed objects and contexts work.

MANAGED OBJECTS AND CONTEXTS

An `NSManagedObject` is essentially a dictionary that provides storage for the *properties* of its associated entity. By default an entity is mapped to an `NSManagedObject`, which is a generic class that implements the behavior necessary for a Core Data model object. To create a managed object class you make it a subclass of `NSManagedObject`:

```
class MyObject < NSManagedObject
  ...
end
```

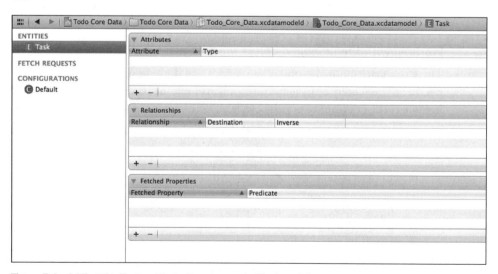

Figure 7.4 Adding the Task entity to the managed object model

The managed objects in an application are managed by an instance of `NSManaged-ObjectContext`.

> **NOTE** When you retrieve a managed object context for a managed object you'll always be returned back the same instance. There can be only one instance of a single managed object in one managed object context.

The managed object context is involved with managing the life cycle of its managed objects. You'll use the managed object context to fetch/retrieve objects and to discard and even commit changes to the persistent store later in this chapter.

The Todo application's `AppDelegate.rb` class already includes the following method, which sets up an instance of a managed object context:

```
def managedObjectContext
  unless @managedObjectContext
    coordinator = self.persistentStoreCoordinator
    if coordinator
      @managedObjectContext = NSManagedObjectContext.new
      @managedObjectContext.setPersistentStoreCoordinator(coordinator)
    end
  end

  @managedObjectContext
end
```

This method returns the application's managed object context. You can see that it's already bound to the application's persistent store coordinator as well. You'll see more of the managed object context in later examples of this chapter.

You can now add properties to the Task entity.

7.2.3 Working with entity properties

When we talk about properties we're talking about the `NSPropertyDescription` class. This class is used to define different properties or attributes of an entity. You can specify the following three property types for a given entity:

- *Attribute* (`NSAttributeDescription`)—Attributes store values for an entity. These attribute values can be represented by an `NSString`, `NSNumber`, `NSDate`, or `NSData`. You also get validation and the option to specify default values.
- *Relationship* (`NSRelationshipDescription`)—Relationships are used to link together multiple objects. There are to-one and to-many relationships.
- *Fetched Property* (`NSFetchedPropertyDescription`)—Fetched properties are similar to relationships except that the objects returned are based on a search predicate or a conditional.

Let's go over each of these in more detail, starting with attributes.

ADDING ENTITY ATTRIBUTES

To access and set properties for managed objects you can either use key-value coding or set the property directly. For example, suppose you want to set a `summary` property for the `Task` managed object. You could do this with the following code (note that this is very difficult to try on your own without running this code in its own Cocoa application):

```
context = NSApp.delegate.managedObjectContext
task = NSEntityDescription.insertNewObjectForEntityForName("Task",
➥ inManagedObjectContext:context)
task.setValue("Take out the trash", forKey:"summary")
```

You first grab the managed object context, and then you create a managed object for the Task entity. You then set the `summary` property using KVC (see chapter 6).

Alternatively, you could set the summary like this:

```
task.summary = "Take out the trash"
```

You'll now add some properties to the Task entity. With the Task entity selected, click the plus (+) button in the Attributes pane, and then add the three properties listed in table 7.2.

Table 7.2   Attribute properties for the Task entity

Attribute Name	Type	Optional	Default Value
summary	String	No	NA
status	String	No	Open
created_date	Date	No	NA

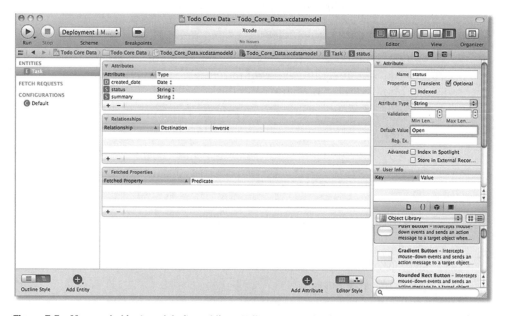

Figure 7.5   Managed object model after adding attribute properties in the Core Data Model inspector

You might not immediately see how to set these attributes as optional or even set their default value using the Core Data Model inspector. To view these attribute settings open the utility area (from the application menu, choose View > Utilities > Data Model Inspector).

You probably noticed that you added an attribute called `created_date`. When you build the Todo List application you'll use this attribute to fetch tasks by date.

After you add these attribute properties your data model should look similar to what's shown in figure 7.5.

Because the Todo application has only one entity, Task, we can't show you how to set up a relationship in the application. To see how relationships work in Core Data let's briefly switch gears.

ADDING ENTITY RELATIONSHIPS

Imagine that you're building a Twitter-like application called MacRuby Twitter. In its most simple form this application has two entities: User and Tweet. When you edit these entities through the managed object model you can add relationships the same way you added attributes to the Task entity. For instance, to represent the many tweets that belong to a given user you can add a to-many relationship on the User entity. You named the relationship tweets (see figure 7.6).

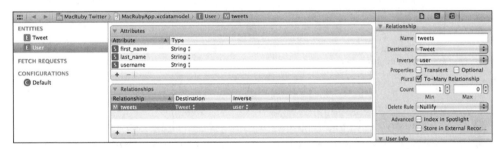

Figure 7.6 Adding a to-many relationship called *tweets* on the User entity and editing its properties

The tweets relationship gives you the ability to retrieve a set of tweets by a given user. What about the inverse relationship?

To retrieve the user who wrote a specific tweet you can add a to-one relationship to the Tweet entity. We named ours user (see figure 7.7).

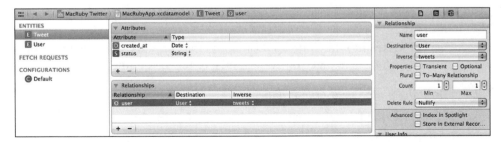

Figure 7.7 Adding a to-one relationship called *user* on the Tweet entity and editing its properties

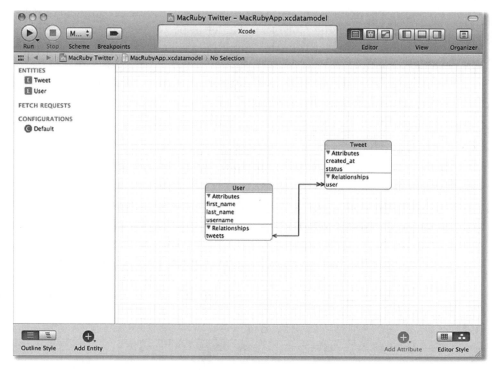

Figure 7.8   In graph mode the Core Data model editor displays a diagram showing the to-one and to-many relationships you created.

After setting up these relationships you can see them when you view the managed object model in graph mode, as shown in figure 7.8.

The arrows in the diagram indicate relationship type. The double arrow from the tweets relationship from a User to a Tweet signifies a to-many relationship, whereas the single arrow from the user relationship from a Tweet to a User signifies a to-one relationship.

ABOUT FETCHED PROPERTIES

Fetched properties are one-way relationships that are calculated using a fetch request. For example, you could make a fetched property on the User entity called `last_tweet`. Because the User has a relationship with the Tweet entity you could write a fetch request that retrieves the last tweet for a given user that populates the `last_tweet` property.

Let's return to the Todo application; before we show you how to create managed objects, you need to make one last change to the Task entity.

7.2.4   Defining a managed object class

From the model editor click the Task entity. In the utility area you'll see that `NSManagedObject` is specified in the Class field. You're going to create a subclass of `NSManagedObject` and point the Task entity to it.

If this were Objective-C you could use Xcode's Core Data model editor to automatically create `NSManagedObjects` from the Task entity. At the time of writing there's currently no way to do the same for MacRuby in Xcode. Still, as you'll see, creating a managed object in MacRuby is no different from anything you've created before.

Create a new Ruby file in the Classes group and save it with the name Task.rb. Add the following code:

```ruby
class Task < NSManagedObject
  attr_accessor :status, :summary

  def complete!
    self.status = "Complete"
  end
end
```

If you were using Objective-C you'd need to specify properties defined for the entities using the `@dynamic` keyword in the implementation. In this case you use `attr_accessor` for the object properties. If you created and retrieved these managed objects through the managed object context you wouldn't need to do this. You also added a `complete!` method that allows you to easily mark a task as complete.

You can now go into the managed object model and change the `Class` property for the Task entity to point to the `Task` class that you just created. You can edit this property in the Data Model inspector in the utility area as shown in figure 7.9.

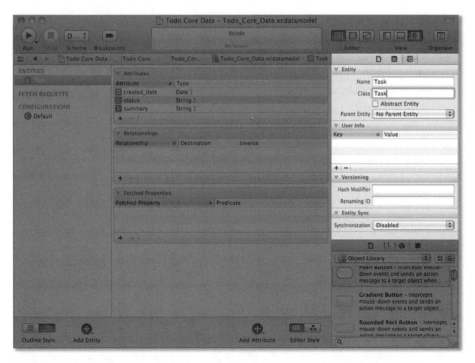

Figure 7.9 Setting the `Class` property for the Task entity in the Data Model inspector

Thanks for hanging in there! Learning the basics and setting up your managed object model was a lengthy process. You're now prepared to learn how to work with managed objects.

7.3   Working with managed objects

Now that you've had some practice creating entities, setting their properties, and creating relationships, you can learn how to do more with managed objects. You haven't had a chance to dive into the code until now. You'll learn how to create, read, update, and delete managed objects in this section.

7.3.1   Creating managed objects and updating properties

When working with an instance of an `NSManagedObject` you need access to your managed object context. In the Todo application you can access it through the `managedObjectContext` method defined by the application delegate:

```
context = NSApp.delegate.managedObjectContext
```

To create a managed object instance you need to know the name of the entity that it represents. For instance, the `Task` managed object class represents the Task entity, which makes it rather easy to remember. There are multiple ways to create an `NSManagedObject`. You could do the following:

```
context = NSApp.delegate.managedObjectContext
managedObjModel = context.persistentStoreCoordinator.managedObjectModel
entity = managedObjModel.entitiesByName.objectForKey("Task")
task = Task.alloc.initWithEntity(entity,
➧ insertIntoManagedObjectContext:context)
```

You first retrieve the managed object context. In the second line you use the context to retrieve the managed object model from the persistent store coordinator. Next, you retrieve the entity by looking it up in the managed object model's dictionary of entities, by name. Last, you allocate a new `Task` instance by using the `initWithEntity:insertIntoManagedObjectContext:` method.

That's quite a bit of work to create an instance of one managed object. Luckily there's a better way. You can use the `insertNewObjectForEntityForName:inManagedObjectContext:` class method in `NSEntityDescription`. This method returns a new `NSManagedObject` instance for the specified entity name and inserts it into the specified managed object context. The following code creates a new instance of the `Task` managed object for the Task entity:

```
context = NSApp.delegate.managedObjectContext
task = NSEntityDescription.insertNewObjectForEntityForName("Task",
➧ inManagedObjectContext:context)
```

You first retrieve the managed object context. You then retrieve a new instance of the Task managed object and insert it into the context. This method automatically matches the entity name to its defined class, which you set in the managed object model.

To update properties in Objective-C you must use the key-value coding techniques that you learned about in Chapter 6. Because Task subclasses NSManagedObject and has an associated entity you have the choice to modify them directly. For instance, you could use either of the following solutions to update the summary property:

```
task.summary = "Pick up dry-cleaning"
```

Or

```
task.setValue("Pick up dry-cleaning", forKey:"summary")
```

Retrieving the value of a property on the managed object works the same way:

```
task.summary
#=> Pick up dry-cleaning
```

Or

```
task.valueForKey("summary")
#=> Pick up dry-cleaning
```

After you set properties on a managed object you'll likely want to save it to the persistent store.

7.3.2 *Persisting changes to managed objects*

Saving and deleting objects with Core Data is simple to do. You perform these actions on the managed object context. You'll come to see that you'll be interacting with the managed object context quite a bit. Without explicitly saving your changes using the managed object context, no changes are persisted with Core Data. We'll first show you how to save a managed object to the persistent store.

SAVING MANAGED OBJECTS

In the previous section you inserted an object into the managed object context when you created a new instance of an NSManagedObject by using the insertNewObject-ForEntityForName:inManagedObjectContext: method. The managed object context keeps track of objects that haven't yet been saved, updated, or deleted. Using the insertedObjects method you can get a set of all unsaved managed objects. Using the updatedObjects method you can identify which objects have been modified but not yet saved. The following example shows both these methods:

```
context = NSApp.delegate.context
not_yet_saved_but_new = context.insertedObjects
previously_saved_but_modified = context.updatedObjects
```

To save these objects to the persistent store you must call the `save:` method on the managed object context. The `save:` method expects a pointer to an `NSError` to be passed in. It returns a Boolean value. Here's the implementation:

```
error = Pointer.new_with_type('@')
unless NSApp.delegate.managedObjectContext.save(error)
  # handle error appropriately
end
```

You first create a pointer with the type encoding of an object. You're using this to represent the `NSError`. You then call the `save:` method on the application's managed object context. If the response is `false` you handle the error in any way that you like. Luckily, you don't have to implement this yourself because the Core-Data-generated application delegate already has this implemented for you in the `saveAction:` method. This method is in the `AppDelegate` class, and looks like this:

```
def saveAction(sender)
  error = Pointer.new_with_type('@')
  unless self.managedObjectContext.save(error)
    NSApplication.sharedApplication.presentError(error[0])
  end
end
```

Weave the managed object context with the following code:

```
NSApp.delegate.saveAction(self)
```

Let's now dig into deleting objects.

DELETING MANAGED OBJECTS

Deleting from the context is similar to saving. It takes one extra step to make sure that the object is removed from the context and then, ultimately, the persistent store.

To delete an object managed by the context call the `deleteObject:` method. The sole parameter it expects is the object that you want to delete. If the managed object that you want to delete hasn't been saved to the persistent store yet, it's removed from the set of managed objects that the context is managing. If the object is already persisted, it's removed after you save the changes to the managed object context. The last step you need to do is call `save:` on the managed object context.

The managed object context allows you to commit changes to the persistent store, but does it support fetching objects from the persistent store that match one or more criteria? That's certainly a feature you'll use heavily in a Core Data application.

Reverting changes to managed objects in a context

Using the `NSManagedObjectContext` class you can revert any uncommitted changes to any of its managed objects. Call the `undo` method to revert any changes that haven't yet been saved.

7.4 Retrieving objects from Core Data

What good is having objects persisted if you can't retrieve them? This section will teach you how to do just that. You'll first learn how to use NSPredicate to create logical conditions to fetch objects. And you'll learn about NSSortDescriptor, which fetches objects in a specified order. You'll then combine your knowledge of predicates and descriptors to fetch objects from Core Data.

7.4.1 Filtering and sorting with predicates and descriptors

It's best to learn first about predicates and descriptors and then learn how to fetch objects. You use predicates to filter results, and you use descriptors to order the results the way you want to view them.

FILTERING WITH PREDICATES

An NSPredicate provides you with the ability to define logical conditions that you can use to search for or fetch results. If you're familiar with SQL-like queries and conditionals, you'll find the string-based conditionals of NSPredicate similar. If you're not used to writing out conditionals, you'll see that it's straightforward. You'll create a few quick examples based on a simple array of objects.

Because you're developing a Todo application, let's experiment on a sample of tasks that you might store in the application. To keep things simple you'll create a new Task class as a subclass of NSObject. Each task will have the same attributes as the existing Task entity. For this example, feel free to follow along in your editor of choice. First, create an empty array and add two tasks to it:

```
all_tasks = []

task_one = Task.new
task_one.summary = "Finish app"
task_one.status = "Completed"
all_tasks << task_one

task_two = Task.new
task_two.summary = "Submit app to App Store"
task_two.status = "Open"
all_tasks << task_two
```

Next, create an NSPredicate to retrieve all tasks with a status of Open:

```
predicate = NSPredicate.predicateWithFormat("status == 'Open'")
```

To apply this filter to the array, use the filterUsingPredicate: method of NSMutableArray, as shown:

```
all_tasks.filterUsingPredicate(predicate)
```

This method filters the all_tasks array and leaves only objects that match that predicate.

If you inspect the array of tasks you'll find that only one task is available—the task with the Open status. Table 7.3 lists some other predicate examples that you can try with the all_tasks array.

Table 7.3   Predicate examples

Predicate	Returned Task(s)
status == 'Completed'	task_one
summary like[c] 'Finish*'	task_one
summary like[c] '*app*'	task_one, task_two
(status ==[c] 'Completed') OR (status ==[c] 'Open')	task_one, task_two

> **TIP** For more predicate examples see Apple's *Predicate Programming Guide* (http://mng.bz/vAHR).

Most of the time using the predicateWithFormat: method is sufficient. If you wish to find out more about the different ways you can use NSPredicate, look up the NSPredicate class in the Apple developer documentation.

Next we'll show you how to use NSSortDescriptor to sort returned objects.

SORTING WITH DESCRIPTORS

Sort descriptors help you sort the results of the objects that Core Data returns. To demonstrate how descriptors work you'll create an instance of NSSortDescriptor to sort the all_tasks array from the previous example.

Suppose you want to sort the all_tasks array by task created_date in ascending order. To create a sort descriptor you allocate a new NSSortDescriptor with the initWithKey:ascending: method. This method takes a key that you want to sort on and whether the order should be ascending, as shown:

```
descriptor = NSSortDescriptor.alloc.initWithKey("created_date",
➥ ascending:true)
sorted_tasks = all_tasks.sortedArrayUsingDescriptors([descriptor])
```

You create a descriptor that sorts on the created date and orders the results in ascending order. Then you call NSMutableArray's sortedArrayUsingDescriptors: method on the all_tasks array. This returns a new array, which is sorted by created_date. To return the results in descending order, change the ascending parameter to false.

Why don't you combine predicates and descriptors to fetch back results?

7.4.2 *Fetching objects from Core Data*

Finally, you've come to fetching objects from Core Data. Although you can get by without knowing much about predicates and descriptors, it's beneficial that you understand how they work and what you can do with them when you can retrieve objects.

To fetch objects you need to be familiar with the `NSFetchRequest` class. What `NSFetchRequest` allows you to do is to create search criteria to retrieve data from the persistent store through the managed object context. When creating a fetch request you provide the following information:

- The `NSEntityDescription` specifies which entity to look up.
- The `NSPredicate` specifies search criteria.
- The `NSSortDescriptor` describes how to order the results.

Let's take this process step-by-step:

NOTE This fetch request won't work in the examples that you've put in place because you have no real data in a persistent store to fetch.

1 Create a new instance of `NSEntityDescription`:

```
context = NSApp.delegate.managedObjectContext
entity_desc = NSEntityDescription.entityForName("Task",
➥ inManagedObjectContext:context)
```

This is the entity description for the Task entity.

2 Create an `NSFetchRequest` and its entity:

```
request = NSFetchRequest.alloc.init
request.entity = entity_desc
```

3 Specify a predicate:

```
request.predicate = NSPredicate.predicateWithFormat("status ==[c]
➥ 'Completed'")
```

4 Create a sort descriptor to sort the results by date created in ascending order:

```
sort_desc = NSSortDescriptor.alloc.initWithKey("created_date",
➥ ascending:true)
request.sortDescriptors = [sort_desc]
```

5 Execute the request.

You'll use the managed object context's `executeFetchRequest:error:` method and supply it with the `NSFetchRequest` and a pointer representing the `NSError`:

```
error = Pointer.new_with_type("@")
results = context.executeFetchRequest(request, error:error)
```

This returns an array of managed objects that match the fetch-request criteria.

The request you've created retrieves every matching result without any limit. If you want, you can apply more constraints to the fetch request. To limit the number of results set the `fetchLimit` property. Also, using this property in conjunction with the `fetchOffset` property can help with pagination. The fetch offset allows you to specify an offset at which to start returning results.

You can now put your knowledge to use and create a Core-Data-backed version of the Todo application.

7.5 Creating a Core Data version of the Todo List application

Throughout this chapter you've been putting together a new version of the Todo List application backed by Core Data. You already created the managed object model and you have an NSManagedObject class for the Task entity.

In this section we'll briefly walk through creating the user interface—you'll use a good amount of code from the previous version of the application (see chapter 3). The difference is that you'll use Core Data to store and retrieve the tasks that are going to be displayed. When the Todo List application is complete you'll feel comfortable enough with Core Data to use it in any of your MacRuby applications.

7.5.1 Building the user interface

The user interface is similar to the previous Todo application. We won't go into too much detail about each user interface element because you've done this before. You could copy the previous interface (MainMenu.xib) but it would be missing some outlets for AppDelegate. The Core Data template, which you used to create this project, generates this class.

Open MainMenu.xib and change the window title to Todo List. Next, add an NSTableView to the window and size it to take up close to 90 percent of the window's height. Make sure the table view has two columns to represent a task's status and its summary. Set the titles of the column headers in the table view to Status and Summary. Make sure to set the identifiers for each column—you'll use the column identifier to

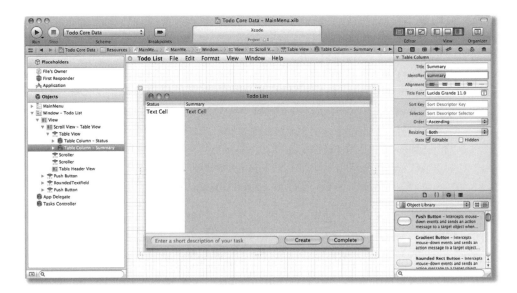

Figure 7.10 Remember to set the column identifiers. You need them to retrieve the correct tasks.

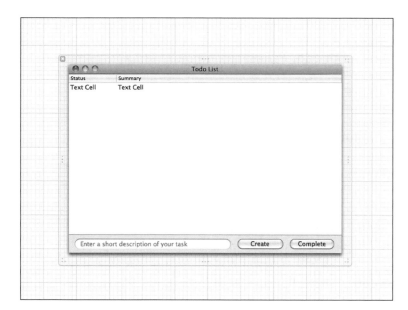

**Figure 7.11
The finished Todo
List interface**

retrieve the appropriate value on the `Task` object. Set the identifier for the Status column to status and set the identifier for Summary to summary (see figure 7.10).

After you have the table view in place, add an `NSTextField` at the bottom-left to represent the area where users type the task description. At the bottom-right add two `NSButtons`: label one Create and the other Complete. Remember to set the auto-sizing properties for each of the UI elements so that they can handle the window being resized. When you're finished you should have an interface similar to figure 7.11.

With the interface in place let's start putting together the controller before you add connections and outlets.

7.5.2 Creating the tasks controller

You'll implement the same methods from the previous application, but you'll also include some new items that you've learned along the way.

Create a new file in the Classes group and save it with the name TasksController.rb. The code shown in listing 7.2 is the list of methods you'll implement in the `Tasks-Controller` class. This provides you with a good starting point.

Listing 7.2   Base for TasksController.rb

```
class TasksController
  attr_accessor :tasks_table_view, :task_text_field

  def awakeFromNib
  end
```

```
  def numberOfRowsInTableView(view)
  end

  def tableView(view, objectValueForTableColumn:column, row:index)
  end

  def create_task(sender)
  end

  def complete_task(sender)
  end

  def fetch_tasks
  end
end
```

You added the necessary outlets for the NSTableView and NSTextField, and you're using the same methods from the previous application, except for one. You added a new method named fetch_tasks which you'll use to retrieve tasks from Core Data.

You'll now fill in each of these methods, starting with awakeFromNib:

```
def awakeFromNib
  @tasks = []
  @context = NSApp.delegate.managedObjectContext
  fetch_tasks
end
```

You first set up an array to hold the tasks. Next, you set an instance variable for the managed object context because you'll be using it in multiple places throughout the controller. After that you call fetch_tasks, which retrieves the tasks from Core Data.

To let the table view know exactly how many rows it needs to display the number-OfRowsInTableView: method returns the number of tasks in the @tasks array:

```
def numberOfRowsInTableView(view)
  @tasks.size
end
```

You can apply your knowledge of key-value coding (see chapter 6) to the tableView:objectValueForTableColumn:row: method. Because the column identifiers match the attributes you can use valueForKey: to return the appropriate value, as shown:

```
def tableView(view, objectValueForTableColumn:column, row:index)
  task = @tasks[index]
  task.valueForKey(column.identifier)
end
```

Before you define the fetch_tasks method you'll implement two IBActions: one to create a task and one to mark a task as complete. You'll start with the createTask: action:

```
def create_task(sender)
  task = NSEntityDescription.insertNewObjectForEntityForName("Task",
➥ inManagedObjectContext:@context)
```

```
  task.summary = @task_text_field.stringValue
  task.created_date = Time.now

  @task_text_field.stringValue = ""
  NSApp.delegate.saveAction(self)
  fetch_tasks
end
```

You first create an instance of the task and insert it into the managed object context. You set the summary property to the value of the NSTextField and then set the created_date property to the current time. You then clear the NSTextField and call the saveAction: method on the application delegate. The last thing you do is call fetch_tasks to retrieve the tasks and populate the table view.

The complete_task: action looks like this:

```
def complete_task(sender)
  return if @tasks_table_view.selectedRow == -1

  @tasks[@tasks_table_view.selectedRow].complete!
  NSApp.delegate.saveAction(self)
  fetch_tasks
end
```

You immediately return if no row is selected in the table view. You then look up the specified task in the @tasks array and mark it as complete. Because that task still belongs to the managed object context you call saveAction: on the application delegate and then re-fetch all the tasks.

You'll finish the controller by defining the fetch_tasks method. This method retrieves tasks using a fetch request and then it reloads the data for the table view:

```
def fetch_tasks
  @tasks = []
  request = NSFetchRequest.alloc.init
  request.entity = NSEntityDescription.entityForName("Task",
  ⇒ inManagedObjectContext:@context)

  sort_desc = NSSortDescriptor.alloc.initWithKey("created_date",
  ⇒ ascending:false)
  request.sortDescriptors = [sort_desc]

  error = Pointer.new_with_type("@")
  @tasks = @context.executeFetchRequest(request, error:error)
  @tasks_table_view.reloadData
end
```

You first reset the tasks array. Then you create a new instance of NSFetchRequest and give it an entity to look up. You then create a sort descriptor that sorts by created_date in descending order, which should bring your newest task items to the top of the table. You then execute the fetch request and, finally, reload the table view.

You're almost ready to try out the application, but first you need to hook together the interface and controller.

7.5.3   *Connecting the interface to the controller*

The first order of business is to add the Tasks Controller as an NSObject, as shown in figure 7.12.

Next select the NSTableView and set its dataSource and delegate to Tasks Controller. Figure 7.13 shows the connections in the Connections tab of the Inspector pane.

Now you can hook up the outlets. Click the Tasks Controller, and go to the Connections tab in the Inspector pane:

- Drag a connection from task_text_field to the NSTextField.
- Drag a connection from tasks_table_view to the NSTableView.

With the outlets connected your Connections tab should look like figure 7.14.

Next drag connections from the actions to the buttons:

- Drag a connection from complete_task: to the NSButton labeled Complete.
- Drag a connection from create_task: to the NSbutton labeled Create.

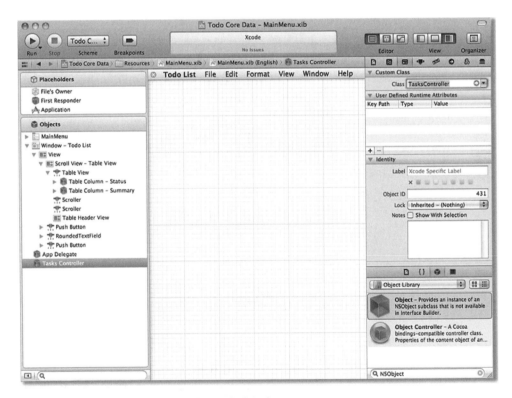

Figure 7.12   Adding the Tasks Controller to the interface

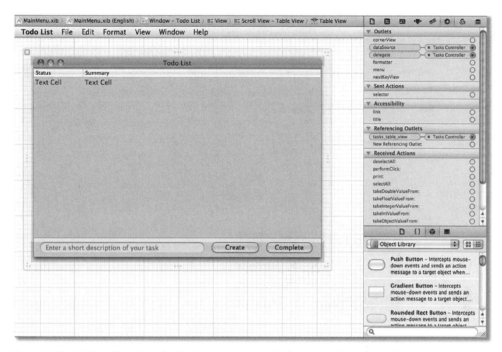

Figure 7.13   Setting the table view's `dataSource` and delegate to Tasks Controller

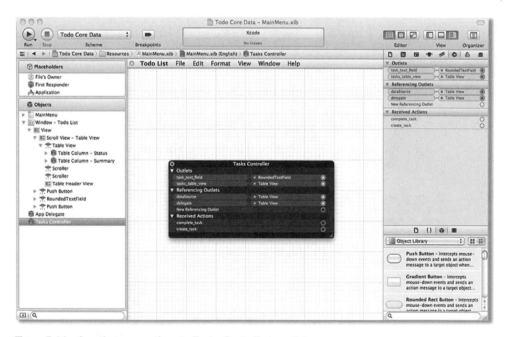

Figure 7.14   Creating connections to Tasks Controller's outlets

Figure 7.15   All connections to outlets and actions

When you've got everything hooked up your Connections tab should look like figure 7.15.

With the connections in place you can finally run the application and see Core Data in action.

7.5.4   *Running the application and inspecting the persistent store*

Run the application and then create a task titled Make my first Core Data application. If all went well you should see the new task listed in the table view.

Quit the application and then relaunch it. The task still appears in the table view (see figure 7.16).

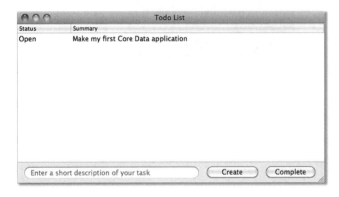

Figure 7.16
The task appears even after relaunching the application.

In the previous version of the Todo List application you chose to store the tasks in memory and didn't persist any of the data that was created. In this version you properly store the task data in Core Data and fetch it directly from the persistent store.

You can now check to see what's actually stored in the persistent store. You used the default XML storage type for the application. This makes the data easy to view. Go to the application's support folder. Typically, this is in ~/Library/Application Support/ *<Application Name>*. In this case the application name is Todo Core Data. In this folder you should see a file named Todo Core Data.xml. Open it in any text editor to view its contents. Your newly created task is listed in this file:

```
<object type="TASK" id="z102">
    <attribute name="summary" type="string">Make my first Core Data
    ➥ application</attribute>
    <attribute name="status" type="string">Open</attribute>
    <attribute name="created_date"
      ➥ type="date">318356622.65318202972412109375</attribute>
</object>
```

Now that you've created your first Core Data application, feel free to mark this task as complete. Add a new task and you'll notice that the newest one always appears at the top of the table view. The sort descriptor you created sorts the data by the date on which each task was created, in descending order.

7.6   Summary

You've now completed a crash course in Core Data. In addition to getting an inside look at the XML persistent store, you learned about managed object models, managed object contexts, and managed objects and their properties. You learned how to save, update, and delete managed objects. You also learned how to use predicates and descriptors to fetch objects from a persistent store. With your newfound knowledge you created a version of the Todo List application that utilizes Core Data.

We covered quite a bit of ground in this chapter, but there's still so much more to Core Data. In one chapter we couldn't cover topics such as migrations, object validations, change management, concurrency, and so on. If you plan on diving deeper we strongly suggest that you look at an in-depth Core Data book.

In the next chapter you'll learn about Core Animation, which provides powerful animation in a simple API.

Core Animation basics

8

This chapter covers

- Cocoa animations
- Using the `CALayer` class
- 2D views in 3D space
- Adding animations to a Twitter client

Great Mac OS X applications not only look beautiful, but also have subtle touches that make them stand out to the user. Think about maximizing and minimizing a window and the associated animation effect: Apple paid amazing attention to detail for that simple, common task. Even hovering your mouse over the dock applies an impressive magnification effect to the application icons.

Apple includes this attention to animation detail throughout most of its applications. As you watch a movie on QuickTime you'll notice that the frame of the window fades away to give you a better viewing experience. Even in the relatively simple System Preferences application you can see a smooth transition when you go from one setting to another. Another great example is Time Machine, which uses Core Animation to zoom you in and out to view different documents that have been backed up.

You might not have paid much attention to the animations you've seen in the past. This is because they're so subtle and effective. When you create MacRuby applications you can take advantage of Core Animation to provide this same kind of experience for your users. Throughout this chapter we'll be taking a close look at Core Animation and how you can use it to enhance your applications.

8.1 Introduction to Core Animation

Core Animation became part of the Cocoa framework with the release of Mac OS X 10.5 Leopard. It was designed to help Cocoa developers easily integrate animations within their applications. In this section we'll examine Core Animation further. You'll learn about what Core Animation provides and look at how it makes your lives easier with a basic animation example.

8.1.1 What is Core Animation?

In a nutshell, Core Animation provides an API that makes it easy to create animated user interfaces. The basic Core Animation classes can be found in the Quartz framework.

Before Core Animation creating animations was too complex for the average developer. Core Animation can help you animate views and windows in your MacRuby application without writing complicated animation code. All you need to do is specify what animation you want to apply on a specific view, and Core Animation's rendering engine takes care of the rest.

When creating animations you'd normally need to think about the time it would take to complete and the frames you'd need to display. Fortunately, Core Animation does this for you. Core Animation pays careful attention to the time specified for an animation; this means Core Animation will drop frames in order to meet the animation time. In addition, the animation's performance will be highly dependent on the type of hardware that is running the application. A machine with a faster CPU and graphics card will obviously handle animations better than a machine with lesser specs.

Core Animation uses OpenGL for rendering processing. It serves as part of the graphics unification layer, which included QuickTime, Core Image, and Quartz, as shown in figure 8.1.

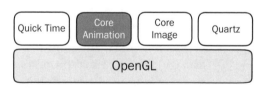

Core Animation introduces a new concept of *layers* for AppKit base views. Let's go over a bit of Core Animation's class structure.

Figure 8.1   Core Animation as part of the graphics unification layer

8.1.2 Class structure

Several types of classes make up Core Animation. Let's do a brief overview of some of the different types, beginning with layers.

Layer classes are essentially the foundation of Core Animation. A layer can be viewed as a 2D surface that can be animated in a 3D space. The 3D space is like a window on your desktop. The depth comes from the layering of all the different windows on your screen. The CALayer class provides the basic layer functionality and is the parent class for all types of Core Animation layers. Layers are responsible for encapsulating all the visual properties of the content that can be displayed.

Animation classes allow you to modify animatable properties of a particular layer. For instance, you can set a layer's hidden property to YES, which can trigger an animation to fade out that layer. We'll go over more about these animatable properties later in the chapter. Core Animation gives you quite a bit of control over your layer animations.

Timing classes are used in conjunction with animations. They let you adjust the pace of a particular animation. You can specify the timing to be linear or dynamic. For example, instead of using a strictly linear animation, you can have an animation slow down as it approaches the end of its specified duration.

Layout Manager classes allow you to create your own managers that can control the position of layers relative to their superlayer. Core Animation gives you this with the CAConstraint class.

Transaction Management classes are required because modifying animatable properties need to be part of a transaction. By using the CATransaction class you can make batch animation changes in a transaction—and even nest transactions.

We're only scratching the surface of Core Animation

Core Animation is such a big topic that we can't cover all aspects of it in this chapter. There are books dedicated to Core Animation that can't cover everything you can do with it. If you want more after this chapter you can find plenty of information (Objective-C specific) online.

8.1.3 *Core Animation's rendering architecture*

Unlike Cocoa views, Core Animation layers don't render directly to the screen. NSView objects play that part of the *view* in the MVC design pattern. Core Animation layers are only model objects. Layers manage different visual properties and provide content that is to be displayed, but displaying the content on the screen isn't the layer's job. In figure 8.2 you can see the structure of the layer tree.

The purpose of the layer tree is to store the object model values for each layer. Each layer tree is also backed by two other trees: a presentation tree and render tree. The presentation tree contains the values that are currently being presented to a user during an animation. This means the values constantly change as the animation occurs. The render tree contains the values that are stored in the presentation layer while the layer is being rendered.

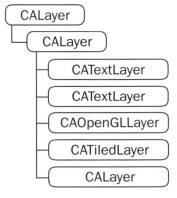

Figure 8.2 Core Animation's layer tree

8.1.4 Creating a basic animation with Cocoa Animation

Before we go any further, let's see what it's like to create a basic animation. This will be a great introduction before we go even deeper into layers and more complex animations. You'll create a new project and use it as your basic animation sandbox. Follow these steps:

1 Create a new MacRuby project called Image Animations. This is a basic application that you'll use to demonstrate a few basic animations that you'll apply to an NSImage.

2 Find a decent-sized image and add it to your Resources group.

3 Add the Quartz Core framework to your project. Go to the rb_main.rb file, and add the following:

```
framework "QuartzCore"
```

You won't use this initially but you'll need it in later examples.

4 Go to the Classes folder and add a new file named AnimationsController.rb. For now, set up your basic class structure with an outlet for an image that you'll add to the interface and a placeholder for an animate action:

```
class AnimationsController
  attr_accessor :image_view

  def start_animation(sender)
  end
end
```

5 Open MainMenu.xib and add an NSImageView (Image Well) to the center of your window. Size it to take up a fair amount of space. In the inspector make sure this NSImageView is set to the image you dragged into your Resources folder. By default, the Image Well has a border property: set it to None.

6 Add a Push Button to the bottom of the window and change its title to Animate. You'll use this button to trigger an animation on your image.

7 Add an NSObject to the interface and set its class to AnimationsController.

8 It's time to hook up your outlets and actions. Drag the image_view outlet you set up in the AnimationsController directly to the NSImageView you just created.

9 Drag the start_animation: action to the Push Button, as shown in figure 8.3. You get bonus points if you somehow end up with the same photo we used!

10 You're ready to add code to AnimationsController, the start_animation: action you created. For now, let's reduce the size of your image by 60 pixels and reposition it whenever you invoke the start_animation: action. You accomplish this by doing the following:

```
def start_animation(sender)
  old_frame = self.image_view.frame
  new_frame = NSMakeRect(old_frame.origin.x + 30, old_frame.origin.y + 30,
  ➥ old_frame.size.width - 60, old_frame.size.height - 60)
  self.image_view.frame = new_frame
end
```

Figure 8.3   Adding an image and a button to the window and connecting its outlet/action

What you're doing here is retrieving the frame for the NSImageView and creating a new NSRect by using the NSMakeRect() function. You then apply this new frame to the NSImageView.

Run the application. When you click the Animate button, the image reduces in size and centers itself. Not much of an animation, is it?

THE ANIMATOR PROXY

This is where you can use something called the *animator proxy* to help spruce things up a bit. Change the last line in the start_animation: method to the following:

```
self.image_view.animator.frame = new_frame
```

All you do here is add a call to the animator for the NSImageView. Try to run the application after applying this tiny change. You should see that your image changes its size and repositions smoothly with an animation. This is much more pleasant and took only one quick modification. All you did was use the animator proxy to make the frame change.

Any NSView or NSWindow can use the animator proxy. The animator proxy is free of Core Animation layers and is really Cocoa Animation, although it's still considered part of Core Animation. The animator proxy belongs to the NSAnimatableProperty-Container protocol. Its purpose is to provide you with an easy way to add animation to an existing class without having to worry about a complicated API.

When the animator proxy notices that one of the animatable properties has been changed, it creates, configures, and fires off the animations. In the previous example, it noticed that the frame property had been changed. It automatically calls the animationForKey: method to retrieve animations for the key/property that's being altered. If an animation is found using this method it's returned. If no animation is returned the property is changed without any animation. The default animation is a CABasicAnimation, which performs a linear interpolation using the fromValue and the toValue. The fromValue in this case is the NSImageView's previous frame. The toValue is the new value, which you sent to the animator proxy.

CHANGING THE ANIMATOR PROXY'S ANIMATION DURATION

In the previous example the animator proxy performed the animation with a predefined duration. No matter how drastically you change the frame of your NSImageView, the animation always takes the same amount of time. The default animation time for the animator proxy is 0.25 seconds. This means the animator proxy will automatically determine how many frames it needs to display to make the animation render properly in this timeframe.

What if you want to change the duration time? You can accomplish this by replacing the last line with the following:

```
NSAnimationContext.beginGrouping
NSAnimationContext.currentContext.duration = 5.0
self.image_view.animator.frame = new_frame
NSAnimationContext.endGrouping
```

When you click the Animate button now, changing the frame of the NSImageView takes five seconds. You have to use the NSAnimationContext to begin a grouping and end it to specify this change.

You'll learn more about grouping and other animations later in the chapter. Next, let's look at Core Animation layers.

8.2 *Core Animation layers*

Layers are the foundation of Core Animation; they're represented by Core Animation's CALayer class. You'll come to see that everything you do with Core Animation has something to do with layers. They're responsible for encapsulating the visual properties (geometry, timing, visuals, and so on) of the content they display.

One of the things that make layers powerful is the fact that their rendering is hardware-accelerated by your machine's GPU. This is useful if you're concerned about performance because the rendering time should be fast.

What makes layers different from NSViews? Layers can be viewed as lightweight versions of NSViews, which can also contain their own layer (also known as *layer-backed* NSViews). Layers can also have sublayers. You'll learn more about layers throughout this section as well as their coordinate system and how to add content to them.

8.2.1 *Layer coordinate systems*

If you've developed for the iPhone or iPad before you probably know that the coordinate system origin (0,0) is located in the upper-left corner of the screen. When you're creating MacRuby applications for Mac OS X the coordinate system origin is in the lower-left corner; see figure 8.4. It's important to remember this when you're laying out layers.

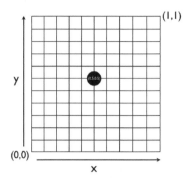

Each CALayer maintains its own coordinate system to which all content is relative. With the possibility of many different sublayers, you can imagine that remembering the coordinates for many content items could get messy. Fortunately, the CALayer

Figure 8.4   The coordinate system origin for a layer is at 0,0.

class provides methods that allow you to convert values from one coordinate system to another. You can use these methods to convert point, rectangle, and size values.

8.2.2 *Layer geometry*

A layer has properties you should be aware of in order to understand the layer's geometry. Many of these properties are expressed as either as a CGPoint or a CGRect. In case you're not familiar with CGPoint and CGRect, let's go over them quickly; feel free to skip ahead if you don't need this introduction.

Both CGPoint and CGRect are structures. A CGPoint contains two float values, one representing the position on the x-axis and one representing a position on the y-axis. A CGRect contains a CGPoint, which represents the origin, and a CGSize, which represents the size of the CGRect. The CGSize has two float values that represent a width and a height.

Table 8.1 lists some of the properties of a layer's geometry.

Table 8.1   Table 8.1 Layer geometry properties

Property	Description
position	Represented by a CGPoint. The position is relative to the layer's superlayer and is expressed in the coordinate system of the superlayer.
bounds	Represented by a CGRect. Contains the size (width and height) and the origin of the layer.
anchorPoint	Represented by a CGPoint. The location in the bounds of a layer that corresponds with the position coordinate.
frame	Represented by a CGRect. The frame value isn't stored but is calculated relative to the position, bounds, and anchorPoint properties of the layer. When a new frame is set, it changes the layer's position and bounds properties.

Thanks for hanging in there through the geometry lesson. With a basic understanding of layers you can go one step further and see how to create and use layers in an application.

8.2.3 *Layer content*

To explore how you can add content to a layer you'll need to create a new application. You'll be adding layers to your view as well as sublayers. Follow these steps:

1 Jump into Xcode and create a new MacRuby application named Layers. Add the Quartz Core framework to the project, and set it up in rb_main.rb.

2 Create a new controller named LayersController.rb. In `LayersController`, add the following code to set up an outlet to your window and set up the `awake-FromNib` method:

```
class LayersController
  attr_accessor :window

  def awakeFromNib
  end
end
```

3 Go back to your interface and set up an `NSObject` that represents your `Layers-Controller`.

4 Connect an outlet from your window to the controller, as shown in figure 8.5.

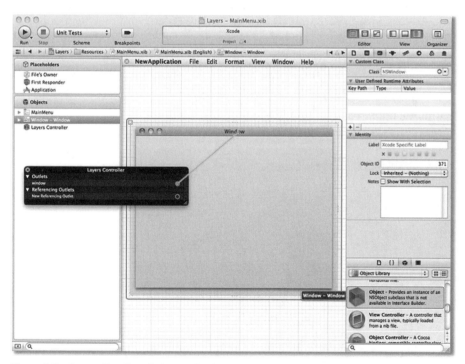

Figure 8.5   Connecting the window outlet from `LayersController` to the `NSWindow`

5 You're ready to jump into CALayers. In the awakeFromNib method add the following line to make sure the main view for the NSWindow is layer-backed:

```
@content_view = self.window.contentView
@content_view.wantsLayer = true
```

6 Add a sublayer: a simple blue box. To do so, add a call to create_blue_box in the awakeFromNib method:

```
def awakeFromNib
  @content_view = self.window.contentView
  @content_view.wantsLayer = true
  create_blue_box
end
```

The create_blue_box method is where you set up and add your CALayer to the layer of your view:

```
def create_blue_box
  blue_box = CALayer.alloc.init
  blue_box.bounds = CGRectMake(0.0,0.0,100.0,100.0)
  blue_box.position = CGPointMake(240.0,200.0)
  blue_box.backgroundColor = CGColorCreateGenericRGB(0.0,0.0,1.0,0.75)
  @content_view.layer.addSublayer(blue_box)
end
```

You create a new instance of a CALayer by allocating and initializing. Next, you set the bounds of the layer using the CGRectMake() function. This creates a CGRect that is 100 pixels wide by 100 pixels tall. You then set the position of the layer using the CGPointMake() function. Next, you set the background color to blue using the CGColorCreateGenericRGB() function with an alpha value of 0.75 (75% percent); this makes the layer partially transparent. Last, you call addSublayer: for the view's layer and pass in the newly created blue box layer.

Run the application and see what you get. You should end up with a blue square in the middle of the window, as shown in figure 8.6.

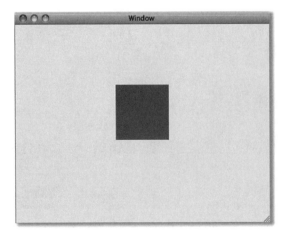

Figure 8.6   The box you created with a CALayer in your view

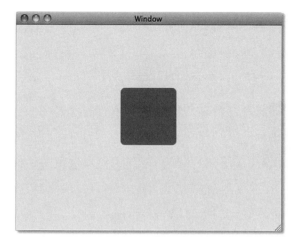

Figure 8.7
The layer with rounded corners

Now that you've created a basic layer you can make some changes. First you'll give it rounded corners. This can be accomplished easily by changing the `cornerRadius` property of the `CALayer`. In the `create_blue_box` method, add the following line just before you add the layer as a sublayer:

```
blue_box.cornerRadius = 8
```

If you run the application you should see that the blue box now has rounded corners, as shown in figure 8.7.

That was extremely simple to do. It goes to show how easy it can be to change certain aspects of a `CALayer`. Next you'll go one step further and add an image to the `CALayer`. You can use the same image that you used in the earlier Cocoa Animation example; add it to the Resources group in your project. Then add the following just below the line where you set `cornerRadius`:

```
file_path = NSBundle.mainBundle.pathForResource("lolcat",ofType:"gif")
file_url = NSURL.fileURLWithPath(file_path)
source = CGImageSourceCreateWithURL(file_url, nil)
image = CGImageSourceCreateImageAtIndex(source, 0, nil)
blue_box.contents = image
```

The name of the file you copied to the Resources folder was lolcat.gif. You use the `pathForResource:ofType:` method to retrieve a string of the file path. Next you create an `NSURL` using this file path. Then you create an empty `CGImageSource` using the `CGImageSourceCreateWithURL()` function. You take the source you just created and retrieve the image by using the `CGImageSourceCreateImageAtIndex()` function. The last thing you do is set the `contents` property of the `CALayer` to the image you just retrieved.

When you run the application you should see your image on top of the blue background in the `CALayer`. It should look similar to figure 8.8, depending on the image you use.

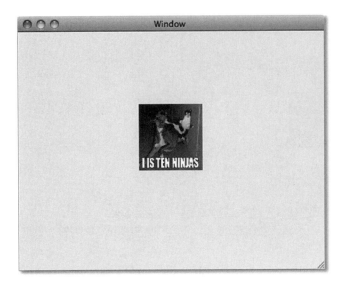

Figure 8.8 Adding an image to your layer contents

You might be asking yourself what happened to the rounded corners. You can make them appear again by changing a property that masks the layer. Add the following line just below where you set your layer's `cornerRadius`:

```
blue_box.masksToBounds = true
```

The entire `create_blue_box` method should now look like the following listing.

Listing 8.1 `create_blue_box` method

```
def create_blue_box
  blue_box = CALayer.alloc.init
  blue_box.bounds = CGRectMake(0.0,0.0,100.0,100.0)
  blue_box.position = CGPointMake(240.0,200.0)
  blue_box.backgroundColor = CGColorCreateGenericRGB(0.0,0.0,1.0,0.75)
  blue_box.cornerRadius = 8
  blue_box.masksToBounds = true

  file_path = NSBundle.mainBundle.pathForResource("lolcat",ofType:"gif")
  file_url = NSURL.fileURLWithPath(file_path)
  source = CGImageSourceCreateWithURL(file_url, nil)
  image = CGImageSourceCreateImageAtIndex(source, 0, nil)
  blue_box.contents = image

  @content_view.layer.addSublayer(blue_box)
end
```

If you run the application you should see that you've successfully masked the layer. As a result the image appears with rounded corners (see figure 8.9).

There's much more you can do with layers, but now you're at a point where you can understand their purpose and how to use them. Let's look next at how you can use Core Animation's `CAAnimation` class to apply animations to your layers.

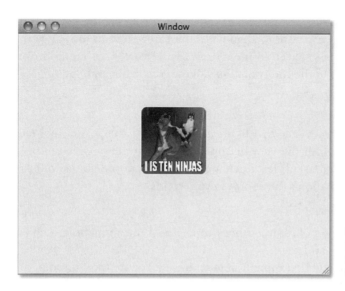

Figure 8.9
The layer content has been masked and the rounded corners are visible again.

8.3   *Animating with Core Animation*

You can use different types of animation depending on the kind of effect you want to showcase. Earlier, you looked at the animator proxy and learned that you don't have much control over the animation it creates for you. Throughout this section you'll learn more about basic animations, keyframe animations, grouping, and transitions.

8.3.1   *Basic animations*

You were introduced to CABasicAnimation in the animator proxy example earlier in this chapter. As the name says, this is a basic animation that allows you to present a change from a current value to a new value linearly. It does this by performing a linear interpolation using the fromValue and toValue, as illustrated in figure 8.10.

Other than their duration, you don't have any control over basic animations. They're useful for quickly presenting simple animations.

You've seen the CABasicAnimation object in action with the animator proxy. Now let's look at how you can create an explicit basic animation without using the proxy.

You'll need to go back to the Image Animations project that you created earlier. In the start_animation: action, you can initialize a new CABasicAnimation by using the animationWithKeyPath: method:

```
animation = CABasicAnimation.animationWithKeyPath("opacity")
```

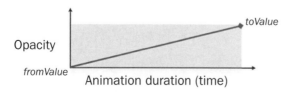

Figure 8.10 CABasicAnimation's linear interpolation for an animation

You create a new instance of CABasicAnimation by specifying the key path of the animatable property that you want to change. In this case you want to change the opacity of your view, so you pass that in to the animationWithKeyPath: method. You're then able to make changes to the interpolation values, fromValue and toValue:

```
animation.fromValue = 1.0
animation.toValue = 0.0
```

Here you're setting fromValue to 1.0, meaning it has full 100% opacity. You want the animation to end up with the view disappearing, so you set toValue to 0. How long should your animation last? If left unchanged, the duration defaults to 0.25 seconds. Let's change the animation's duration to two seconds:

```
animation.duration = 2.0
```

You also have the option of setting other properties of the animation, such as repeat-Count, autoreverses, and so on.

Next you need to add this animation to your view. You do this by adding the animation to a layer on the view. Normally the NSImageView isn't layer backed. Do the following to make sure the NSImageView *is* layer backed:

```
image_view.wantsLayer = true
```

If you want to, you can also cover this when you're working with your interface. Figure 8.11 shows how to check whether your NSImageView needs layer backing: in the inspector you select the Image View check box. We'll go deeper into layers in the next section.

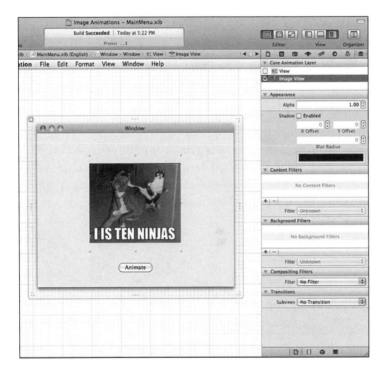

Figure 8.11 Adding layer backing in the interface in Xcode

The next thing you need to do is add the new animation to this layer by using the addAnimation:forKey: method:

```
image_view.layer.addAnimation(animation, forKey: "opacity")
```

By doing this you're executing the animation. Let's see how this looks in the start_animation: method you created in the last section:

```
def start_animation(sender)
  animation = CABasicAnimation.animationWithKeyPath("opacity")
  animation.fromValue = 1.0
  animation.toValue = 0.0
  animation.duration = 2.0

  image_view.wantsLayer = true
  image_view.layer.addAnimation(animation, forKey:"opacity")
end
```

When you run the Image Animations application and click the Animate button the image should fade out after two seconds. Now, what if you want to do more with your animation? Instead of linearly going from full opacity to none, you can use a different type of animation that allows you to use keyframes.

8.3.2 *Keyframe animations*

Keyframe animations are similar to basic animations, but you have more control over the values of properties over the course of the animation. If you've ever done any video editing you may be familiar with keyframes; they're specific points during the animation, as illustrated in figure 8.12.

To create a keyframe animation you use the CAKeyframeAnimation class and initialize it using the animationWithKeyPath: method. To see how a basic keyframe animation works, let's try to replicate the previous CABasicAnimation example using keyframes. Here's how you use a keyframe animation in the startAnimation: action:

```
def start_animation(sender)
  animation = CAKeyframeAnimation.animationWithKeyPath("opacity")
  animation.values = [1.0,0.0]
  animation.keyTimes = [0.0,1.0]
  animation.duration = 2.0

  image_view.wantsLayer = true
  image_view.layer.addAnimation(animation, forKey:"opacity")
end
```

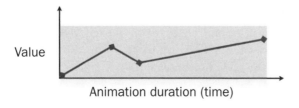

Value

Animation duration (time)

Figure 8.12 Keyframe animation allows for different values at different key times.

Let's break this down. You first initialize a new `CAKeyframeAnimation` using the `animationWithKeyPath:` method. Next, instead of specifying a `fromValue` or `toValue`, you pass an array of values that correspond with a specific key time. Because you're trying to replicate the previous example you use only two values. The first value (1.0) represents the opacity at the beginning of the animation, and the second value (0.0) represents the opacity at the end.

You may notice on the next line that the key times specified are from 0 to 1. The key times are a percentage of the progress of the animation. If your animation has a duration of 2 seconds, then a key time specified at 0.5 represents the time when the animation has been rendering for 1 second.

You set the duration of the animation on the next line. Also you assume that the `NSImageView` isn't currently layer-backed, and you make sure to call `wantsLayer`. Finally, you add this animation to the layer of the `NSImageView` with the `add-Animation:forKey:` method.

Running the animation should yield the same results as the `CABasicAnimation` example. The opacity of the `NSImageView` should fade out after two seconds.

How about taking advantage of keyframes and making it go from full opacity to half and then back to full again? To do this, you only need to change `values` and `key-Times` to the following:

```
animation.values = [1.0,0.5,1.0]
animation.keyTimes = [0.0,0.5,1.0]
```

If you make this change and run the animation you'll see that at the beginning of the animation the image remains at full opacity. At the one-second mark, the image is at half opacity. From then to the completion of the animation, the image returns to full opacity.

Keyframe animations allow you to do many exciting things, such as moving a view along a nonlinear path, rotating, and much more. Next you'll learn about grouping animations.

8.3.3 *Grouping animations*

If you want to bundle multiple animations together you can do so by using animation groups. For example, you can have one animation that changes the opacity of a view and another animation that resizes it. To do so you need to create a `CAAnimation-Group` and give it an array of the animations that it should group together.

Unlike previous examples, where you've had to add an animation to a layer for a specific key path, you add the group animation to the `animations` property of your view. The animation is started once one of the key paths you specify during the initialization of the animation (using `animationWithKeyPath:`) is triggered. You'll stick with the same `NSImageView` you've been animating and try to group two different animations together. Listing 8.2 shows the code for this example.

Listing 8.2   Grouping multiple animations together

```
def start_animation(sender)
  image_view.wantsLayer = true
  image_view.layer.addAnimation(animationGroup, forKey:nil)
end

def animationGroup
  group = CAAnimationGroup.animation
  group.animations = [scaleAnimation, opacityAnimation]
  group.autoreverses = true
  group.duration = 2.0
  group
end

def scaleAnimation
  scale = CABasicAnimation.animationWithKeyPath("transform")
  scale.fromValue = NSValue.valueWithCATransform3D(
  ➥ CATransform3DIdentity)
  scale.toValue = NSValue.valueWithCATransform3D(
  ➥ CATransform3DMakeScale(0.1,0.1,0.1))
  scale
end

def opacityAnimation
  opacity = CABasicAnimation.animationWithKeyPath("opacity")
  opacity.fromValue = 1.0
  opacity.toValue = 0
  opacity
end
```

Having trouble compiling this example?

If Xcode is complaining that `CATransform3DIdentity` is undefined it may be because you don't have BridgeSupport installed. BridgeSupport for MacRuby allows you to access non–object-oriented ANSI C symbols such as constants, enumerations, structures, and other functions. You can download BridgeSupport at http://bridgesupport.macosforge.org/.

Let's walk through this code. You begin by assuming that you didn't set the `NSImageView` to have layer-backing through your interface and are setting it programmatically. The next line in the `start_animation:` method calls the `animationGroup` method, which returns a `CAAnimationGroup` that contains two separate animations. Also notice that you don't need to specify a key when adding this animation to your layer.

In the `animationGroup` method you first initialize a new `CAAnimationGroup`. On the next line you store an array, which contains two animations in the `animations` property. These animations are created and returned in the `scaleAnimation` and opacityAnimation methods. Next you set the autoreverses property to true to have the animation reverse after completion. You set the duration of the group animation to two seconds and on the last line of the method return the CAAnimationGroup.

The goal of the scaleAnimation method is to create and return an animation that scales your view. You first create a CABasicAnimation and set the key path to transform. On the next line you set the fromValue property to an NSValue created with a CATransform3D. This is the first time you're using the CATransform3DIdentity constant. In this case the CATransform3DIdentity is a matrix that has no scale, rotation, skewing, or any kind of perspective applied to it. Next, you set toValue to an NSValue created with a CATransform3D: specifically, a CATransform3DScale, which you create using the CATransform3DMakeScale() C function. You're using this function to scale by 0.1 for the x-, y-, and z-axes. This will cause your animation to make the image shrink in size. You then return the animation.

The last method is opacityAnimation. The contents of this method should look familiar because you've done this before. You create an animation that changes the opacity of your view and return it at the end of the method. On the first line you create a CABasicAnimation and specifying the opacity key path. Next you set the fromValue opacity to 1.0 and toValue to 0. On the last line you return the animation you've created.

Let's run the application and give it a whirl. When you click the Animate button the image begins scaling to a smaller size and reduce its opacity at the same time. You should see something similar to figure 8.13.

After the image finishes scaling down and disappears the animation will automatically reverse. This is because you specified autoreverses to be true when you created your animation group. Specifying this on a specific animation in a group won't have any effect: it only works when applied to the group containing all the animations. Then the image animates back to its original opacity and size, as shown in figure 8.14.

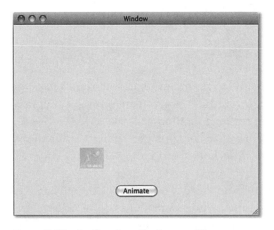

Figure 8.13   Scaling down the image while reducing the opacity

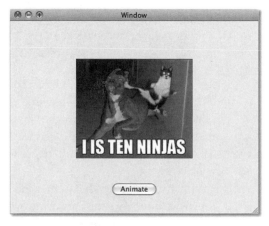

Figure 8.14   The animation reverses to its original opacity and size.

Feel free to change some of the properties of the animation to experiment and see how your changes affect the outcome.

8.4 *Summary*

As we said at the beginning of this chapter, there's quite a bit of ground to cover with Core Animation. Even though we've just scratched the surface you should have a good understanding of the Core Animation basics. You learned about how Core Animation can help you create eye-catching animations in your MacRuby applications, similar to the ones Apple uses.

We went over Core Animation's rendering architecture and also ventured into a bit of Cocoa Animation. Next you discovered Core Animation's `CALayer` class and experimented with creating and modifying your own layers. Last but not least, you created animations of your own using basic and keyframe animations.

If you want to go one step further, think about how you can use Core Animation in some of the applications you've built in previous chapters. How can you use what you've learned to enhance the application visually as well as the overall user experience?

In the next chapter we'll leave Xcode and examine how to create MacRuby applications using HotCocoa.

Part 3

MacRuby extras

Part 3 explores some advanced and alternative uses of MacRuby. We'll talk about testing, scripting with MacRuby, and using tools like HotCocoa. We'll also go over packaging your applications for the Mac App Store.

HotCocoa

9

This chapter covers

- HotCocoa mappings
- Creating UI components
- Porting an app to HotCocoa

Interface Builder is the de facto standard for building user interfaces for all manner of Cocoa applications (whether you're using Objective-C, MacRuby, Nu, or whatever other exotic language that talks to Cocoa), but sometimes it's nice to have a more accessible way to persist your user interface code. You can probably think of plenty of instances where you've wanted to look at the code that Interface Builder was generating but couldn't. For developers who don't like to use a visual tool like Interface Builder or would rather create their UI programmatically, there's an easy solution called HotCocoa. HotCocoa is a library written by Rich Kilmer that gives you that access by letting you specify your UI (and more) in Ruby.

9.1 Introducing HotCocoa

If you've looked at much Ruby code you can probably remember at least one moment when you stood back and admired its beauty. Ruby's flexible syntax allows you to build some useful and elegant domain-specific languages (DSLs). For example, the Sinatra web framework helps you create web applications with a simple DSL:

```
get "/hotcocoa" do
  "HotCocoa is still awesome at #{Time.now.strftime('%D %T')}"
end
```

This little snippet creates a web application that lives at http://localhost/hotcocoa and that renders something like "HotCocoa is still awesome at 03/02/2011 13:31:12," but you could probably figure that out from reading the code.

DSLs are typically most useful for expressing complex ideas specific to a certain problem set in an accessible way in order to reduce the cognitive load for the developer. MacRuby goes a long way to provide a nice set of Ruby wrappers around Cocoa's mechanisms, but sometimes your code ends up looking a bit un-Rubyish. For example, to create a simple window the code looks like this in bare MacRuby:

```
win = NSWindow.alloc.initWithContentRect(yourFrame,
➥ styleMask:NSTitledWindowMask,
➥ backing:NSBackingStoreBuffered,
         defer:false)
```

The code has a lot of idiosyncrasies for Ruby code: the Objective-C-ish `alloc/init-With` pair, the use of constants as values passed into methods, and so on. HotCocoa gives you the tools to wrap these sorts of eyesores into a nice Ruby shell—and it has most of the common ones built in. For example, the previous code can be expressed with HotCocoa as follows:

```
win = window(frame: yourFrame,
             style: :titled,
             backing: :buffered)
```

As you can see, the code reads much better, takes fewer lines, and looks more Rubyish by comparison.

9.1.1 Getting started

The first thing you need to do is install HotCocoa on your machine. Because HotCocoa is available as a gem for MacRuby installation is extremely simple. Go to your Terminal application and type the following line:

```
sudo macgem install hotcocoa
```

Now that you have HotCocoa installed you can get started. You normally don't want to stub out boilerplate stuff out every time you want to start a basic application, so HotCocoa ships with a bin script to generate it for you. You can use it as follows to create a brand-new HotCocoa project:

```
hotcocoa YourProjectName
```

Running this script generates an application skeleton in a directory named for your project (in this case, the very descriptive `YourProjectName`). There you'll see a few source files, a Rakefile that will build your application (with the help of a build configuration in config/build.yml), and an icon resource. Here's a list of the files created for you:

```
./lib/application.rb
./lib/menu.rb
./config/build.yml
./resources/HotCocoa.icns
./Rakefile
```

To build your application's skeleton run `macrake` in Terminal.

If you decide to dive into the code the source files may be a little overwhelming at first, but fear not! We'll cover all those methods and mappings in the next section.

9.2 Built-in mappings

HotCocoa has mappings for about 45 different pieces of Cocoa, but we're only going to cover the most important ones here. If you'd like to learn about the other mappings we suggest you head over to the code at GitHub (http://github.com/HotCocoa/hotcocoa) and look in lib for the other mappings; most of the files have an example in their headers.

9.2.1 Applications and menus

Setting up an application with HotCocoa requires a single call to `application`. The smallest possible HotCocoa application looks like the following:

```
require "rubygems"
require "hotcocoa"
include HotCocoa

application do |app|
end
```

This, of course, does nothing but create a run loop, but it's fun to see that you can write a MacRuby app in just a couple lines of code with HotCocoa. You'll need to dive deeper to get a better understanding, though.

Looking in your newly generated HotCocoa application will provide a better example. The first bit of code in lib/application.rb probably looks something like the following listing.

Listing 9.1 Generated lib/application.rb

```
require 'rubygems'
require 'hotcocoa'

class YourProjectName
  include HotCocoa

  def start
    application name: 'YourProjectName' do |app|
      app.delegate = self
```

```
    window frame: [100, 100, 500, 500], title: 'HotCocoa Demo' do |win|
      win.will_close { exit }

      # We'll discuss the window more in the next section...
    end
  end
end
# Other delegate methods
end
```

```
YourProjectName.new.start
```

This code is much closer to what a real HotCocoa application should look like. You wrap the application logic into a class that you instantiate and call `start` on. The `start` method creates an application instance using the `application` mapping in Hot-Cocoa and runs the code inside.

Try to run this by entering the following from the base of your application directory in Terminal:

```
macrake run
```

You end up with a window that looks like figure 9.1.

The other piece that composes a typical Mac application is the application menu. Your gen-

Figure 9.1 Window from the basic HotCocoa example

erated application's menu lives in lib/menu.rb; if it's available, this file is loaded automatically by HotCocoa when running your application. When you open this file you should see code that looks something like this:

```
module HotCocoa
  def application_menu
    menu do |main|
      main.submenu :apple do |apple|
        apple.item :about, :title => "About #{NSApp.name}"
        # More items in the Apple menu....
      end

      # More menus....
    end
  end
end
```

Creating a menu structure with this little DSL is simple. The call to the `menu` method creates a menu instance which you can then assign submenus to with calls to the `sub-menu` method (as the generated file snippet does with `:apple`).

To insert a menu separator call `separator` on a menu object (for example, in the previous code you might call `apple.separator`). To add an actionable menu item like Open or Copy you use the `item` method. In the example, you create an About YourApp menu item using the `item` method. Behind the scenes HotCocoa has created an action for you named `on_about` (it names the action `on_whatever_the_first _agument_is`). You can override this behavior by providing an explicit action like so:

```
menu.item :open, :title => "Open...", :action => :on_open_a_file
```

You can further modify the menu item by adding a shortcut-key combination. Two option keys control the shortcut functionality: `:key` and `:modifiers`. The `:key` option lets you specify a shortcut key for accessing that action. So if you wanted the comma key (,) to pop open a new tweet window in your hot new Twitter client, you would do something like the following:

```
menu.item :tweet, :title => "New tweet...", :key => ","
```

You can add a modifier key (for example, rather than just a comma, it could be Command+,) to the menu item with the `:modifiers` key. HotCocoa has mapped the Objective-C constants to sensible Ruby symbols, so you can address them like so:

```
menu.item :tweet, :title => "New tweet...", :key => ",",
➥              :modifiers => [:command]
```

You can assign other modifier keys (such as `:control`, `:alt`, and `:shift`) and even combine them (for example, `[:command, :shift]`).

Now that you have a good grasp of how to create the big-picture infrastructure for your application, let's look at making it do something useful.

9.2.2 *Windows and controls*

Windows are the fundamental interaction pieces of a Mac application. They contain all the logical pieces of your UI and provide structure and organization for everything, and fortunately HotCocoa makes it easy to conjure them and tweak them to your liking. For example, the following is one of the smallest examples you can write with a window:

```
application(:name => "HotCocoa!") do |app|
  window(:frame => [100, 100, 500, 500], :title => "Hello!")
end
```

With this code you'll get a window that is 500 pixels wide by 500 pixels tall, positioned 100 pixels away from X and Y baselines; it has the title "Hello!". These are the same dimensions as the generated HotCocoa example you first saw in figure 9.1. The simple example here shows exactly how readable HotCocoa makes MacRuby UI code.

HotCocoa has a fair bit of flexibility when it comes to tweaking a window's style. For example, the following code is the same window, but styled a little differently:

```
application(:name => "HotCocoa!") do |app|
  window( :frame => [100, 100, 500, 500],
    ➥ :title => "Hello!",
    ➥ :style => [:textured, :titled]) do |win|
  win.contentView.frame_color = color(:name => "green")
  end
end
```

This will make the window textured and with a green frame color, as shown in figure 9.2.

Of course, you probably wouldn't want to style your window exactly like that (the searing green border may annoy some users), but you can change these and a number of other properties of the basic window layout. We won't cover those here because you generally won't use them, but you can check out the code on GitHub to see what the options are.

DELEGATE METHODS

To make your window (or any control in a HotCocoa app) do something useful, you need to have its delegate methods map to some-

Figure 9.2   Textured window with a green border after modifying the window's properties

thing. HotCocoa maps all the common delegate methods to an elegant API; one of the most common examples you'll see involves the `windowWillClose:` delegate method:

```
application(:name => "HotCocoa!") do |app|
  window :frame => [100, 100, 500, 500], :title => "Window" do |win|
    win.will_close { exit }
  end
end
```

As you can see, HotCocoa has mapped the `windowWillClose:` delegate method (called when the window is closing) to a nice method that takes a block (in this case, you exit the app if the window closes). We'll look at two more forms for this same logic in the next section.

HotCocoa provides mappings for a number of common delegate methods, for actions such as state changes (for example, for windows you have `did_resize`, `will_move`, and so on), and more. Each mapping has a set of these delegations, typically situated at the bottom of the file. Now that we've looked at windows, let's start putting something in them!

BASIC CONTROLS

We'll begin by looking at some simple controls you can add to your windows and then move on to special-purpose UI elements. First, let's return to the code generated by HotCocoa; your application block should look something like the following:

```
application :name => "Basic Control" do |app|
  app.delegate = self
  window :frame => [100, 100, 500, 500], :title => "Window" do |win|
    win << label(:text => "Hello from HotCocoa",
    ➡ :layout => {:start => false})
    win.will_close { exit }
  end
end
```

To add controls to a window you use the << operator. In this case, the call to the `label` mapping creates a new `NSLabel` instance, which you then append to the window. Running this code will display a simple window with a text label that says "Hello from HotCocoa."

If you're not familiar with common programmatic GUI layout paradigms, the way HotCocoa/Cocoa flows controls in its windows may be a little surprising. For example, consider the following code:

```
application :name => "Labels" do |app|
  app.delegate = self
  window :frame => [100, 100, 500, 500], :title => "Window" do |win|
    4.times do
      win << label(:text => "Hello from HotCocoa",
      ➡ :bordered => true,
      ➡ :layout => {:start => false})
    end

    win.will_close { exit }
  end
end
```

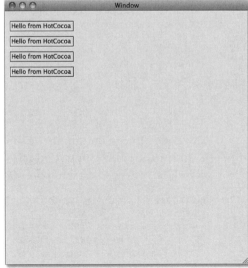

Running this code will produce a window with four labels stacked vertically (see figure 9.3).

You may have been expecting them to be overlapping in the corner or perhaps floated against one another at left. But in our experience this setup tends to make it easier to build usable GUIs more quickly with code.

Figure 9.3   Four labels stacked vertically in the application's window

HotCocoa has mappings for a lot of the common delegate methods on text fields. For example, let's say you want to keep track of how many characters you've typed into a text field. Your code may look something like the following:

```
application :name => "Text Field" do |app|
  app.delegate = self
  window :frame => [100, 100, 500, 500], :title => "Window" do |win|
    my_label =  label(:text => "0",
    ➡ :layout => {:start => false,
    ➡ :expand => [:width]})
    win << my_label

    field = text_field(:layout => {:expand => [:width]})
    field.did_change { my_label.text = field.stringValue.length }
    win << field

    win.will_close { exit }
  end
end
```

As you can see, you use the did_change delegate mapping to track when there's a change in the text field and update the label accordingly.

> **NOTE** Note the use of :expand => [:width] in the :layout argument. This makes the fields auto-expand to the width of the containing window. Otherwise each text field will be about one character wide, and the label will only be as wide as the text you initially assign it! We covered auto-sizing views when working on interfaces in Interface Builder.

The last basic control we'll look at is the button. Adding buttons is similar to adding labels. For example, let's add a button to the previous label example:

```
application :name => "Booktest" do |app|
  app.delegate = self
  window :frame => [100, 100, 500, 500], :title => "Window" do |win|
    win << label(:text => "Hello from HotCocoa",
    ➡ :layout => {:start => false})

    win << button(:title => "Click me!")

    win.will_close { exit }
  end
end
```

This code places a button on the window, but if you follow its lead and click the button it currently does nothing. Code to assign an action to the button can be written two ways. First, you can add it as part of the call to the button:

```
application :name => "Booktest" do |app|
  app.delegate = self
  window :frame => [100, 100, 500, 500], :title => "Window" do |win|
    win << label(:text => "Hello from HotCocoa",
    ➡ :layout => {:start => false})
```

```
   win << button(:title => "Click me!",
     ➥ :on_action => proc {
     ➥ alert :message => 'You clicked me!!' })

   win.will_close { exit }
 end
end
```

Clicking the button now shows a silly alert dialog about being clicked, as shown in figure 9.4.

This form is great for convenience or calling out to other methods, but putting complicated logic in it would make the code difficult to read. Fortunately, another form makes writing readable and complicated code much easier. This form involves using an on_action method to attach logic the same way you did with the will_close delegate method:

```
btn = button(:title => "Click me!")
btn.on_action { alert :message => 'You clicked me!!' }
win << btn
```

Either form will yield the same results, but the latter gives you a lot more flexibility to create code that works but is also readable.

Let's put all these controls together. Suppose you want to write a text-filtering utility. For this example you'll downcase and reverse the text entered in a text field, as shown in the following listing.

Figure 9.4 Clicking the button shows a simple alert dialog.

Listing 9.2   Text-filtering utility in HotCocoa

```
application :name => "Booktest" do |app|
  app.delegate = self
  window :frame => [100, 100, 500, 500], :title => "Window" do |win|
    my_label =  label(:text => "Waiting...",
    ➥ :layout => {:start => false,
    ➥ :expand => [:width]})
    win << my_label

    field = text_field(:layout => {:expand => [:width]})
    field.did_change { my_label.text = "Text changed..." }
    win << field

    btn = button(:title => "Filter!")
    btn.on_action do
      field.text = field.stringValue.downcase.reverse
      my_label.text = "Filtered!"
    end
    win << btn

    win.will_close { exit }
  end
end
```

First you create a label that will be a status indicator of sorts. Next you create a text field with a did_change delegate handler that sets the status label's text to indicate you've changed the text. Finally you add a button that lowercases and reverses the text entered in the text field and sets the status label's text to indicate the text is filtered. If you try it the code will, for example, change "Hello COCOA!" to "!aococ olleh."

9.2.3   *More advanced layouts*

You've been using some of the default options for laying out windows and views. Let's see how you can achieve more control over what you're displaying to the user. First let's examine how you've been creating windows:

```
window :frame => [100, 100, 500, 500], :title => "Window" do |win|
  # ...
end
```

You normally don't want your window to be positioned 100 pixels to the right and 100 pixels from the bottom of the user's screen. You want it to be centered. One way to accomplish this would be to determine the resolution of the screen and do some math to figure out how to position the 500 x 500 window in the center. Luckily you don't have to do this. You can change the previous code to center the window:

```
window :size => [500,500], :centered => true, :title => "Window" do |win|
  # ...
end
```

Instead of specifying the frame of the window, you're only specifying its width and height by using :size. The other important change you make adds :centered => true, which centers the window within the user's screen.

Because you're building your layout in code you want laying out views to be ridiculously easy. You can already see that HotCocoa makes this simple, but there's one binding that you should pay attention to: layout_view.

By default, when you create a new window, a LayoutView is appended to the view. LayoutView is a subclass of NSView, which means you have access to any of the NSView methods. You can manually create your own LayoutView to gain more control over the elements it contains.

When you create a new window you can pass in the option :view => :nolayout. You might want to do this because you can manually create your own LayoutView and add it to the view yourself.

Here's a simple example of how you can use layout_view:

```
layout_view(:layout => {:expand => [:width, :height],
  :padding => 0, :margin => 0}) do |layout|
  # ...
end
```

This LayoutView will auto-resize to the width and height of the window. You also specify no padding and no margin.

It's important to note that by default a LayoutView's mode is set to vertical. This means any controls (buttons, text fields, and so on) added to it are stacked on top of each other. An example of this was shown in figure 9.3. What if you wanted to lay things out horizontally?

```
layout_view(:layout => {:expand => [:width, :height],
  :padding => 0, :margin => 0},
  :mode => :horizontal) do |layout|
  # ...
end
```

You can do this by passing :mode => :horizontal as shown here.

You can pass in many different options to modify the layout of a view. These are shown in table 9.1.

Table 9.1 Layout options

Option	Description
:mode	:vertical or :horizontal. Specifies whether contained elements should be laid out vertically or horizontally.
:margin	Margin for the layout, specified as an integer.
:padding	Padding for the layout, specified as float values.
:align	:top, :bottom, :left, or :right. Specifies the alignment of items contained within the layout.
:spacing	Spacing for items contained within the layout.
:expand	:height, :width, or [:height, :width]. Auto-expands (resizes) the view.

Let's now let's take on a simple HotCocoa application. You'll get a chance to see layout_view in action.

9.3   *Building a speech application using HotCocoa*

A simple but fun application that you can build takes advantage of Cocoa's NSSpeech-Synthesizer class. This quick application allows you to type in a text field and have NSSpeechSynthesizer speak the text out loud for you. Let's walk through creating a new HotCocoa project called Speak.

9.3.1   *Laying out the views*

Before you can work on layout views you need to create the new HotCocoa project. In Terminal type the following:

```
hotcocoa speak
```

Now that the application has been generated continue with these steps:

   1 Open lib/application.rb in your favorite text editor. Change the window's dimensions and remove some of the generated code in the start method:

```
def start
  application :name => "Speak" do |app|
    app.delegate = self
    window :size => [400, 80], :center => true,
➥   :title => "Speak" do |win|

      # Adding horizontal layout here

    end
  end
end
```

Here you specify the size of the window and make sure the window appears in the center of the screen.

   2 Add a horizontal layout to the window which you'll use to contain the text field and button. Add this code within the new block you've created:

```
horiz = layout_view(:frame => [0, 0, 0, 40],
➥ :mode => :horizontal,
➥ :layout => {
➥ :padding => 0,
➥ :margin => 0,
➥ :start => false,
➥ :expand => [:width]}) do |horiz|

  # Adding text field and button here

end
win << horiz
```

This creates a horizontal layout with no padding or margin, 40 pixels tall, with auto-expanding width.

3 Add the following code inside the block:

```
@field = text_field(:layout => {:expand => [:width]})
horiz << @field

@button = button(:title => "Speak", :layout => {:align => :center})
@button.on_action { speak }
horiz << @button
```

If everything's set up properly your window should look similar to figure 9.5.

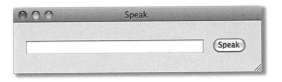

Figure 9.5 The text field and button in the application's window

You might have noticed that you call `speak` on the button's `on_action` method. You'll set this up in the next section.

9.3.2 Making your application speak to you

The last thing you need to do is have the application say whatever is in the text field. This is easily accomplished using the `NSSpeechSynthesizer` class. You'll do this by creating the `speak` action that you specified in the last code snippet.

Add the following code to make the application speak to you:

```
def speak
  synth = NSSpeechSynthesizer.alloc.init
  synth.voice = "com.apple.speech.synthesis.voice.Vicki"
  synth.startSpeakingString(@field.stringValue)
end
```

You've used the `NSSpeechSynthesizer` before in this book, in the Pomodoro application. The code in this method is standard MacRuby that you should be familiar with. You first initialize a new instance of `NSSpeechSynthesizer`, specifying the voice you want and then feeding it a string to speak.

This is all you need for the Speak application. The application.rb file should look like the following listing.

Listing 9.3 Finished lib/application.rb

```
require 'rubygems'
require 'hotcocoa'

class Speak
  include HotCocoa

  def start
    application :name => "Speak" do |app|
      app.delegate = self
```

```
          window :size => [400, 80],
          ➥ :center => true,
          ➥ :title => "Speak" do |win|
            horiz = layout_view(:frame => [0, 0, 0, 40],
            ➥ :mode => :horizontal,
            ➥ :layout => {
            ➥ :padding => 0,
            ➥ :margin => 0,
            ➥ :start => false,
            ➥ :expand => [:width]}) do |horiz|

              @field = text_field(:layout => {:expand => [:width]})
              horiz << @field

              @button = button(:title => "Speak",
              ➥ :layout => {:align => :center})
              @button.on_action { speak }
              horiz << @button
            end

            win << horiz
            win.will_close { exit }
          end
        end
      end

  def speak
    synth = NSSpeechSynthesizer.new
    synth.voice = "com.apple.speech.synthesis.voice.Vicki"
    synth.startSpeakingString(@field.stringValue)
  end
end

Speak.new.start
```

Run the application, type something in, and click the Speak button. You should hear
Vicki saying whatever you typed. Cool, isn't it? In this one small file you've put
together the layout of an application and added the functionality to make your application speak to you.

9.4   *Summary*

In this chapter, we ran through the process of creating interfaces and went over some
of the built-in mappings. You worked with windows and various controls and created a
basic application. HotCocoa makes it easy for you to create MacRuby applications
without having to use Xcode or Interface Builder.

   Many developers don't grasp the idea of using a tool like Interface Builder or
would rather have more control over their UI. Using the standard Cocoa APIs can be
tiring because it takes a lot to do a little. This is where HotCocoa shines, although it
offers much more than just UI helpers. In the next chapter you'll learn how to test
with MacRuby.

MacRuby testing

This chapter covers

- Software testing
- The MiniTest framework
- Building test suites

Software testing may not have the glamour and glory associated with building shiny and polished Mac apps, but it can save you headaches down the road. The expressiveness of Ruby and its rich testing frameworks and tools can help you with this process.

If you've done much Ruby development in the past, you've encountered the Ruby community's fervor toward testing. There are multiple testing frameworks and many camps regarding strategies and methodologies. Rather than try to cover all the different tools available, we're going to focus on the MiniTest framework and go over a few tips and tricks. We'll take you through an introduction to Mini-Test, setting it up in your project, choosing worthwhile things to test, and building MiniTest tests. By the end of this chapter, you'll have a firm grasp on how to design and build test suites for more robust applications.

10.1 Testing MacRuby applications with MiniTest

MiniTest is a testing library written by Ryan Davis and the folks of the Seattle Ruby Brigade (www.zenspider.com/Languages/Ruby/Seattle). It's a fast testing framework with syntax similar to Ruby's standard Test::Unit library. If you prefer RSpec syntax, there's a spec library that bridges the syntax. We'll cover an example of using MiniTest's spec-syntax bridge later this chapter. MiniTest also includes a built-in mocking component to allow you to decouple your tests from external systems.

As we mentioned, Ruby comes with a testing framework in its standard library called Test::Unit. Many of the concepts we'll cover for MiniTest also apply to Test::Unit and other testing libraries. We chose to cover MiniTest because it's a small library and close in form to Test::Unit. MiniTest is smaller than the standard library because it doesn't include unneeded external libraries; at the same time, it adds several features of newer testing libraries while staying in the spirit of the standard library. But if MiniTest isn't your cup of tea, rest assured that your favorite testing framework will likely work with MacRuby soon if it doesn't already.

One big player that's missing from the MacRuby testing field is RSpec. It has worked intermittently on different versions of MacRuby, but if you look at the bug reports, it's clear that your mileage may vary depending on the version of RSpec, and the version of MacRuby.

By default, MiniTest looks a lot like Test::Unit. The following listing shows a hypothetical example of how to test the Cat class.

Listing 10.1   Testing Cat using MiniTest

```ruby
require "minitest/autorun"
class CatTest < MiniTest::Unit::TestCase
  def setup
    @cat = Cat.new
  end

  def test_loves_lasagna
    assert @cat.favorites.include? "lasagna"
  end

  def test_weight_threshold
    @lasagna = Food.new(name: "lasagna", weight:7)
    assert_raises(Cat::OverweightException) do
      @cat.eat(@lasagna)
    end
  end
end
```

Even without knowing the implementation of Cat, it's easy to follow the intent of these tests. The MiniTest API is easy to keep in your head and doesn't involve any clever magic. The subject under test is the Cat class. Each method beginning with test defines a new test relating to the subject. When you run this test suite, the tests are run and the test assertions are verified to ensure that the code is working as you expect. Before each test, the optional setup method is run to set up any objects needed by the test. In this case, you're instantiating a new Cat object for every test. Similarly, overriding the optional teardown method is useful to do any cleanup that may affect other tests.

Suppose your system only handles cats weighing less than 6 pounds. If you were to introduce a new method on `Cat`, which inadvertently fattened the model beyond the specified limits, the MiniTest example would catch it, and a catastrophic system failure would be avoided. Although this example seems contrived, real software can grow out of control at an alarming pace in a complex system. By having a complete test suite, your software will be more robust, and fewer regressions will appear when you add new features.

As mentioned, if you prefer RSpec's more English-like syntax, MiniTest includes a spec library that lets you use RSpec style expectations to write your tests. The same `Cat` test can be rewritten as shown in the next listing.

Listing 10.2 Rewritten `Cat` test

```
require "minitest/spec"
describe "Cat" do
  before do
    @cat = Cat.new
  end

  it "should love lasagna" do
    @cat.favorites.should include("lasagna")
  end

  it "should throw an exception when it's overweight" do
    lambda { @cat.eat(@lasagna) }.must_raise(Cat::OverweightException)
  end
end
```

Now that you've had this general overview, let's dive into MiniTest.

10.2 *Installing and configuring MiniTest*

Installing MiniTest for MacRuby is extremely simple. You can install the latest Mini-Test library through macgems. Open your Terminal application, and run the following line:

```
sudo macgem install minitest
```

Next, you need to create a new group named `test` to hold your tests. By convention, the test filenames should end in _test.rb. You'll likely have helper methods to set up your test or custom assertions. A good place to put those helpers is in test_helper.rb. When you create your test files, you can require this single helper file at the top.

The minimum helper file will load the MiniTest library:

```
require "rubygems"
require "minitest/autorun"
```

Rather than run the tests one file at a time, you'll create a Rakefile to have all the tests run at once. The MiniTest gem comes with `rake` tasks to help you do this. The following code is a skeleton Rakefile that runs all your tests:

```
require "rake"
require "rake/testtask"
```

```
Rake::TestTask.new do |t|
  t.libs << File.dirname(__FILE__)
  t.test_files = FileList["**/*_test.rb"]
  t.verbose = true
end

desc "Run all tests"
task :default => :test
```

Traditionally, Rubyists would put their test files in a test subdirectory for organization. Xcode doesn't like this approach and prefers to have everything in the top-level directory. That's why the rake task assumes everything is at the top level. You add the Rakefile's current directory to the load path so that when your test attempts to load test_helper.rb, the test can find it on the load path. Without this line, you would see an error that test_helper.rb couldn't be found when you tried to invoke your tests. To organize your code, it's best to use Xcode's group feature and not worry about where Xcode keeps the files in the build process.

To test that you have the gem and configuration correctly set up, let's create a blank test class with a trivial assertion and add it to the test group. Here's a dummy blank test:

```
require "test_helper"
class BlankTest < MiniTest::Unit::TestCase
  def test_true
    assert true, "I should pass"
  end
end
```

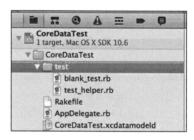

When you're finished setting up the project, your project inspector should look something like figure 10.1.

To test that everything is working, open your Terminal and jump to your project directory. Then, run the command macrake test. You should see your tests passing, a summary of the time it took, and the results, as shown in figure 10.2. Congratulations: you've written your first test in MacRuby!

Figure 10.1 Project inspector with test_helper.rb and blank_test.rb in a test group

Figure 10.2 Running macrake test from the command line

Removing test files from your build target

When you're creating a Deployment build, it's harmless to leave the tests with your app; but if you have a lot of tests and would like to cut down on the size of your app bundle, you can create a new build target that doesn't copy the test files. The following figure shows a duplicated build target with the test files removed from the Copy Resources build phase.

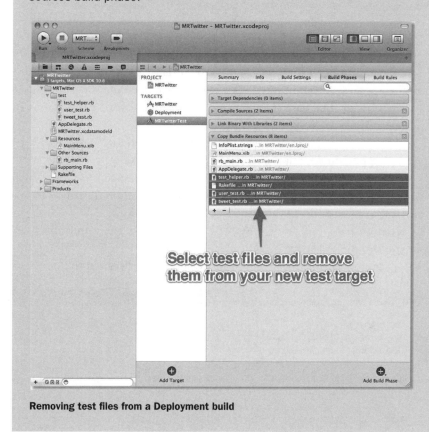

Removing test files from a Deployment build

10.3 Application vs. logic testing

At this point, you're ready to write your first real tests. Let's revisit the Core Data version of Todo List application you built in chapter 7. You want to make sure that when you call `TaskController#create_task`, a new task is created and inserted into the data store. This is the most important part of the Todo application, and there's no excuse for it to not be tested. The following listing shows a test you can use for this.

> **Listing 10.3 Testing task creation and storage for the Todo application**

```
require "test_helper"
require "tasks_controller"
```

```
class TasksControllerTest < MiniTest::Unit::TestCase
  def setup
    @tasks_controller = TasksController.alloc.init
  end

  def test_create_task
    tasks_count = @tasks_controller.tasks.count
    @tasks_controller.create_task(nil)
    assert_equal tasks_count + 1, @tasks_controller.tasks.count
  end
end
```

Unfortunately, if you tried to run this, you would get an error claiming that the application delegate wasn't initialized. The problem is that you're invoking the test suite before the application is initialized. As a result, the Core Data stack hasn't been initialized, none of your nibs have been loaded, and none of your connections have been connected.

There are two categories of tests: application tests and logic tests. *Logic tests* are tests that don't depend on your application to be running. Examples include tests on external systems and tests on calculations and other logic. *Application tests*, on the other hand, need to be run within the context of your application. Listing 10.3 is an example of a test that depends on the context of the application.

In order to run application tests, you need to have the application fully set up before you run the test suite. A good place to inject the tests is in your application delegate's `applicationDidFinishLaunching:` callback, as shown in the next listing.

Listing 10.4 Running tests in `applicationDidFinishLaunching:`

```
class AppDelegate
  def applicationDidFinishLaunching(a_notification)
    if ENV["PWD"] =~ /Debug$/
      $LOAD_PATH << File.dirname(__FILE__)
      Dir["**/*_test.rb"].each do |path|
        require File.basename(path, File.extname(path))
      end
      MiniTest::Unit.new.run
    end
  end
end
```

This chunk of initialization code looks daunting at first, but let's go over it line by line to see how it works. The `if` conditional on the third line specifies that the test suite will only be run when the build is in the Debug profile. Right after that, you add the directory of the current file to the load path; you do so for the same reason you had to add the current directory to the load path of the Rakefile. Every subclass of `Mini-Test::Unit::TestCase` is tracked by MiniTest and will be run. All you have to do is make sure you require all the test files, which is what is accomplished next. The code looks for filenames ending in _test.rb and requires them. Finally, after all test suites have been loaded, you execute `MiniTest::Unit.new.run` and have the test output to the Xcode console. After adding the snippet of test-loading code to `application-DidFinishLaunching:`, you can run your tests by running the application in Debug mode by pressing Cmd-R.

Load path problem

If your project was generated with Xcode 3, the directory structure for files that are copied over to the final build is slightly different than in Xcode 4. As a result, even if your tests run fine in the Terminal, they may fail to load when invoked from `applicationDidFinishLaunching:`. To fix this, append the current directory to the load path before you require other files:

```
$: << File.dirname(__FILE__)
```

Let's now look at how you can further integrate your tests into Xcode.

10.4 *Where to start testing*

With MiniTest installed and configured, your project is ready to be tested. It can be difficult at first to decide what's worth testing. You don't want to make trivial assertions that bring little value to your codebase. If you do, your tests will get in your way when you're trying to write real application code. You'll get frustrated and toss out your tests. Following the same reasoning, you don't want tests that are more complex than the code they're testing.

In general, you shouldn't test functionality that is part of the Cocoa APIs. Instead, focus on code that you've written and that is part of your application code base. In this section, we'll go over some good starting points for testing, using a stripped-down Twitter client as an example.

10.4.1 *Application initialization*

The actual application run loop is usually hidden from the developer. The evented GUI nature of a desktop application makes it hard to understand what is calling what. But thanks to Cocoa's pervasive use of delegates, you can focus your testing efforts on making sure a delegate knows what it's supposed to do. You can verify that connections are set up properly, instance variables are instantiated properly, and the return values for the delegate methods are what you expect for various different scenarios.

For starters, you can verify that the `AppDelegate` is attached to the application. You'll also be using the `AppDelegate` instance frequently in other tests, so you can add a helper method in test_helper.rb to save some typing:

```
def app_delegate
  NSApp.delegate
end
```

Next, create a test file called app_delegate_test.rb as shown here:

```
require "test_helper"
class AppDelegateTest < MiniTest::Unit::TestCase
  def test_app_delegate
    assert !app_delegate.nil?, "AppDelegate not properly attached to our
    ➥ main application"
  end
end
```

If the test fails, then you're trying to run your tests outside of your main application run loop. Go over the explanation in section 10.3 to see how to set up your project so your tests run within the same process as your application.

10.4.2 *Core Data*

Core Data was introduced in chapter 7 as a technology to store your application's data, as well as a way to manage and query that data. With its entities, relationships, and predicates, Core Data is a perfect candidate for unit-testing your model data to prevent inconsistencies. You can also test your predicates to guarantee that your query fetches results that you expect. In chapter 7, we talked about how to model your data for a Twitter application. There were two entities, User and Tweet, and a to-many relationship from User to Tweet. You'll revisit this example now to see how to test the various parts of Core Data.

In order to test Core Data, you'll need to initialize the data store before you can use it. You can manually initialize the store, but we prefer to run these tests after applicationDidFinishLaunching: and use the AppDelegate's methods for accessing the Core Data stack. By accessing the stack via the delegate, you can exercise the code the main application uses for initializing the stack and verify that it works. If the Core Data initialization fails for your test, then you know it will fail for your main application as well.

To test that you're successfully connected to Core Data, you'll next create a test to ensure that you can create Users in the data store. To make the test more interesting, you'll add a requirement to the User model that the email field is required. Instead of making the code changes first, you'll write the tests first. This style of programming is called test-driven development (TDD) and is popular in the Ruby community. By writing the tests first, you'll know at each step of the way that you haven't broken any previous code you've written, and you'll also know you're finished when all the tests pass.

The following listing shows the two tests to check whether a User is valid.

> **Listing 10.5   Two tests for valid Users**

```
require "test_helper"

class UserTest < MiniTest::Unit::TestCase
  def setup
    @context = NSApp.delegate.managedObjectContext
    if @user
```

```
      @context.deleteObject(@user)
    end
    @user = NSEntityDescription.insertNewObjectForEntityForName("User",
➥     inManagedObjectContext:@context)
  end

  def test_user_missing_email
    success = @context.save(nil)
    assert !success, "user should not be valid without email"
  end

  def test_user_valid
    @user.email = "foo@bar.com"
    success = @context.save(nil)
    assert success, "user should be valid with email"
  end
end
```

The setup method is run before each of the two test methods. This lets you have a fresh User instance to test with so the tests are independent of one another. The first test asserts that a User won't be saved to the data store because its email field isn't filled in. The second test checks that a User can be successfully saved after its required email attribute is assigned.

When you run this test, you get a test failure as shown in Figure 10.3.

Figure 10.3   User test failure in the Xcode console

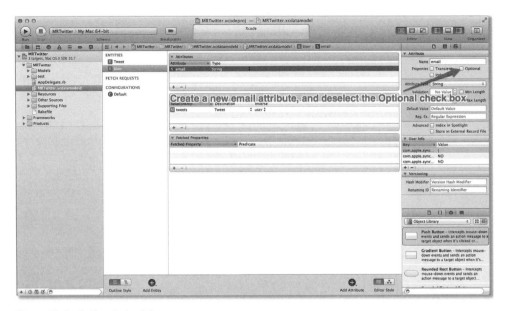

Figure 10.4   Optional check box

Because the original model doesn't require the email field, the `User` is successfully saved even if they don't have an email assigned. To remedy this, first create a new version of the modeling file, because you'll be making a change to the schema. In the project navigator, expand the modeling file and select the managed object model. Then go to Editor > Create Model Version, and save the new version. Select the new model version, create a new `email` attribute, and deselect the Optional check box for the attribute, as shown in figure 10.4.

After you save this change, run the test again; all the tests will now pass.

10.4.3   *Managing persistence store for testing*

Core Data offers you flexible strategies for persisting data. You can store your data in a human-readable XML format, in a binary format, in SQLite, or in memory. There are tradeoffs in performance for these different stores, and deciding which one to use depends on your application. In addition to these, you can write your own custom persistence store to fit any specific needs of your application.

It's best to test in an environment that is as similar to your actual application as possible. Although the different persistence stores should offer the same behavior, it's painful to find out that your tests are passing but your actual application isn't working because of a difference in configuration. By making no code changes and accessing the Core Data stack through your application delegate, you'll use the same persistence store as your normal application.

If you find that your test suite runs unbearably slowly, you can speed up Core Data–related tests by switching to an in-memory data store. You'll only realize the benefits if you're doing a lot of heavy operations through Core Data. If you have a small dataset, then the extra time needed to initialize and clear a SQLite persistence store is out-weighed by the extra maintenance overhead of having a different store type for your test suite.

Whichever store you choose to use, remember to reset the data before a test. Otherwise, you may receive nondeterministic test results where one test affects the results of another test. For example, suppose you want to make sure an entity is successfully persisted in the data store by checking the number of fetch results for that entity. If you don't clear the context after each test, then other tests that create the same entity will cause the fetch request to produce an indeterminate number of results. To make it easier to tear down and reinitialize the persistent store, you can introduce a new helper instance method in AppDelegate.rb, as shown in the next listing.

Listing 10.6 `initializePersistentStore` method in AppDelegate.rb

```
def initializePersistentStore
  directory = NSURL.alloc.initWithString "file://localhost" +
➥ ENV["PWD"].sub(" ", "%20")#, relativeToURL:
➥ NSURL.alloc.initWithString("file://localhost/")
  error = Pointer.new_with_type("@")
  url = directory.URLByAppendingPathComponent("MRTwitter.storedata")

  unless persistentStoreCoordinator.addPersistentStoreWithType(
➥ NSXMLStoreType, configuration:nil, URL:url, options:nil, error:error)
    NSApp.presentError(error[0])
    return nil
  end
end
```

Having a helper method for adding a new persistent store isn't enough. The existing old persistent store still exists. In order to have a clear test, you need to add one more helper method to AppDelegate.rb, as follows.

Listing 10.7 `removePersistentStores` method in AppDelegate.rb

```
def removePersistentStores
  persistentStoreCoordinator.persistentStores.each do |store|
    error = Pointer.new_with_type("@")
    unless persistentStoreCoordinator.removePersistentStore(store,
    ➥ error:error)
      NSApp.presentError(error[0])
    end
    unless NSFileManager.defaultManager.removeItemAtPath(store.URL.path,
    ➥ error:error)
      NSApp.presentError(error[0])
    end
  end
end
```

Now, whenever one of the test suites needs to manipulate the Core Data stack, you call the appropriate helper methods to tear down and reinitialize the Core Data stack as needed.

10.4.4 *Testing predicates*

After verifying the validity of your entities, it's a good idea to make sure any fetch requests you create return the results you expect. Suppose you want a helper function that returns the latest tweets. If you follow TDD, the implementation of how the fetch requests are written will be hidden by the interface you design. This will leave you with a clean and well-tested method that you can reuse throughout the rest of the application.

You want this method to return an array of tweets sorted in descending order by creation date. You'll create it as a class method on the `Tweet` class. Before you do this, let's write the test to translate your intent into test code that you can use to verify the application code.

Listing 10.8   Translating the intent into test code

```ruby
require "test_helper"
class TweetTest < MiniTest::Unit::TestCase
  def setup
    @context = NSApp.delegate.managedObjectContext
    app_delegate.removePersistentStores
    app_delegate.initializePersistentStore
  end

  def test_latest_tweets
    tweets = Tweet.latest_tweets
    assert tweets.empty?,
    "Tweets should be empty initially, but has #{tweets.count} instead"

    t1 = NSEntityDescription.insertNewObjectForEntityForName("Tweet",
    ➡ inManagedObjectContext:@context)
    t1.createdAt = Time.now - 1000
    t2 = NSEntityDescription.insertNewObjectForEntityForName("Tweet",
    ➡ inManagedObjectContext:@context)
    t2.createdAt = Time.now
    assert @context.save(nil)

    tweets = Tweet.latest_tweets
    assert_equal [t2, t1], tweets, "Tweets out of order"
  end
end
```

In the `setup` method, you use the helper methods from listings 10.6 and 10.7 to tear down and reinitialize the Core Data stack and ensure that the tests are independent of one another. Next, the `test_latest_tweets` method verifies that the results should be empty when there are no tweets in the store, and that the results should be sorted by the `createdAt` date attribute in a descending order.

Now that the tests are written, let's fill out the implementation. First you need to update the model file to add a `createdAt` attribute to the `Tweet` entity. Its type should be set to `Date`. Also change the entity class for `Tweet` to be the `Tweet` subclass instead of the default `NSManagedObject`. Then you can write the `Tweet` subclass, as shown in the following listing.

Listing 10.9 Tweet subclass of NSManagedObject

```
class Tweet < NSManagedObject
  def self.latest_tweets
    context = NSApp.delegate.managedObjectContext
    tweets = []
    request = NSFetchRequest.alloc.init
    request.entity = NSEntityDescription.entityForName("Tweet",
    ➥ inManagedObjectContext:context)

    sort_desc = NSSortDescriptor.alloc.initWithKey("createdAt",
    ➥ ascending:false)
    request.sortDescriptors = [sort_desc]

    error = Pointer.new_with_type("@")
    tweets = context.executeFetchRequest(request, error:error)
    tweets
  end
end
```

The `latest_tweets` class method constructs an `NSFetchRequest` for entities of the `Tweet` class. In addition to matching on the entity name, you also add an `NSSort-Descriptor` on the `createdAt` attribute in descending order to the fetch request. After executing the fetch request, you return the resulting tweets.

10.5 *Summary*

Using a combination of logic and application tests with MiniTest will help you get the test coverage you want. In addition to these basic tools, a great benefit of MacRuby is the ability to use all the existing testing frameworks and ideas from both the Ruby community and the Objective-C community. By taking the time to write tests up front, you save yourself a lot of headache and frustration when you need to expand your application.

The Mac App Store provides a new medium for application distribution for Mac OS X. In the next chapter, you'll learn how to take advantage of this App Store, including review guidelines, provisioning, and the submission process.

MacRuby and the
Mac App Store

11

This chapter covers:

- Understanding the Mac App Store
- Knowing the App Store rules
- Submitting a MacRuby app

Creating MacRuby apps to solve your problems can be both fun and rewarding. But let's face it: most of us want others to enjoy the fruits of our labor. For a long time, there wasn't a standardized way to distribute desktop applications. You had to create a product web page and distribute the app via a link, which required users to figure out how to install it themselves. Luckily, most people who knew their way around a Mac knew how to install an application.

Many developers struggled with spreading the word about their apps. Even with the many social media outlets today, letting people know about your application and getting them to your website to download the app can be difficult.

There's now a new way to distribute Mac OS X MacRuby applications: Apple's Mac App Store. You can list your application in a centralized location that allows for easy discovery and installation. Throughout this chapter, you'll learn about the Mac App Store, its benefits and limitations, and the steps to list your application.

11.1   Introducing the Mac App Store

The Mac App Store was announced as a distribution platform for Mac OS X applications. Apple had tremendous success with the iOS App Store and wanted to bring the same method of distribution to Mac OS X. The Mac App Store was released in early 2011 as part of the Snow Leopard 10.6.6 update.

What are the benefits of releasing a MacRuby application on the Mac App Store? What limitations will you face? What other requirements are there? Let's go over each of these questions in detail.

11.1.1   Benefits of releasing on the Mac App Store

The iOS App Store has shown that releasing applications on a widely used distribution platform can be beneficial to developers. Developers previously faced the issue of finding ways to get the word out about their applications. Imagine all the great applications you've never tried because you've never heard of them!

The Mac App Store, just like the App Store for iOS, places applications in categories, listed by Featured, rating, popularity, and so on. This allows users to easily sift through thousands of applications. Also, because everybody who has the latest version of OS X has the Mac App Store installed, applications are accessible to potentially millions of users. Figure 11.1 shows the Featured section of the Mac App Store.

Figure 11.1   Featured section of the Mac App Store

Installing applications through the Mac App Store is easy. In the past, applications were packaged as zip archives or disk images. Many nontechnical people had issues trying to install apps. With the Mac App Store, when a user chooses to install an app, it's installed and placed in the Applications folder automatically. This is especially great if your application is intended to be used by a wide audience.

Formerly, if your application wasn't free, you had to set up a system to validate licenses to determine the authenticity of an individual's purchase. You also had to set up a payment system through the application or through a website. Now this is all handled for you by the Mac App Store. This arrangement has its downsides, though, as we'll discuss in the next section.

Let's not forget the stories of people striking it rich through the iOS App Store. As you can imagine, this is also possible with the Mac App Store. Granted, only a small percentage of developers ever reach the amazing level of success you may have read about in the news, but you can make a respectable amount of money. Now, before you start dreaming up ways to customize your future mega-yacht, let's go over some of the limitations of the Mac App Store.

11.1.2 *Limitations of the Mac App Store*

Most great things don't come without a price, and the Mac App Store is no exception. Full control over your application is the price you pay to distribute the app on the Mac App Store. After reading this chapter, you may decide that the benefits outweigh the limitations; it's important, though, that you know about these drawbacks before releasing your MacRuby application on the Mac App Store.

First is the well-known application review process. You can't just submit your application and have it appear on the App Store right away. Your application may take a few days—or a few weeks—to be approved. Also, if you wait two weeks and your application isn't approved, you have to resubmit your application and repeat the review process. This can be a major issue if you're trying to meet a specific release date for your application.

The same review process applies for updates to your application. If you find a major bug, you'll still need to wait for the update to be approved before it reaches your users. You can imagine how catastrophic this could be if you let a bad release go out to the public.

> **Becoming part of Apple's Mac Developer Program**
>
> Before you can submit to the Mac App Store, you need to be part of Apple's Mac Developer Program. This program allows you to access the latest OS X development builds, developer forums, and technical support, and of course it lets you submit applications to the Mac App Store. Enrolling in the Mac Developer Program costs $99 per year. You can enroll at http://developer.apple.com.

Developers who have struck it rich in the App Store have helped Apple earn a pretty penny at the same time. Any paid application that is released on the Mac App Store requires that Apple receive a 30% cut. Thus if your application costs $0.99, you pocket only $0.69. This can be seen as a small price to pay for not having to set up a payment system, which would most likely take a small percentage of the sale as well.

11.2 Knowing the App Store rules

Before we jump into how you can unleash your MacRuby app onto the masses, you should know what you can and can't do. Luckily, Apple provides a lengthy set of review guidelines that you can go by. It's important that you meet these guidelines to get your application approved.

You must abide by more than 90 different review guidelines. We won't discuss all of them because most are obvious. For instance, if your application doesn't work, it won't be accepted (please make sure your app works before you submit it). You can view the full list of review guidelines at http://mng.bz/6Wjr. We'll go over a select few from some sections we think are important.

11.2.1 Functionality

The most important rule is that applications that crash or exhibit bugs will be rejected. Even well-tested applications can have bugs, but make sure they don't inhibit the use of the application. Applications also can't be labeled as beta, demo, trial, or test versions.

You can't use any method of updating your application outside of the App Store. For instance, many Mac applications use the Sparkle framework to provide application updates. Using a framework such as Sparkle to update your application and circumventing Apple's update process is prohibited.

11.2.2 Metadata

When you submit your application, you use iTunes Connect. (We'll discuss this when we talk about the process of submitting your MacRuby app.) The application title should match the name of the application you're submitting. In addition, the app icon and attached screenshots should match and should always adhere to the 4+ age rating.

11.2.3 Location

If your application requires the use of a user's location, you need to ask for their consent before using it. You also can't submit applications that use location-based APIs for autonomous control of any kind of vehicle or device.

11.2.4 User interface

Make sure your application conforms to Apple's Human Interface Guidelines (HIG) for Mac. You can see these guidelines at http://mng.bz/N6Yd.

Apple also doesn't want apps that look similar to its own applications. For example, you shouldn't submit an application that looks identical to iChat or iTunes. Another important thing to note is that your application shouldn't change the native UI elements or behaviors of standard Mac OS X applications.

11.2.5 Privacy

If your application needs to transmit private information about a user, it must do so with the user's permission. Also, Apple doesn't allow applications that require users to share personal information in order to function. For instance, you can't require a user to share their email address and date of birth.

11.2.6 Charities and contributions

If your application is for a charity, it needs to be free. You're also not allowed to collect donations within the app: you must load a separate web browser.

11.2.7 Legal requirements

Be sure to abide by all legal requirements in any location where your app is available to users. You're also not allowed to submit an application that enables users to share files illegally. For example, Napster wouldn't have been allowed into the Mac App Store.

Apple's review guidelines for the Mac are always changing, so always check the official list of rules. Next, we'll walk through submitting an application to the Mac App Store.

11.3 Submitting a MacRuby application

We know you've been waiting to get to this part, and we applaud you for being patient. In this section, we'll discuss the steps you need to take to submit a MacRuby application to the Mac App Store. If you're lucky, your app may end up being your ticket to early retirement! Probably not, but if so, please be sure to send us a check (we're just kidding—kind of).

11.3.1 Creating certificates

Before you submit your application, you must create two certificates. These certificates will be used to sign your application bundle and installer. Let's quickly run through the steps to create them:

1 Point your web browser to the Developer Certificate Utility at http://mng.bz/5DWS, and click the link to create your certificates. You should be presented with a page that looks similar to figure 11.2.

2 The form asks for a certificate signing request. It's up to you to create this signing request using the Keychain Access application. Open the Keychain Access application from within the Utilities folder in Applications. Then, choose

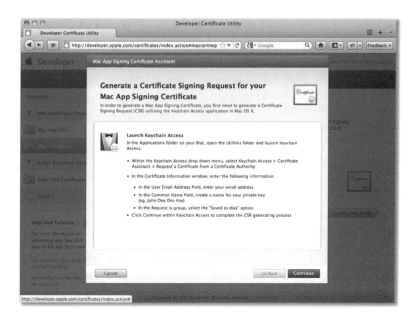

**Figure 11.2
Creating
certificates using
the Developer
Certificate Utility**

Keychain Access > Certificate Assistant > Request a Certificate from a Certificate Authority (see figure 11.3).

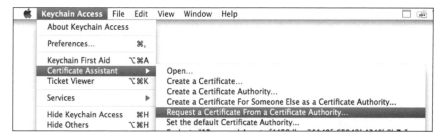

Figure 11.3   Keychain Access menu to request a certificate from a certificate authority

3 Enter your email address in the User Email Address field. In the Common Name field, enter a name for your certificate. Select Saved to Disk instead of having the certificate signing request emailed to you. See figure 11.4.

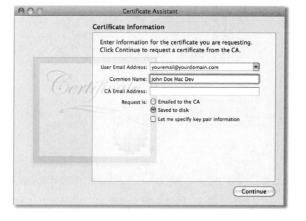

Figure 11.4   Creating your certificate signing request

4 Click Continue. You're asked to save the signing request somewhere on your Mac. Save it in a location you'll remember, because you'll need to use it again soon.

5 Go back to your web browser, click Continue on the form, and upload your newly created certificate signing request by clicking Generate (see figure 11.5).

6 It may take a few minutes for the certificate

Figure 11.5   Uploading your certificate signing request

to be created. When it's ready, download it and then double-click it to install it into your Keychain.

7 You're asked to repeat the process to create a new certificate for the installer. Create a new certificate signing request for the installer and go through the same steps.

8 When both certificates have been created, the Developer Certificate Utility should list them as shown in figure 11.6.

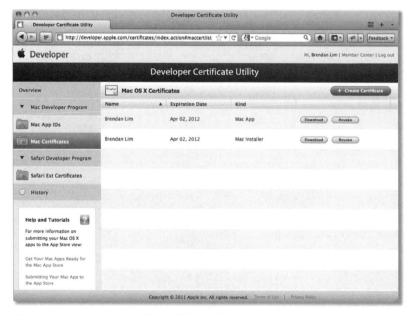

Figure 11.6   Developer Certificate Utility listing your newly created certificates

Next, let's look at how you can create your App ID.

11.3.2 Registering your Mac App ID

The next step is to register an App ID, also known as the bundle identifier. This ID will be used to identify your application for any future updates. You might have noticed this in the Info.plist file in your MacRuby application, specified under CF Bundle Identifier. This needs to be a unique identifier and can't be shared with any other Mac or iOS application.

To create your Mac App ID, follow these steps:

1 Go back to the Developer Certificate Utility page. You should see an option to create a new App ID. You're asked for an App ID Name or Description; this is the name of your application.

2 The next step is to specify your App ID. Because it should be unique across iOS and Mac applications, you may want to consider namespacing your identifier. For example, feel free to use something like com.*yourcompanyname*.mac.*appname*. Figure 11.7 shows how you might choose to name the bundle identifier for an application called Awesome App.

Figure 11.7   Registering your Mac App ID

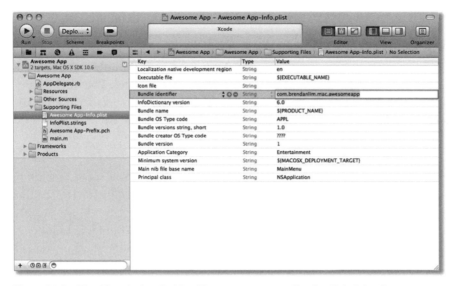

Figure 11.8   Matching the bundle identifier to your new application ID in Info.plist

3   Make sure you match the App ID to the Bundle Identifier in your Info.plist file. Without this, your application won't be recognized properly when it comes time for submission. See figure 11.8.

Now that your Mac App ID is registered, you can get your application ready for submission.

11.3.3   *Preparing icons and screenshots*

Your application can't be submitted without an icon. (We discussed how to create an icon in chapter 2.) Apple provides a helpful tool for creating application icons: the Icon Composer, located in /Developer/Applications/Utilities. You can drag in a large image file, and the Icon Composer will create an icon for your application. Then, add the icon to your application by dragging it to the Resources folder and then specifying its name in the Icon property of Info.plist.

You'll also need an icon that is 512 pixels wide by 512 pixels tall, which will be used when you prepare your application for submission in iTunes Connect. It's important that this image matches the icon used for your application. If it doesn't match, you application could end up being rejected.

Finally, you'll need screenshots of your application. Apple requires that you submit at least one screenshot, which should have an aspect ratio of 16:10 and be at least 1280 pixels wide by 800 pixels tall. You can easily take one by using the keyboard shortcut Cmd+SHIFT+4: this turns your mouse into a crosshair and allows you drag the bounds of the screenshot you want to capture. The resulting image is then saved onto your desktop.

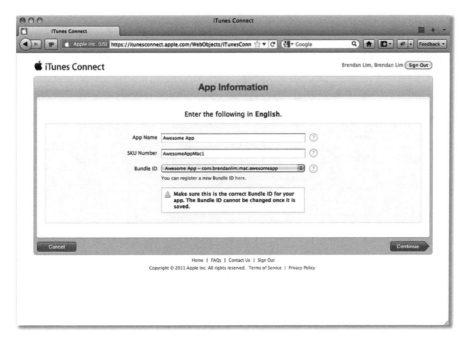

Figure 11.9 Specifying your application information in iTunes Connect

11.3.4 Adding your application to iTunes Connect

You're ready to prepare your application for submission on iTunes Connect. This is where you can manage your application's profile, modify billing information, and view sales statistics. Here are the steps:

1 Go to iTunes Connect in your web browser: http://itunesconnect.apple.com.
2 Log in with your developer credentials, and click Manage Applications.
3 Click Add New App. You're presented with the form shown in figure 11.9.
4 Enter the name of your application in the App Name field. For the SKU, enter something to help you identify your application; it will be used to represent your application in your sales statistics. In the Bundle ID field, choose the App ID you created previously. Click Continue.
5 On the next screen, specify the date you'd like your application to go on sale and the app's price. Click Continue.
6 On the next screen, you're asked to provide detailed information about your application, which will be used for the app's profile (see figure 11.10). Make sure the version number and category match what you set in your application's Info.plist file; if they don't match, the app won't submit properly.
7 Next you're asked questions about your application's content to determine its rating.
8 Submit screenshots of your application, as instructed.

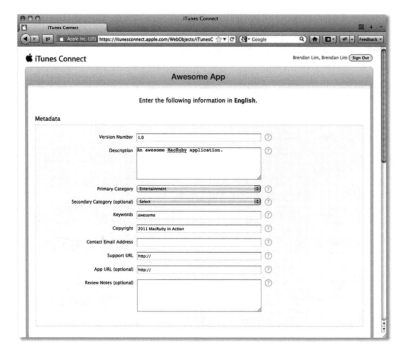

**Figure 11.10
Filling out your
application
information**

9   You're presented with a screen that shows you an overview of your application.
    The app's status should be set to Prepare for Upload. Click your application
    and then click the Ready to Upload Binary button shown in figure 11.11; the
    application profile's status changes to Waiting for Upload.

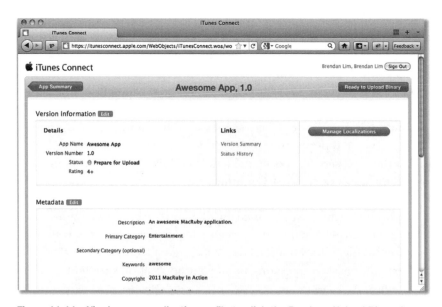

Figure 11.11   Viewing your application profile to click the Ready to Upload Binary button

Let's get your application ready to be uploaded.

11.3.5 *Packaging and submitting your application*

You're just about ready to submit your application for approval. But before you can package your application for submission, you must make a few changes. Follow these steps:

1 The Mac App Store requires that you not support PowerPC processors or 32-bit Intel (i386) processors. By default, the supported architectures include i386 and x86_64; so, you need to remove i386 from your project's build settings. To do this, go into Build Settings, double-click Valid Architectures, and remove i386, as shown in figure 11.12.

2 While you're still in Build Settings, go to the Code Signing section and set Code Signing Identity to the certificate that you created and installed into your Keychain. If you did this properly, it should appear in the pop-up; select it before proceeding (see figure 11.13).

3 Add a build target to your deployment setting so you can package the MacRuby framework in your application. To do this, first edit your Deployment scheme by clicking the Deployment drop-down and choosing Edit Scheme, as shown in figure 11.14.

Figure 11.12   Removing i386 from Valid Architectures in Build Settings

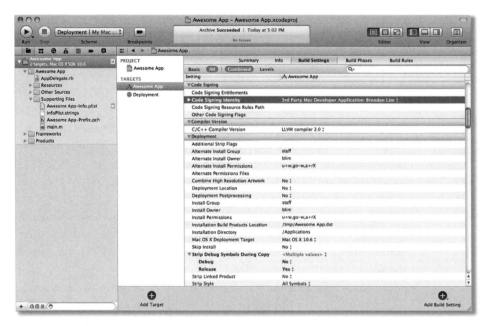

Figure 11.13   Selecting the proper code signing identity

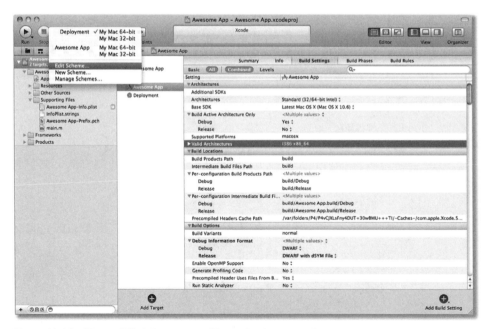

Figure 11.14   Choose Edit Scheme to modify the Deployment scheme.

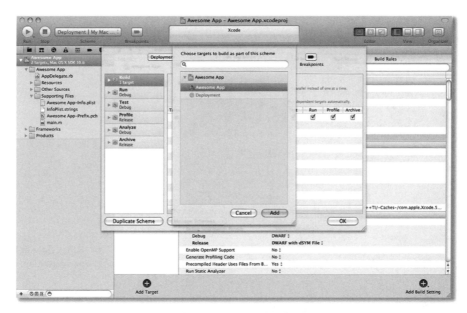

Figure 11.15   Adding your application's target to the build phase

4 In the screen that opens, choose the Build phase, and click the + arrow to add a new target. Then, choose your application's target, as shown in figure 11.15.

5 Change the order by dragging your application's target above the Deployment target. Your Build phase should look like figure 11.16.

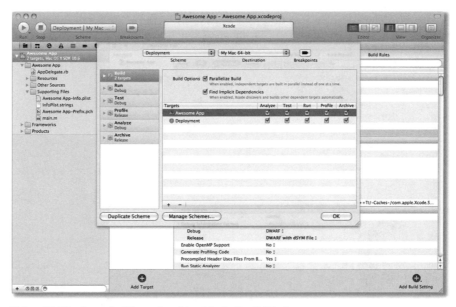

Figure 11.16   Arranging the order of targets in the Build phase

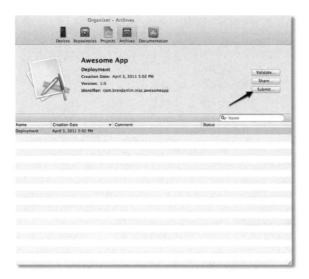

Figure 11.17   Click Submit in Xcode Organizer's Archive section.

This completes the changes you need to make to your application. You're now ready to archive the application and submit it to the Mac App Store:

1   To archive your app, choose Product > Build For > Build For Archiving.
2   Once that's finished, choose Product > Archive. Doing so adds your application's archive to Xcode's Organizer in the Archive section.
3   Submit your application to iTunes Connect by clicking the Submit button, as shown in figure 11.17.
4   You're asked to log in with your developer credentials upon submission. iTunes Connect then tries to determine what application you're submitting based on its bundle ID. Verify this, as well as your certificate, as shown in figure 11.18.

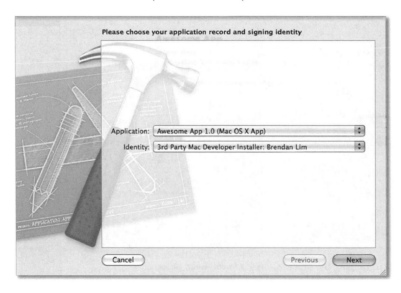

Figure 11.18 Submitting your application through Xcode's Organizer

Congratulations! If you've followed the steps correctly, your MacRuby application should be submitted for review. This will also be reflected in your application's profile on iTunes Connect. Your application's new status should be Waiting for Review.

Although the review process can take some time, you can periodically check on your application in iTunes Connect; its status will change to In Review when it's being reviewed. If you're lucky, you'll hear back after a few days. Don't be surprised, though, if you don't get a response for up to two weeks. It's a waiting game.

11.3.6 *Dealing with application rejection*

Having your application rejected can definitely ruin your day. It can be even worse when you realize that you can't meet a deadline because the app wasn't approved in time. The truth is, this happens to many developers—don't feel as though you're the only one. You can find many famous app-rejection blog posts online.

If your application is rejected you'll receive an email telling you so. It will normally explain why the application was rejected. If you need further explanation, you can reply to the email. Apple is also open to you contesting the rejection: if you think your application should have been approved, you can reply and explain why, although most of the time the reviewers are right.

To resubmit your application, you'll need to fix the problem the reviewers found. Then, ready your application for submission on iTunes Connect, and submit through Xcode the same way that you did previously. The last step is to wait—again.

11.3.7 *Submitting an update*

When you're ready to update your application, you'll find the process much quicker than the initial submission. The first and most important thing to do is to update your application's version in your Info.plist file. For example, if you were on version 1.0, you might want to change it to 1.1 if the update isn't major.

Next, go to your application's profile in iTunes Connect and add a new version to the app. You're asked questions about the new version, including the version number and what changes you're made. Once you've supplied this information, upload a new binary the same way you did with the original release.

Updates are subject to the same review guidelines and approval process. You should expect to wait up to two weeks for an update to be approved, although updates do tend to be approved more quickly than initial releases.

11.4 *Summary*

Sadly, this chapter marks the end of our journey together into the world of MacRuby. You've come far throughout the course of this book and become a full-fledged MacRuby developer who has learned many aspects of Cocoa development and much more.

Now you have the skills to create amazing Mac OS X applications using MacRuby. We hope you'll continue your journey by venturing deeper into the world of MacRuby and OS X development. We also fully expect to see your MacRuby application on the top-10 list in the Mac App Store!

appendix A:
Scripting with MacRuby

Sometimes a window-based Cocoa application is too much for what you need to accomplish. Ruby developers are accustomed to using the language to write quick scripts that perform occasional lightweight tasks that don't need a graphical interface. MacRuby is no different and lets you accomplish the same thing while being able to interact with Mac OS X applications that conform to Apple's Open Scripting Architecture (OSA) through the Scripting Bridge framework.

AppleScript is Apple's language for interacting with applications that are OSA compliant. For a long time, AppleScript has been the language of choice for scripting on the Mac. With Apple's continued Ruby and MacRuby support, we wouldn't be surprised to hear that MacRuby was AppleScript's replacement. Throughout this appendix, you'll learn more about AppleScript, Apple Events, and how to interact with other applications using MacRuby.

A.1   Before, there was AppleScript

OSA allows for inter-application communication by using Apple Events. Apple Events are standardized data formats used to send information to compatible Mac applications. Until recently, most people used AppleScript to interact with Apple Events. Apple made all this available through the *Scripting Bridge* framework released with Mac OS X 10.5.

AppleScript was created to aid users by letting them automate repetitive tasks. Let's take a quick look at AppleScript to better understand what it is and how it's used. We'll get to MacRuby scripts after we quickly go over some of the reasons you wouldn't want to use AppleScript.

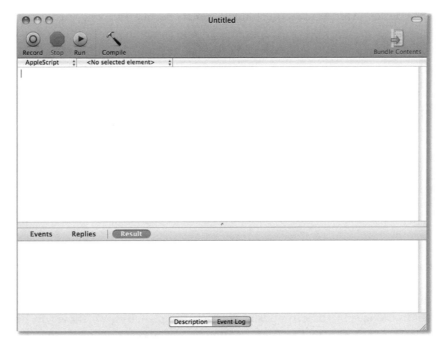

Figure A.1   The main AppleScript Editor window

A.1.1   *Introduction to AppleScript*

Developers have written many AppleScript scripts over the years to easily automate tasks using a syntax that was supposed to mimic natural language. Oddly enough, the problem with AppleScript was its syntax.

Before we jump into a few quick examples, open the AppleScript Editor, which is in Applications in the Utilities folder. The window is similar to figure A.1.

You enter the code for AppleScripts and run them from this window. Enter the following basic "Hello World" script:

```
tell application "Finder"
  display dialog "Hello World"
end tell
```

You first declare a `tell` block for the Finder application. Whatever is executed in this block is directed toward the Finder. The second line instructs Finder to display a dialog box that contains the string "Hello World." Finally, you close the dialog box using `end tell`.

Plug this script into the AppleScript Editor and click the Run button. A dialog appears with the words "Hello World" and two buttons, as shown in figure A.2.

That was pretty easy to understand. The problem comes when you try to do something

Figure A.2   "Hello World" AppleScript example

more complex. The AppleScript syntax tries to be like English, but it *isn't* English. This makes it hard for many people to read and understand. The following example retrieves the current playing track and artist from iTunes and displays the information in a dialog:

```
tell application "iTunes"
  try
    if not (exists current track) then return
    set current_artist to (get artist of current track)
    set current_track to (get name of current track)
  end try
end

tell application "Finder"
  display dialog current_artist & " - " & current_track
end tell
```

Here you create a `tell` block for iTunes and return if no track is currently playing. You use the `set` function to set the variables `current_artist` and `current_track`. You then take this and use it to create a dialog in Finder.

As things become more complicated, the code gets much harder to read—we'd rather use MacRuby to accomplish the same thing. Before we show you how to do that, let's see where you can find documentation about how to interact with other applications.

A.1.2   *AppleScript dictionaries*

Many Mac OS X developers document ways to interact with their applications with AppleScript. You haven't done this for the applications you've built in this book, but you're more than welcome to do the same for your MacRuby apps. To find available dictionaries, go into the AppleScript Editor and choose File > Open Dictionary. Doing so opens a list of applications on your machine that have dictionaries (see figure A.3).

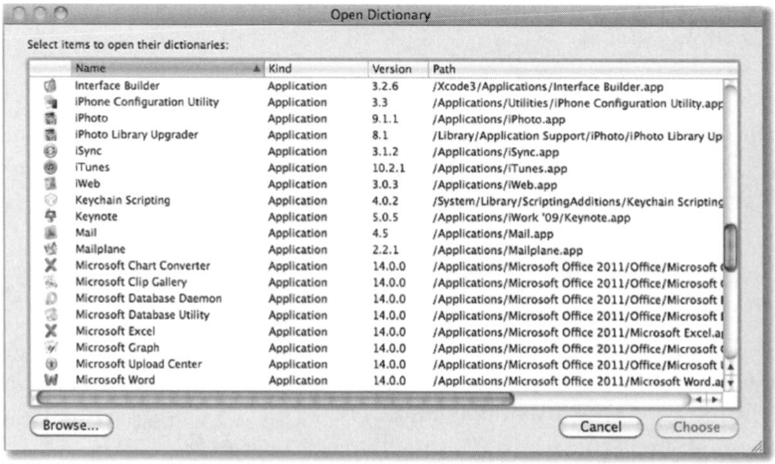

**Figure A.3
List of available
dictionaries in
the AppleScript
Editor**

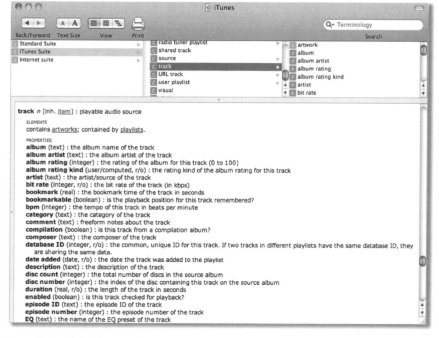

Figure A.4   Diving into the iTunes dictionary documentation

We all have iTunes on our machines, so let's look at the iTunes dictionary. Scroll down the list in the Open Dictionary dialog, select iTunes, and click Choose. In the previous example, you retrieved the artist and the name of the track that was playing. To find this in the iTunes dictionary's documentation, go into iTunes Suite and choose Track. You'll see the properties, such as `artist` and `name`, as shown in figure A.4.

The list includes all the properties you can access for a specific track in iTunes. Feel free to browse and look at the cool things you can retrieve and manipulate from other applications.

Next, we'll discuss ways you can interact with other applications with MacRuby scripts.

A.2   MacRuby scripting

Armed with what you've learned so far, you can now try scripting with MacRuby. We'll first go over how to create a custom BridgeSupport file. In some cases this is necessary, and it's good to know how to manually create such a file yourself. You'll then create scripts that interact with iTunes and with iChat.

A.2.1   Creating a BridgeSupport file

BridgeSupport files are XML files that describe C functions, structures, Objective-C methods, and their encodings. They're used to make these items available at runtime. You used a BridgeSupport file in chapter 8 when you were working with C functions in

Core Animation. You'll use them throughout this section to interact with other applications with your MacRuby scripts.

It's not always necessary to create a BridgeSupport file, although it's good to do so just in case—some APIs described in an app's Apple Event dictionary may use non–object-oriented items such as constants and enumerations. Luckily, Apple provides a simple way to create BridgeSupport files. First let's look at how you can retrieve the definitions for an application without going through the AppleScript Editor. Go to Terminal, and type in the following:

```
$ sdef /Applications/iTunes.app
```

The output is a long XML representation of what was shown in figure A.3. You can use this output to create a BridgeSupport file:

```
$ sdef /Applications/iTunes.app | sdp -fh --basename iTunes
```

This command uses the XML output to create an Objective-C header file with the name iTunes.h. The sdef command creates a scripting definition for iTunes, and the sdp command is used as a scripting definition processor.

Next, run gen_bridge_metadata to create your BridgeSupport file:

```
$ gen_bridge_metadata -c "-I." iTunes.h > iTunes.bridgesupport
```

This command creates the iTunes.bridgesupport file, which you can manually load in your scripts. The gen_bridge_metadata command generates bridging metadata for a given framework or set of headers.

Now that you have this ready, you can start working on an iTunes script using MacRuby.

A.2.2 *Controlling iTunes With MacRuby*

In this section, you'll write a MacRuby script using the Scripting Bridge framework. Using iTunes is a great way to demonstrate some of the cool things you can do.

PLAYING ITUNES WITH MACRUBY

The following simple script turns on iTunes and then plays one of your songs:

```
framework "Foundation"
framework "ScriptingBridge"

app = SBApplication.applicationWithBundleIdentifier("com.apple.itunes")
load_bridge_support_file "iTunes.bridgesupport"

app.stop
app.playpause
```

You first load the Foundation and the Scripting Bridge framework. Next you call the applicationWithBundleIdentifier: method on the SBApplication class. You pass in the bundle identifier for iTunes, which happens to be com.apple.iTunes. You don't need to, but you load your own BridgeSupport file (keep in mind that this particular example would work fine without this line). Make sure you either specify the full path of the .bridgesupport file you created or have the file in the same directory as your MacRuby script. You then tell iTunes to stop playing the current track, if there is one. The last line calls playpause, which either plays or pauses iTunes. This is why you call stop before executing this line: otherwise, each time you ran this script, it would either play or pause the current track. With the way it's set up, the script should always play a track.

You can have some more fun with this script. What if you want to automatically change the track after a certain length of time? All you need to do is add the following to the bottom of the script:

```
loop do
  sleep(30)
  app.nextTrack
end
```

This makes iTunes proceed to the next track every 30 seconds.

You could get really creative: how about creating an alarm clock that plays iTunes?

ITUNES ALARM CLOCK

You can make a few changes to the previous script and use it as an alarm, with the help of iCal:

1 Add the UNIX shebang notation to the top of your script; it's used to specify your MacRuby path and execute your script. Let's also have the script switch tracks every 10 seconds, to make the alarm a little more annoying:

```
#!/usr/local/bin/macruby
framework "Foundation"
framework "ScriptingBridge"

app = SBApplication.applicationWithBundleIdentifier("com.apple.itunes")
load_bridge_support_file File.dirname(__FILE__) + "/iTunes.bridgesupport"

app.stop
app.playpause

loop do
  sleep(10)
  app.nextTrack
end
```

2 Save this file as iTunesAlarm without any extension. It's important to save it without an extension so it will be properly executed when you specify which script to run.

3 Load Terminal, go to the directory where you saved iTunesAlarm, and modify its permissions by typing in the following line:

```
$ chmod a+x iTunesAlarm
```

This allows groups to execute this script.

4 Open iCal, and create a new event for the time you'd like to wake up. Double-click the event you just created, and click the Edit button.

**Figure A.5
Setting up
iTunesAlarm to
be executed for
your Alarm event
in iCal**

5   Under the Alarm setting, choose Open File. On the line below, choose Other, and find your iTunesAlarm script.

6   Set the number of minutes before the specified event time you'd like the script to be executed. Figure A.5 shows the script set to 0 minutes before so it will run at the time you specified for the Alarm event.

Next, let's see how you can use a script to update your iChat status.

A.2.3   *Updating your iChat status*

Some chat clients allow you to automatically update your status to whatever song you're playing in iTunes. iChat currently doesn't allow you to do this automatically. You'll make a script that will solve this by automatically updating your status with the iTunes song you're listening to.

If you look at the dictionaries for iChat in the AppleScript Editor, you'll see that you can access the statusMessage property. You'll use this property as well as the currentTrack property for iTunes in your script:

```
#!/usr/local/bin/macruby
framework "Foundation"
framework "ScriptingBridge"

itunes = SBApplication.
➥ applicationWithBundleIdentifier("com.apple.iTunes")
```

```
ichat = SBApplication.
➡ applicationWithBundleIdentifier("com.apple.iChat")

loop do
  ichat.statusMessage = "#{itunes.currentTrack.artist} -
  ➡ #{itunes.currentTrack.name}"
  sleep(5)
end
```

You first call `applicationWithBundleIdentifier:` and pass in com.apple.iTunes to get a reference to the iTunes scripting bridge. Then you do the same for iChat and specify com.apple.iChat as its bundle identifier. In the loop, you create a string from the artist and track name and set that as your iChat status message. On the last line in the loop, the script sleeps for five seconds before repeating.

If you run this script, it will update your status to whatever you're currently listening to. Figure A.6 shows an example.

You can easily modify this script to update something other than

Figure A.6　The script updates your status in iChat.

iChat to let people know what you've been listening to. Try digging around to see what other applications you can interact with.

index

X

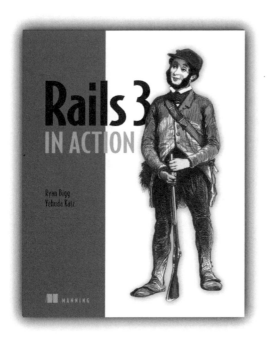

Rails 3 in Action
by Ryan Bigg and Yehuda Katz

   ISBN: 978-1-935182-27-6
   592 pages
   $49.99
   September 2011

MongoDB in Action
by Kyle Banker

   ISBN: 978-1-935182-87-0
   312 pages
   $44.99
   December 2011

For ordering information go to www.manning.com

MORE TITLES FROM MANNING

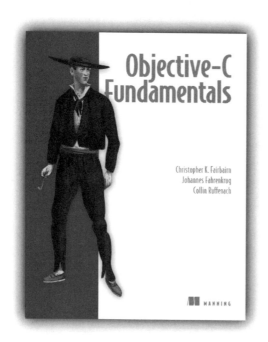

Objective-C Fundamentals
by Christopher K. Fairbairn,
   Johannes Fahrenkrug,
   and Collin Ruffenach

ISBN: 978-1-935182-53-5
368 pages
$44.99
September 2011

iOS 4 in Action
Examples and Solutions for iPhone & iPad

by Jocelyn Harrington,
   Brandon Trebitowski,
   Christopher Allen,
   and Shannon Appelcline

ISBN: 978-1-617290-01-5
504 pages
$44.99
June 2011

For ordering information go to www.manning.com

Well-Grounded Rubyist
Covering Ruby 1.9
by David A. Black

ISBN: 978-1-933988-65-8
520 pages
$44.99
May 2009

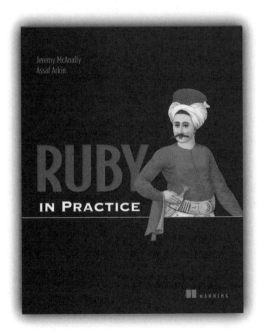

Ruby in Practice
by Jeremy McAnally and Assaf Arkin

ISBN: 978-1-933988-47-4
360 pages
$39.99
March 2009

For ordering information go to www.manning.com

Erlang and OTP in Action
by Martin Logan, Eric Merritt,
  and Richard Carlsson

ISBN: 978-1-933988-78-8
432 pages
$49.99
November 2010

The Quick Python Book, Second Edition
by Vernon L. Ceder

ISBN: 978-1-935182-20-7
360 pages
$39.99
January 2010

For ordering information go to www.manning.com